ON STRIVING TO BE A MUSLIM

Prof. Col. (Rtd.) ABDUL QAYYUM
Staff College, Quetta

Foreword By

GENERAL MUHAMMAD ZIA-UL-HAQ
Chief of Army Staff

Preface

ABDUL HAMEED SIDDIQUI

☆

Kazi Publications

CHICAGO, ILL. (USA)

DEDICATED TO

THE CAUSE OF ALLAH

Reprinted with the kind permission of the Author

Printed in U.S.A.

بِسْمِ اللّٰهِ الرَّحْمٰنِ الرَّحِيْمِ

In the name of God, the Beneficent, the Merciful

وَالْعَصْرِ ۝١

By the declining day ;

اِنَّ الْاِنْسَانَ لَفِيْ خُسْرٍ ۝٢

Lo ! Man is in a state of loss ;

اِلَّا الَّذِيْنَ اٰمَنُوْا وَعَمِلُوا الصّٰلِحٰتِ وَتَوَاصَوْا بِالْحَقِّ ۝٥

Save those who believe and do good
works and exhort one another to Truth,

وَتَوَاصَوْا بِالصَّبْرِ ۝٣

And exhort one another to Endurance.

(Quran, Surah 103)

CONTENTS

FOREWORD

THIS book presents in one compact volume, through the medium of the printed word, some of a series of lectures on Islam which I have had the pleasure of listening to in the living voice. Professor Abdul Qayyum undertook to deliver these talks at my behest and he has been heard with much joy by a large number of officers of the Pakistan Army. There has been an insistent demand from many of those who have heard him that these talks be committed to writing to facilitate that individual, personal study and reflection in peace which alone promote true understanding. I am glad this book will meet that need and go beyond, reaching those who have not heard him, with its call to inquiry in a field which is central to our lives as individuals and as a community.

For his book, the author has chosen the title : "On Striving to be a Muslim". Having known him for many years, I also know that this choice is as significant as it is deliberate. He has repeatedly stated that he is no "authority" on Islam but a common, sincere seeker in quest of the truth. What he presents are, as he says, glimpses of the joy that has been his in this never-ending quest : a search for knowledge, backed by practice, racing towards that vision and experience of Islam which is the goal of all who strive to be Muslims. In this endless drive towards perfection, he feels an intimate kinship with us all : "a pilgrim among pilgrims in our common quest of Islam." And this awareness of a shared bond and a common goal compels him, as he says, to share with his fellowpilgrims such of the joys of understanding as he has experienced during the course of his personal inquiry.

I commend this book to all who seek to understand Islam not on the basis of any blind allegiance to *Taqlid* but through the exercise of their own sufficient reason, and that personal inquiry which is incumbent on each one of us in our effort to understand and practise the teachings of the Qur'an and the Sunnah. I, for one, have found these talks refreshingly candid and sincere, a spur to further study and reflection. I trust that those who read this book will have adequate reason to largely share my evaluation of it.

GENERAL M. ZIA-UL-HAQ
Chief of Army Staff
G. H. Q. Rawalpindi

PREFACE

A Muslim is one who strives hard to be in spiritual accord with the demands of the Divine Will, which humanity has come to learn through the Prophets of Allah and finally through the last of the Prophets, Muhammad (peace and blessings of Allah be upon him). Prof. Abdul Qayyum gives a very interesting account of the honest strivings of a believer for the achievement of this noble end. He has attempted to furnish a rational basis for this sacred struggle, which is the need of the modern youth. Religion is defined as the elevation of the human spirit into union with the Divine. It is, therefore, in its root a matter of soul. We are religious not in virtue of thinking accurately or willing rightly but simply and essentially in virtue of a certain state of feelings and affections towards God. This is all true, but in order to elevate it from the religion of subjective caprice, we have to look to the objective standards in religion, which in Islamic terminology are called the laws of Shari'ah. These laws are rational, universal, and Divine and their value can be judged from their immense appeal to reason. Prof. Abdul Qayyum while explaining the nature of Islamic thought and the framework of Shari'ah and the infinite wisdom that lies behind them has clearly delineated the natural bounds of reason and the transgressions which it has made from time to time in the course of history.

This book is an interesting and thought-provoking study. The learned author has written it in a chaste, lucid, scholarly style. It is a valuable addition to the existing stock of Islamic literature.

ABDUL HAMEED SIDDIQUI

20 Muharram, 1398 H.
1 January, 1978.

AUTHOR'S NOTE

This book is a compilation of the edited transcripts and notes of some lectures on Islam which I have had the privilege of delivering before a fairly wide circle of officers of the Pakistan Army, particularly between the years 1973-76. They represent, in the external world, a reflection of my own inner pilgrimage in quest of the Truth.

I have greatly hesitated in bringing out this book and would, in truth, have never dared to do so were it not for the constant insistence of many friends and some strangers. The testimony of friends, though agreeable, is not always reliable; and I have been more than conscious of the fact that this is a field in which innumerable men of infinitely greater knowledge and piety have already spoken and written. And yet, I have at last dared to bring out this book. The reasons are only a few, but compelling.

Many great voices in this field are today stilled by the hand of death. They echo in the books that they have left behind but their echoes are drowned in the din of our everyday 20th Century life. There are several living voices also, muffled by circumstance or stifled by the arrogance of authority. In such a situation, it seems to me, that every voice that can be raised, however feeble, must be raised: with the prayer that our collective effort, drawing inspiration from the effort of the splendid few both dead and alive, may at last find acceptance with the Lord. This, in itself, is reason and obligation enough for a small man to join the chorus of the great, singing with full-throated ease:—

"I live for Him, Who loves me;
Who knows me true:
For the Cause that lacks assistance,
For the Wrong that needs resistance,
For the Future in the distance,
And the Good that I can do. . . . ."

God created us tier upon tier, and all men are not born equal. Precisely for this reason, we have as little cause to be awed by the brilliance of the great as we have to be contemptuous of the limitations of the small. Since everything stands out or falls relative to other things around it, the great are great only because of the smallness of the small around them. Yes, we, the small, have also a role to play! By lighting our little lamps we compel those who are better gifted to do their bit; and equally important: when the small refuse to be smaller than they are, they prevent the mediocre from becoming great!

Most of us are small men, whether we like it or not; but we greatly err when the lamp within us remains unlit for fear that it will never match the sun. Away with such fears! Let history forget the thousand little lamps and commemorate the flashing few. Our reward is with our Lord; and no flame, however feeble, misses the benediction of His Light!

Even the brilliance of the sun is so much candle-power, and no more. So, let us light our little candles! Within the bounds of our own country, in the Army, within the little organisation to which we belong, within our radius and inside our own little circles, let us light our little lamps! Who does not know that the mightiest of flashes, originate from the tiniest of sparks?

Let us, then, be honest! Let us not dream of a world-illumination without striking the first flickering flame! Let us not uselessly wait for that great contribution and allow our little contributions to die in the embryo! Today we live: to light a little candle, to make a little contribution, to perform a small act of prayer and sacrifice. Today we live, tomorrow may be too late. . .

It is thoughts such as these that have persuaded me to bring out this book—fearfully, with hope. To three men my special thanks are due: Brigadier Muhammad Iqbal (Chief Instructor, Command and Staff College, Quetta) who provided me the time and the facilities to complete this undertaking; Brigadier

Muhammad Aslam, Artillery (ex-DS, Staff College) who enjoyed as much as he questioned what I wrote; and Lt. Col. Tanwir Hussain Naqvi, AC (still a DS at the Staff College) who nagged me into believing that what I had written was, despite its several flaws, worth the Printer's time and effort. Havildar Abdul Rashid and Naik Muhammad Hanif did the laborious task of typing the manuscript. Naib Subedar Abdul Rehman, ACC and his team joined in to complete this first phase of the venture.

To Parveen, Naila and even little Munier—my wife, daughter and son—this book owes its existence in more ways than I can count. They have been the field in which this spirit has grown, these thoughts crystallised, this faith sprung to life. In the background, eternally present, have been the foundations of faith so lovingly (and at times, sternly) laid by a wise father and a mother so good as to be beyond the reach of any verbal tribute.

In the end, I am grateful to General Zia-ul-Haq for having written the Foreword and to Professor Abdul Hamid Siddiqui for having written the Preface. Mr. Muhammad Saeed, my Publisher, has shared my pain and now shares my joy in this closing act of placing the book before its readers.

Our reward is with our Lord; and this labour completed, together we pray:—

> "Our Lord!
> Accept (of us) this act (of prayer and service) performed.
> Lo! Thou, only Thou,
> Art the All-Hearing, All-Knowing." (*Quran*, 2: 12)

Staff College, Quetta,
1 January, 1978.

ABDUL QAYYUM.

THE RELIGIOUS IMPULSE

Introductory Remarks

1. I have said before, my friends, that what spills over in the external world as a series of lectures on Islam is, in truth, a continuous throb deep within me, a joy that I have experienced and cannot contain, a joy that bursts the dams, over-flows, inundates. And I seek of you no more and no less than that supreme privilege of sharing with you *this* joy that is as much *your* heritage as it is mine—a joy that is our *common* heritage. And in sharing this joy with you, my purpose—I made it clear —is *not* to *motivate* you; but to merely state the *Truth*, regardless of consequences ; and yet, not without the hope and the prayer that something of its *splendour* may draw you to it with its noose of light, even as it has drawn me to it a captive bemused. In this effort at *communication*, I also ṣaid, I stand here *not* to lecture, *not* to teach, *not* to instruct, *not* to preach, *not* to sermonise—but I speak *as* one of you *for* all of us : a pilgrim among pilgrims in our common quest of *Islam*. And since it is *knowledge* that we seek about this *all-pervading way of life*, this *Din* that is Islam, let us pray that our quest may be a *joyous* (and not a dreary) one.

2. You would recollect that occasion when *Ubayy Bin Ka'b* recited the *Ayatul Kursi* to the Prophet (peace be upon him), and the Prophet struck him on the breast with his open palm, saying : "*Al-ḥamdolillah* ! May your quest, O *Abul Mundhir*, may your quest of knowledge be a *joyous* one !"[1]

3. Permit me, my friends, to recite to you the *Ayatul Kursi* even as *Ubayy Bin Ka'b* had done, so that you and I *together* may feel the hand of the Prophet strike us on the breast, praying for

---

1. *Mishkat*, vol. 2, p. 449. In the context of recitations from the Qur'ān, also see : *Ibid.*, Chapter on "The Excellent Qualities of the Qur'ān".

us even as he prayed for *Ubayy Bin Ka'b* : "May your quest of knowledge, my friends, may your quest of knowledge be a *joyous* one !"....

"Allah ! There is no ilah but *He*.." (2 : 255)

4. And now, having recited the *Ayatul Kursi*, having fixed the fixed end of our compass on the *Qur'ān*, let us stretch out as far and wide as we possibly can, "even unto China", going East, going West, going everywhere—gathering every crumb of understanding that we can gather, from everywhere :

"To Allah belongeth the East and the West;
Withersoever ye turn, *there* is Allah's countenance.
Lo ! Allah is All-Embracing, All-Knowing." (2 : 115)

This, my friends, is the frame-work, that broad universal canvas on which we shall attempt to paint our understanding of Islam as a way of life.

5. Only a fool would dare to choose so vast a subject as Islam for a single one-hour talk. Let us then begin at the beginning, with a reference to that universal God-consciousness which we, in everyday language, identify as the *Religious Impulse* in man. Historical experience confirms that man does not and cannot live by bread alone. But caught as we are in the scientific—materialistic *din* of the 20th Century, many of us scoff at this truth. But Truth *cannot* be scoffed at, save in ignorance ; and since it *must not* be scoffed at, permit me to say a few words on this issue as a prelude to our subsequent enquiry into some of the many facets of Islam.

The Prevailing Notion

6. There is a common notion prevalent in our times that *Religion* is an out-dated, out-moded, antiquated thing ; that religion has always been something of a personal-individual opiate with a limited social role ; perhaps relevant to ancient and medieval times, but it is a force that is now expended, overtaken by the march of history and rendered irrelevant to the needs of modern man.

7. This, I submit, is a hasty, superficial, false notion. It betrays a lack of understanding of the fundamentals of human nature and a failure to grasp the lessons of history. *Religion*, as an impulse and an orientation towards the divine rising above the beast in man, is *inherent* in human nature : an eternal and inextinguishable urge, a universal phenomenon as old as the rise of self-consciousness in man.

The Universal Urge

8. As for the universality of religion, consider what *Plutarch* wrote many centuries ago :

> "In wandering over the earth, you can find cities without walls, without science, without rulers, without palaces, without treasures, without money, without gymnasium or theatre ; but a city without temples to gods, without prayer, without oaths and prophecy—such a city no mortal has yet seen and will never see."[2]

9. The many centuries that have gone past since *Plutarch* bear added historical testimony to the *universality* of *Religion* as an inextinguishable force inherent in and relevant to the nature of man. *William James*, one of the greatest modern psychologists, observes :

> "It seems probable that in spite of all that science may do to the contrary, men will continue to pray to the end of time, unless their mental nature changes in a manner which nothing that we (so far) know should lead us to expect. The impulse to pray is a necessary consequence of the fact that whilst the innermost of the empirical selves of a man is a self of the social sort, it yet can find its only adequate *socius* (its great companion) in an ideal world...most men, either continually or occasionally, carry a reference to it in their breasts...I say 'for most of us', because it is probable that men differ a good deal

---

2. Plutarch, quoted by W. M. Urban, *Humanity and Deity*, p. 15. Quoted by Pervez, *Islam : A Challenge to Religion*, Chapter 1.

in the degree in which they are haunted by this sense of an Ideal Spectator. It is a much more essential part of the consciousness of some men than of others. Those who have the most of it are possibly the most religious men. But I am sure that even those who say they are altogether without it, deceive themselves, and really have it in some degree."[3]

From Consciousness to Awareness or Forgetfulness

10. The *Religious Impulse*, then, is *inherent* in the nature of man. None of us is without it ; and none of us can deny it without being guilty of falsehood, asserting that which is contrary to the very foundation of our being.[4] God-consciousness is a consequence of the breath that the Lord breathed into the breast of mankind (*Qur'ān*, **15** : 29). This consciousness is in effect an after-glow, a residual memory in the mind of the human race of that first pre-eternal covenant between man and God, when man recognized his Creator and swore to worship and to serve none but Him. (*Qur'ān*, **36** : 60-61). It is this consciousness which is the motive force behind what we call the "Religious Impulse". It is, of course, true that there are some who, exercising their free will, go on to nourish this consciousness till it matures into an awareness of God ; while there are many who choose to leave it untended as a vague stirring in the soul. Between them, these two categories comprise the overwhelming bulk of mankind. There is, of course, yet a third category : those who deliberately choose to deny, to forget, to warp, mutilate or simply turn away from this natural conscious-

---

3. William James, *Varieties of Religious Experience.* Quoted by Iqbal, *The Reconstruction*, p. 89.

4. For an understanding of the temporal consequences of the neglect or violation of man's natural religious impulse, study Carl Gustav Jung's exposition on the role of the "religious function" in what he calls the "Individuation Process". See : Frieda Fordham, *An Introduction to the Psychology of Jung.*

ness of God within them; and in so doing, they violently violate the very foundation of their own being. Such unnatural men are few and it is against the danger of falling into this category that the Qur'ān warns mankind:

> "And be not ye as those who forgot Allah, so that *He* (then) caused *them* to forget *their own* souls. Such are the evil-doers." (*Qur'ān*, **59** : 19).

God-forgetfulness is self-forgetfulness, an unnatural denial of the universal nature of man. And it is remaining true to this God-created nature that is the true religion. The Qur'ān says :

> "So set thy purpose for religion as a man by nature upright—the nature (framed) of Allah, in which He hath created man. There is no altering (the laws of) Allah's creation. That is the right religion, but most men know not." (*Qur'ān*, **30** : 30).

The *Religious Impulse*, then, springs from an eternal source *within* the breast of man and is *not* an *external acquisition* or a passing phenomenon of history. To deny its existence or to ignore its presence is *un-natural*, contrary to human nature and natural law.

The Inextinguishable Urge

11. Individuals (in their own lives) and mankind (in various epochs of history) have no doubt, from time to time, chosen to ignore or smother this *Natural Religious Impulse*. This violation, far from extinguishing *Religion* as a living force, has created cruel contradictions in their lives and eventually paved the way for an unavoidable return to and a resurgence of the *Religious Impulse.*[5] *Will Durant*—Historian, Philosopher and Sage—

---

5. In this context, 20th Century Russia and China are often cited as examples to refute this contention. I think we take too limited a view, confining our vision to the present and the immediate future. What is privately present, is not non-existent merely because it is suppressed or fails to find immediate social expression. The coercive powers of the modern state are great but

[*Contd. on page* 6

commenting on contemporary times, writes : "The propaganda of Patriotism, Capitalism or Communism succeeds to the inculcation of a supernatural creed and a moral code. Holy days give way to holidays. Theatres are full even on Sundays ; and even on Sundays churches are half empty. In Anglo-Saxon families religion has become a social observance and a protective coloration ; in American Catholic families it flourishes; in upper and middle class France and Italy religion is 'a secondary sexual characteristic of the female'...."[6]

12. Many of us in the Third World, wistfully fix our gaze on the material progress of the West, and by a queer twist of Logic assume even this *turning away from religion* as a *cause* of their success. We could be like *them*, many of us say, if only we would break away from the shackles of *Religion* ! What a naïve conclusion ; what cruel blindness *not* to see the dead-end impasse, the confusion, the decay, the multiplication of human folly that this inevitably leads to.[7] We shall presently make a brief reference to the crisis in Western civilisation as a consequence of the unbridled pursuit of material progress as an end in itself ; but here it would be sufficient to note that such progress, far from rendering *Religion* anachronistic, paves the

---

Contd. from page 5]

cannot, when seen in the perspective of history, indefinitely perpetuate systems contrary to human nature. Even in periods of social repression, the religious impulse not only finds private-individual expression but must be substituted by the state through alternative modes of worship. Communism, as we all know, has its own twisted modes of "sublimation" and the very necessity of this sublimatory process confirms our contention. In assessing such issues, we need to tune our ears to what Will Durant calls "the slow heartbeat of the social organism, the vast systole and diastole"—that cosmic "breathing" which ushers in the rise and fall of nations.

6. Will and Ariel Durant, *The Lessons of History*, Chapter 7 (Religion and History).

7. *Ibid.*, Chapters: 6 (Morals and History), 8 (Economics and History), 9 (Socialism and History), 10 (Government and History), 12 (Growth and Decay).

way for a *resurgence* of it. Human ingenuity cannot do away with God ; and when crisis comes, whether in our individual or collective lives, the *Religious Impulse* inherent in human nature compels us to return to God and religion as the only way out of the futility and weariness of human solutions. This is no dogmatic assertion but an objective observation. *Will Durant* writes :

> "One lesson of history is that religion has many lives, and a habit of resurrection. How often in the past have God and religion *died* (or been killed) only to be *re-born*!...There is *no* significant example in history before our time of a society successfully maintaining moral life without the aid of religion."[8]

The Decay of the Religious Impulse

13. The *moral crisis* is the most haunting crisis of our times, polluting whatever progress we make in other fields and ticking away like a time-bomb in the heart of whatever we build. Having forsaken the religious impulse within us, we have landed ourselves in a paradoxical world in which the very material achievements which we point to with pride threaten to destroy us. *Northrop* writes:

> "It would seem the more civilised we become the more incapable of maintaining civilisation we are."[9]

What human intelligence, devoid of the religious impulse and the restraints that emanate from God-consciousness, creates, the human intelligence also capriciously destroys. Even that agnostic, *Bertrand Russell*, found himself compelled to observe:

> "To describe man as a mixture of god and beast is hardly fair to the beasts...No beast and no yahoo could commit the crimes committed by Hitler and Stalin. There seems

8. *Ibid.*, Chapter 7.

9. F. S. C. Northrop, *The Meeting of East and West.* Quoted by Khurshid Ahmed in his Preface to Maududi, *The Ethical Viewpoint of Islom.*

> no limit to the horrors that can be inflicted by a combination of scientific intelligence with the malevolence of Satan...Human imagination long ago pictured Hell, but it is only through recent skill that men have been able to give reality to what they had imagined...Sometimes, in moments of horrors, I have been tempted to doubt whether there is reason to wish that such a creature as man should continue to exist."[10]

Transition and Resurgence

14. The crisis of our times is the crisis of ever-increasing *Power* along-side an ever-diminishing sense of *moral responsibility*. Talking of "the invisible break-down in our civilisation", *Lewis Mumford* refers to "the erosion of values, the dissipation of humane purposes, the denial of any distinction between good and bad, right or wrong, the reversion to sub-human levels of conduct".[11]

Having forsaken the *religious impulse* our exclusive and ferocious concentration on the *material* has dragged us below the level of the beast. This fall is the greater because, unlike the beast, we had and still have the option to cultivate the divine in us. We had and still have the option to become the "crown of God's creation". That goal, freely chosen, can be attained only by a *rational* cultivation of the *natural religious impulse* inherent in us all. If this is *not* done, 20th Century civilisation will sink lower into the morass of its own creation. If the past history of the human race may be taken as a reliable guide for a projection into the future, I would surmise that we shall probably survive through a resurrection and a resurgence of the *religious impulse*. There is cause, I believe, *not* to give way to *Russellian* despair but to hope with *Pitirim A. Sorokin* that we shall emerge out of the painful chaos of the present era and

10. Bertrand Russell, *Human Society in Ethics and Politics*. Quoted by Khurshid Ahmed, *Ibid.*
11. Lewis Mumford, *The Conduct of Life*. Quoted by Khurshid Ahmed, *Ibid.*

step into a new epoch more worthy of mankind. *Sorokin* writes :

> "Every important aspect of the life, organisation and the culture of Western society is in the most extraordinary crisis...Its body and mind are sick and there is hardly a spot on its body which is not sore, nor any nervous fibre which functions smoothly...We are seemingly between two epochs : the dying Sensate culture of our magnificent yesterday and the coming Ideational culture of the creative tomorrow. We are living, thinking and acting at the end of a brilliant 600-year long Sensate Day. The oblique rays of the sun still illumine the glory of the passing epoch. But the light is fading and in the deepening shadows it becomes more and more difficult to see clearly and to orient ourselves safely in the confusions of the twilight. The night of the transitory period begins to loom before us, with its nightmares, frightening shadows, and heart-rending horrors. Beyond it, however, the dawn of a new great Ideational culture is probably waiting to greet the men of the future."[12]

Staring Over the Edge of the Precipice

15. These, gentlemen, are ideas that we ought to ponder over—long and long. They are not the ramblings of ordinary men. They represent the deepest reflections of some of the finest minds soaked in the Western tradition: *modern* minds that have lived through and know the pulse of 20th Century Western civilisation. They speak from their various standpoints, from a wide variety of disciplines : as psychologist, historian, philosopher, educationst, scientist, sociologist and what have you. I have given you only a random sampling and a limited one at that. But the conclusion is clear. The great voices of the modern, thinking West have joined in a chorus warning mankind of the

---

12. Pitirim A. Sorokin, *The Crisis of Our Age*. Quoted by Khurshid Ahmed, *Ibid*.

futility and the impending disaster staring in the face of a material and materialistic civilisation. This is a warning strewn over the pages of the Qur'ān and I could well have cited some relevant verses to you. But I have, at this stage, deliberately refrained from doing so. I wanted you to hear some voices from *within* the Western fold itself, so that you and I might better understand that it is only distance and a superficial glance that lend enchantment to the view.

16. The modern West has had its chock full of material security and comfort. Its seemingly endless drive towards "a higher standard of living" (what a vulgar and barbarous phrase!) has only intensified its mental, emotional and spiritual insecurity. Happiness and fulfilment have been sacrificed at the altar of the gods of Wealth, Power and Sensual Pleasure. And the result of it all is clear for the perceptive eye to see : "meaninglessness in philosophy, insecurity in policy, exploitation in economy, immorality in society, distortion in art, frustration in literature, chaos in poetry"—knowledge running wild and gone amok for want of any moral moorings, innovation piled upon innovation for innovation's sake; "in short, supremacy of techniques but the eclipse of man".[13]

17. And now the wise men of the West would put a brake on this headlong plunge towards disaster. Staring over the edge of the precipice, they now call for an agonizing reappraisal of what *Prof. Conklin* terms as "the meaning of life, the nature of the world in which he (man) lives, and the kind of life he wants to live with his fellows".[14] What should these words mean, if they be not a reference to the *Religious Impulse* inherent in man, a call for a return to *Religion* ? For, *Religion*, in its most comprehensive sense (*Din* as it is called in Islamic terminology), "includes a world-vision (*Weltanschaung*), a daring belief, a set of absolute obligations; a range of imaginative,

13. Khurshid Ahmed, *Ibid.*

14. E. G. Conklin, *Man : Real and Ideal.* Quoted by Khurshid Ahmed, *Ibid.*

emotional and practical experience that is denied to the non-religious mind. It is an interpretation of the universe, of both Nature and History; it is an answer in ultimate terms to the torturing difficulties which we compendiously call the problems of life. And it is a *Way of Living* which, with that interpretation, is both noble and rational, both theoretical and practical. How theoretical it can be is evident from the volume and difficulty of theology. How practical it can be is evident from history."[15]

18. And talk of the historical role of *Religion*, consider what *H. G. Wells* wrote in his *Outlines of History* :

> "The over-riding forces that hitherto in the individual soul and in the community have struggled (against) and prevailed (over) the ferocious, base and individual impulses that divide us from one another, have been the powers of religion...Those clearly inter-twined influences have made possible the greater human societies...They have been the chief synthetic forces throughout this great story of human co-operation."[16]

Conclusion

19. And so, my friends, we could go on with our enquiry into that master question: *Why Religion ?* The deeper we go into it, the clearer comes the reply : the *Religious Impulse* is inherent in the nature of man. It is a universal, inextinguishable urge. What is more, all that has been fruitful and of abiding value in human civilisation has been the product of a *rational cultivation and an application in the concrete* of this *natural Religious Impulse.* A turning away from this impulse creates cruel contradictions in life and the ensuing pain, conflict, sorrow, confusion and chaos force a resurrection and resur-

15. Fazalur Rahman Ansari, *Foundations of Faith*, pp. 1-2. For an interesting collection of definitions of "religion", see : Pervez, *Op. cit.*, Chapter on "What is Religion?"

16. Ansari, *Ibid.*, p. 2.

gence of it. Far from being a dead or dying force, an anachronistic or antiquated thing — *Religion* is the crying need of our times and, hopefully, there are signs of the coming of what *Sorokin* called the great "Ideational culture of the creative tomorrow".

SELECTED BIBLIOGRAPHY

1. Marmaduke Pickthall, *The Meaning of the Glorious Qur'ān : Text and Explanatory Translation.* Accurate Printers, P.O. Box : 1338, Lahore.
2. *Mishkat al-Masabih,* Translation by Dr. James Robson. Sheikh Muhammad Ashraf, Kashmiri Bazar, Lahore.
3. G. A. Pervez, *Islam : A Challenge to Religion.* Idara Tulu-e-Islam, Lahore.
4. Mohammad Iqbal, *The Reconstruction of Religious Thought in Islam.* Sheikh Muhammad Ashraf, Kashmiri Bazar, Lahore.
5. Frieda Fordham, *An Introduction to the Psychology of C. G. Jung.* A Pelican Book.
6. Will and Ariel Durant, *The Lessons of History.* Simon and Schuster, New York.
7. Abul A'la Maududi, *The Ethical Viewpoint of Islam.* Translation by Professor Khurshid Ahmed, Islamic Publications, Lahore.
8. Dr. Fazalur Rahman Ansari, *Foundations of Faith.* World Council of Islamic Federations Publications, Nazimabad, Karachi.

THE RELIGIOUS IMPULSE

Passages from the Quran

(Ref. Page 2)

Allah ! There is no God save Him, the Alive, the Eternal. Neither slumber nor sleep overtaketh Him. Unto Him belongeth whatsoever is in the heavens and whatsoever is in the earth. Who is he that intercedeth with Him save by His leave ? He knoweth that which is in front of them and that which is behind them, while they encompass nothing of His knowledge save what He will. His throne includeth the heavens and the earth, and He is never weary of preserving them. He is the Sublime, the Tremendous. (2 : 255)

٢٥٥- اَللّٰهُ لَآ اِلٰهَ اِلَّا هُوَ ۚ
اَلْحَیُّ الْقَیُّوْمُ ۚ
لَا تَاْخُذُهٗ سِنَةٌ وَّلَا نَوْمٌ ؕ
لَهٗ مَا فِی السَّمٰوٰتِ وَمَا فِی الْاَرْضِ ؕ مَنْ
ذَا الَّذِیْ یَشْفَعُ عِنْدَهٗۤ اِلَّا بِاِذْنِهٖ ؕ
یَعْلَمُ مَا بَیْنَ اَیْدِیْهِمْ وَمَا خَلْفَهُمْ ۚ
وَلَا یُحِیْطُوْنَ بِشَیْءٍ مِّنْ عِلْمِهٖۤ
اِلَّا بِمَا شَآءَ ۚ
وَسِعَ كُرْسِیُّهُ السَّمٰوٰتِ وَالْاَرْضَ ۚ
وَلَا یَـُٔوْدُهٗ حِفْظُهُمَا ۚ
وَهُوَ الْعَلِیُّ الْعَظِیْمُ ○

Unto Allah belongs the East and the West, and whithersoever ye turn, there is Allah's Countenance. Lo ! Allah is All-Embracing, All-Knowing. (2 : 115)

١١٥- وَلِلّٰهِ الْمَشْرِقُ وَالْمَغْرِبُ ۗ
فَاَیْنَمَا تُوَلُّوْا فَثَمَّ وَجْهُ اللّٰهِ ؕ
اِنَّ اللّٰهَ وَاسِعٌ عَلِیْمٌ ○

(Ref. Page 5)

And be not ye as those who forget Allah, therefore He caused them to forget their souls. Such are the evil-doers. (59 : 19)

١٩- وَلَا تَكُوْنُوْا كَالَّذِیْنَ نَسُوا اللّٰهَ
فَاَنْسٰىهُمْ اَنْفُسَهُمْ ؕ
اُولٰٓئِكَ هُمُ الْفٰسِقُوْنَ ○

So, set thy purpose (O Muhammad) for religion as a man by nature upright—the nature (framed) of Allah, in which He had created man. There is no altering (the laws of) Allah's creation. That is the right religion, but most men know not. (30 : 30)

٣٠- فَاَقِمْ وَجْهَكَ لِلدِّیْنِ حَنِیْفًا ؕ
فِطْرَتَ اللّٰهِ الَّتِیْ فَطَرَ النَّاسَ عَلَیْهَا ؕ
لَا تَبْدِیْلَ لِخَلْقِ
اللّٰهِ ؕ ذٰلِكَ الدِّیْنُ الْقَیِّمُ ۙ
وَلٰكِنَّ اَكْثَرَ النَّاسِ لَا یَعْلَمُوْنَ ○

REASON, KNOWLEDGE AND FAITH

Introductory Remarks

1. I speak to you, my friends, as one of you, for all of us : a pilgrim among pilgrims in our quest of Islam. On our way to that vision and experience of Islam that we together seek, Knowledge has a crucial and indispensable role to play. And so, today, as a prelude to our enquiry into *Taqwa*, *Imān* and the Basic Attributes of a Muslim, we shall begin with that all-important subject of Reason, Knowledge and Faith. I consider this necessary because all that we shall inquire into in the subsequent talks hinges on the conclusions arrived at in this one on Reason, Knowledge and Faith : their nature, their inter-relationship, their scope, function and role in the shaping of a Muslim's comprehension and practice of Islam. Let us proceed.

Blind Faith : A Contradiction in Terms

2. How often, my friends, have we heard the phrase: "Blind Faith!" How often have we heard it asserted that Faith is a matter of acceptance without questioning, that Reason has no role to play in the acquisition of Faith. So much and so often have we heard this asserted, that many of us now take it for axiomatic that the highway of Faith runs a course which at its very start-point displays the sign in bold, block capitals : "*No reason beyond this point*!" And on the sign it is also written, cruelly in small print : "No knowledge either! All drivers to drive blind-folded!" Alas, here is the Autobahn of Faith, where the lower speed limit is 80 mph and the Military Police detachments, Allāh alone knows on Whose orders, thoughtlessly put up the thoughtless sign: "*No reason beyond this point*! *All drivers to drive blind-folded*!" Little wonder, then, that the Highway of Faith should be littered with fatal accidents : the odd, lucky

freak gets through; the many of mankind lie bleeding wrecks on the way-side. And 20th Century man, wise only in the ways of the world, shakes his head intellectually at this impossible poster, veers away into one or the other of the narrow, dusty lanes to the left or the right of the Autobahn of Faith. And then, they come to a dead end in the middle of a forest; night descends, and they are lost for ever. The alleys are choked, vehicles nose to tail, bumping into one another; and lo! the Highway of Faith: broad, clean, straight, bathed in light for those who have the courage to defy and disobey those thoughtless signs of those thoughtless Military Police detachments. But such men (so it would seem) are few; and lo! the Highway of Faith: empty, deserted, forlorn and forsaken, her lamps burning uselessly in the wilderness of the ignorant.

3. "Blind Faith", they say! Whoever heard of a more flagrant contradiction in terms? A little common sense, a little reflection, a little time to stop and think, a little Logic and Scientific Method however late in the day, and we would see that this ("Blind Faith") is a phrase which consists of two contradictory and mutually exclusive terms. Here is an idea ("Blind Faith") that is conceptually false; and being conceptually false, it cannot be actualised. Here is an idea as arbitrarily self-contradictory as: a "square circle", a "round triangle", "light-shedding darkness", "diseased health". The *blindness* of Ignorance lies at one end of the spectrum and the *vision* of Faith at the other end of the spectrum; and any effort to conjoin the two is a cruel, criminal negation of all knowledge. Blindness lies buried fathoms below the water-line at the base of the ice-berg and Faith is its very summit, the pinnacle bathed in sunlight. What ignorance or what absurd, perverse reasoning would conjoin the two? What worm at the base of the ice-berg would leap to the summit, in one blind leap? No, sir: Blindness is to Faith, as Squareness is to a Circle or Roundness to a Triangle; as Darkness is to Light, and Disease is to Health. These are contradictory, mutually exclusive

terms; they cannot co-exist. No, sir: there *is* no such thing (there is *no* such thing) as "Blind Faith".

4. And yet, some insist: "No, no, Abdul Qayyum. Don't be so emphatic! Be good! Let us compromise. Let us say there is *some* "blind faith"! Some? Well, then it must be like an army with its GHQ sent en-bloc on permanent leave, a formation without headquarters, a college without professors, a hospital without doctors, a 10-megaton atomic device without a trigger mechanism—as dead as the Dodo; as empty, barren, sterile, denuded of life as Death itself. Of what use is such a faith? It can work no wonders here; and in the Hereafter, the Lord will consign it to the dust-bin.

5. No, my friends, I submit that "Blind Faith" is a contradiction in terms; it is a meaningless, non-existent, un-real concept. It is the entry of this unreality into the Reality of Islam that is to my mind, the primary, the foremost cause of the decadence that we now see around us among the vast majority of the Islam-professing peoples. And, in Pakistan at least, we the so-called "educated" lay the burden of this guilt on the head of him whom we contemptuously and derogatorily designate as the "Mullah". How convenient! How very convenient!

6. But are we guiltless of the guilt that we so contemptuously dump on the Mullah's head? We rile at the Mullah and yet we are tied to his apron strings: not in the merriness of our daily lives but when crisis comes. Without the Maulvi Sahib coming to our rescue, we would be at a loss to conduct a marriage ceremony, to recite the *Adhān* in the ears of a newly-born child, to say the funeral prayer over a dear departed. Having missed our own education, we need him to teach our children how to read the Qur'ān and even the form of the canonical prayer. For us religion has become a matter of social convenience, conformity without conviction, intermittent observance divorced from the main-stream of life, an appendage that we cannot do without and yet are too indifferent to enquire into.

7. What a sorry state of affairs, my friends! And who is responsible, the Mullah or I and you—we? *We* have condemned the Mullah to the status of an ignorant *Padri* and *we* remain even more ignorant ourselves. We say we are Muslims. We say we follow a *Din* (a way of life) that makes no distinction between matters secular and matters religious, and yet we are the very ones to perpetrate and perpetuate this cruel dichotomy in our lives. And if some day (and I pray that that day may come soon) Allāh should give us the vision and the strength to close this yawning gap in our lives, this crevasse, this gash down the middle—we shall do so, using the Mullah as a bridge. For he, the Mullah, has kept at least the husk of Islam alive, and we (the so-called "educated") have neither husk nor substance. And if some day (and I pray that that day may come soon) we should get to the substance of Islam, we shall do so rising on the shoulders of the Mullah; and when we so scale the heights of Islam, Allāh knows, the shoulders that we step on and leave behind will not be without reward for that indispensable service that they perform. The keeper of the base is not any the humbler than the climber who climbs to the summit.

8. And how many are there among us who would really climb—to the summit? God has given us the gift of education, freedom from the grinding worry of unrequited basic material needs, better opportunities, better prospects in life. Shall we not use these to become Muslim soldiers, Muslim engineers, Muslim doctors, Muslim officers and Muslim *men*? Or shall we go the way of all flesh, and say Islam is not our profession ; we are only professional soldiers, engineers, doctors etc. If we, who have the gift of education, abandon Islam leaving it to the mercies of the ignorant, we shall not escape the bitter consequences of such a betrayal. If we abandon Islam, Allah will abandon us—as surely as night followeth day.

9. But if we should want to emerge from our long, long night towards the dawn of a new day, we the so-called educated must wash away the stains on our souls through a life-long

ablution in the waters of Islam. And having done that, we must don the mantle of Islam; we must resolutely wield the temporal power that comes to us to establish the Kingdom of God on earth : each one of us, within the radius of his own circle and the perimeters of his own God-given trust, a trust that some of us mistakenly call "my command". Not your "command", my friends, but your "trust"—a trust reposed in you by the Lord of all the worlds : a trust to be lived upto, *not* a command to be exercised.

10. But if from this trust we shy away, leaving the field to the ignorant, arrogant Bramble Bush, then our days are numbered regardless of our claims to distinction as Olive, Fig, Vine or Cedar tree. I refer you, my friends, to the parable of the trees in the Book of Judges in the Old Testament:

> Once upon a time the trees decided that they must appoint a king to rule over them. And so the delegation of the trees went to the *Olive Tree* and said : "O, Olive, come thou and rule over us ! " And the Olive replied : "What, shall I give up the oil wherewith men light the lamps in the temples, and come to be promoted over the trees ?"
>
> And so the delegation went to the *Fig Tree* and said : "O, Fig, come thou and rule over us ! " And the Fig tree replied : "What, shall I give up the sweetness of my fruit which feedeth man's hunger and come to be promoted over the trees? "
>
> And so the delegation went to the *Vine* and said : "O, Vine, come thou and rule over us !" And the Vine replied : "What, shall I throw away the nectar that they press out of me wherewith men quench their thirst and come to be promoted over the trees ?"
>
> And so, at last, the weary delegation went to the *Bramble Bush* and said : "O, Bramble Bush, come thou and reign over us !" And the Bramble Bush replied : "Indeed, indeed I shall come ! Indeed, if ye would

anoint me king over thee, then come: Place thy trust in my shade; and if ye do not, then let the fires issue forth from the Bramble Bush and devour the Cedars of Lebanon!"[1]

11. The message is clear, my friends. My plea, my appeal is to the Olive, the Fig, the Vine and the Cedars among us to come forth and don the mantle of Islam (*not* to shy away from it), so that we may all be saved from the fires of the Bramble Bush. And when I refer to the Olive, the Fig, the Vine and the Cedars among us, please note that being any one of these is not a function of age, length of service or rank but a matter of intrinsic human worth. My appeal is to the good and the competent among us, regardless of age or rank. It is we who must light within ourselves and then carry forth the torch of Islam—to the outermost limit of the radius of our circle. And it must be a radiant faith, an illumined and a luminous faith, a faith lit and aflame; *not* a dark, dusty, dingy faith, not an ignorant faith, not "Blind Faith".

12. "Blind Faith", I said, is a contradiction in terms, conceptually false and, therefore, incapable of actualisation. To this thesis we shall now turn for an examination-in-detail.

Reason and Faith

13. Faith is supra-rational; but it is *not* ir-rational. Reason and Faith are complementary, *not* contradictory. The correct application of Reason will, with God's grace, lead to a clear, sound, stable faith; admitted, that false and perverse reasoning will lead to a false and perverse faith or no faith at all.

14. The Rational Intellect cannot, of its own, discover what Revelation reveals. But the rational intellect can apprehend (directly perceive to some extent and logically infer the rest) the truths presented before it by Revelation. It can *a-Posteriori*

---

(1) *The Holy Bible*, Book of Judges; Chap. 9, Verses 8-15; pp. 294, 295. Free rendering.

grasp what Revelation *a-Priori* reveals.[2] Without Reason, Revelation cannot be apprehended; without Revelation, Reason cannot unveil the ultimate mysteries of life. Denied the faculty of reasoning, the beast cannot interpret the Revelation designed for human beings. For the beast, Instinct is enough for the conduct of life at the animal level; for man, the rational animal, Revelation is necessary for the conduct of life at the human level. Reason, interpreting Revelation, makes for humanity. Without the exercise of Reason, man remains on the level of the beast—unable to comprehend or indifferent to the value-structure relevant to man.

Through Reason to Faith

15. But because the Rational Intellect operates in "serial time" (the temporal sequence of Past, Present and Future), it cannot grasp in one go what Revelation, transcending serial time, instantly reveals.[3] In its effort to apprehend Revelation, the Rational Intellect proceeds haltingly, by stages, through a connected chain of reasoning: the familiar processes of Analysis, Synthesis and Evaluation. It strives to understand any given Revelation, to the extent it can, through a *tri-phase process* :

(*a*) Breaking up the whole of the Revelation into discrete components, and then studying these *individual components in isolation.*

(*b*) That done, it seeks to understand the *relationship between these components*, grouping allied components together into a coherent and smaller number of larger idea-packets.

(2) Parvez, *Islam: A Challenge to Religion.* See the Chapters on: "Divine Guidance", "Reason and Imān" and "Role of Reason in Din". Here is an elaboration of : Iqbal, *Reconstruction of Religious Thought in Islam.* Particularly see the portions on : Reason, Philosophy and Religion (pp. 112, 113); Finite and Ultimate Ego (pp. 126, 127); Religion and Science (pp. 127, 128); Human Ego: Freedom and Immortality (pp. 143-154).

(3) For a brief exposition of the concept of "time", See: Iqbal, *The Reconstruction of Religious Thought in Islam*, pp. 120-126.

(*c*) These fewer and larger idea-packets are then examined for an *identification of those Guiding Principles* which integrate the parts into the unity of the whole of that Revelation.

16. This tri-phase process enables the Rational Intellect to distinguish a "false" Revelation from a "true" one. It judges a particular Revelation (as a whole) as :

(*a*) "*False*". If the Guiding Principles do not appeal to Reason; or there appear a large number of inconsistencies in the individual components and their inter-relationship.

(*b*) "*True*". If the Guiding Principles are eminently rational, and the inconsistencies that appear in the individual components and their inter-relationship are either none or so few that these may be reasonably attributed to the feebleness, the incompleteness and the inadequacy of the Rational Intellect to independently grasp every detail of Revelation.

17. Once, however, the Rational Intellect has brought the human mind to this point of judgement, rejecting several systems and accepting one (as a whole), the further function of the Rational Intellect legitimately narrows down to an effort at understanding (*Not* questioning) those individual components and their inter-relationship where its comprehension was previously perceived to be inadequate or incomplete. There are, then, two clear phases in this process of acquiring faith :

(*a*) *Phase* 1. Decision-making with regard to a revealed system (as a whole): a progressive and eventually massive negation of *All* ("La ilaha"), followed by a full and unconditional acceptance of *One* ("illa Allah"). The attitude of mind necessary for this phase of the operation is one of *Vigorous Questioning*.

(*b*) *Phase* 2. Personal clarification of the accepted system : reducing the areas or points of inadequate comprehension. The attitude of mind necessary for this phase of the operation is a vigorous, passionate, prayerful attempt at *Understanding*—understanding with a view to eliminating the part-shadowlands that persist, *not* questioning what has already been vigorously questioned and fully accepted as a whole.

18. *Phase* 1 completed in the full light of rational consciousness, marks the *beginning of Faith*; *Phase* 2 pertains to the *consolidation and expansion* of the Faith already acquired in Phase 1. Phase 1 is the "assault crossing across the obstacle" of Human Understanding; Phase 2 is the "consolidation in the bridgehead" (01-03 line) and the subsequent "break-out" into the realm of Faith. Without Phase 1, Phase 2 cannot begin; the more conscious, deliberate, meticulous the crossing in Phase 1, the easier is the task of consolidation and expansion in Phase 2. And the eventual quality of the Faith attained depends on the quality of the consolidation in Phase 2: "consolidation" (clarification, deepening, strengthening, fortification, expansion), in which acts of obedience to His commandments, even in the face of partial understanding or doubt, has a "revealing" role to play.

Agreed Premises, Contrary Conclusions

19. Please note that in this march towards the initial acquisition and the subsequent perfection of Faith, the exercise of the Rational Intellect is indispensable. The supra-rational leap into Faith can be meaningful, valid and assured of increasing certainty, only when it proceeds from an adequate base of conscious reasoning. The Spirit cannot clearly and perspicuously behold a truth without some preliminary "staff work" having been done on it by the faculty of Reason. This is true of the vast, vast majority of us—a rule which we cannot but the more assiduously observe when we consider the exception: the Prophets. Infallible, a-priori, supra-rational reception of the Truth and perception of the Reality are an exclusive privilege of the Prophet. To him, Revelation reveals in a flash, through

an act of Divine grace, truths which the mind of ordinary man cannot by personal exertion discover. What is more, the Rational Intellect's a-posteriori understanding of these revealed truths can never match the felicity of the Prophet's understanding of them, because he has, so to say, "beheld" (directly perceived) what, in our case, can only be indirectly "inferred". These are, by and large, agreed premises; and yet, I draw from them conclusions quite the opposite of what the votaries of "blind faith" advocate. I proceed as follows :

(*a*) The absolute certainty of the Prophet's faith is a product (or corollary) of his absolute knowledge.[4]

---

(4) I would define "Knowledge" as the clear and perspicuous understanding of that way of life (*Din*) which enables the human spirit to so conduct its life Here in this world as to successfully transcend the shock of Death, leading it on to a higher state of existence (ascending and unceasing bliss) in the eternal Hereafter.

For an interesting and educative discourse on the subject, see : *Great Books of the Western World*, Vol. 2, p. 377. Knowledge is not "secular" learning, but understanding life in its totality (Here + Hereafter), unravelling the secrets of life with reference to fundamental questions of human destiny. In this context, consider the following excerpt from the "Great Books" :

"One opinion from which there is hardly a dissenting voice in the great books is that education should aim to make men good as men and as citizens ..Thus it would seem to be a common opinion in all ages that education should seek to develop the characteristic excellences of which men are capable and that its ultimate ends are human happiness and the welfare of society....If happiness cannot be fully achieved on earth, then whatever temporal ends education serves must themselves be ordered to eternal salvation, and the whole process of human development must be a direction of the soul towards God. 'What did it profit me,' *Augustine* asks in his *Confessions*, 'that all the books I could procure of the so-called liberal arts, I, the vile slave of vile affections, read by myself and understood?....For I had my back to the light, and my face to the things enlightened; whence my face, with which I discerned the things enlightened, was not itself enlightened. Whatever was written, either on rhetoric or logic, geometry, music and arithmetic,

[*contd. on p.* 23

(*b*) Though we shall never attain this level of Knowledge and Faith (because we are *not* prophets), the same relationship and ratio between these two elements hold good in our case also.

(*c*) The clearer our Understanding, the firmer will our Faith be. In proportion as we understand, so shall we believe.

(*d*) Now, given Divine Revelation, there is no gap to be bridged between prophetic Understanding and prophetic Faith. Total understanding leads to instant and total faith. In the case of the Prophet, then, there is no passage from Understanding to Faith. There is no "leap" to be taken from the one to the other; the two occur instantly, simultaneously; they coincide.

(*e*) In our case, however, denied prophetic revelation and with only the ordinary intellect to go by, there is a gap between our Understanding and our Faith. This gap, the product of incomplete undertanding, has to be bridged by what logicians call the "Inferential Leap" and we may call the "Leap of Faith".

(*f*) Now, it is obvious that the narrower this gap and the shorter this leap from understanding on the "home bank" (rational perception), the firmer and surer will our landing be on the "far bank" (Supra-rational perception) of Faith.

---

contd. from p. 22]
by myself without much difficulty or any instructor, I understood, Thou knowest, O Lord my God; because both quickness of understanding and acuteness in discerning is Thy gift; yet did I not then sacrifice to Thee.' Wherefore, Augustine concludes concerning this stage of his learning, 'it served not to my use but to my perdition.'. . . ."

Also see: Abu Bakr Kalabadhi, *Doctrine of the Sufis*. Kalabadhi quotes Al-Jonaid of Baghdad: "*Taubah* implies that you should be unto Him a face without a back, even as you have so long been to Him a back without a face."

Cf. Plato's parable of the Cave. See: Bertrand Russell, *History of Western Philosphy*, Chapter on "Plato".

20. What does all this add up to? Simply this :

(*a*) For the human mind (Prophets excluded), the exercise of the Rational Intellect is necessary for the acquisition of Faith. Its function, however, is preliminary : restricted to preparing the mind and narrowing the gap antecedent to the leap of faith. It has also a consolidating function: clarifying, deepening and fortifying Faith subsequent to the leap.

(*b*) For the human mind (Prophets excluded):
Reason + *Knowledge* = *Faith*
For the Prophet, the equation is :
Knowledge (absolute) = *Faith* (absolute).

(*c*) For the human mind (Prophets excluded), the element of the "unknown" (in the Prophet there is *no* unknown) in *Faith* cannot be meaningfully asserted as having been perceived, unless the individual making the assertion can trace its roots to some "Knowns" in the ground of his personal reflection and experience.

(*d*) Where no such link or circuit can be traced, the assertion "I believe" is either a lie or wishful thinking, meaning in actual fact no more than: "I am merely stating what someone else believes or has asked me to believe." Where is the "I" in this "I believe"? In this declaration of Faith, the "I" is missing. Beyond the verbal proclamation, there is no substance in this faith; and lacking the substance, it does not merit the nomenclature.

(*e*) Finally, I repeat: the clearer our Understanding, the firmer will our Faith be. In proportion as we understand, so shall we believe.

Three Vexing Questions

21. Having said what I have said so far, I now turn to three questions (pertaining to Reason, Knowledge and Faith) which have long vexed my mind and which may be vexing some of

your minds also. I shall take them one by one, presenting before you my answer to them. I wish, however, to make it clear that I claim neither completeness nor infallibility for these answers—not even for myself and, therefore, even less for you. They represent my understanding of these issues within my painfully restricted study of the Qur'ān as of today; but on the Qur'ān they are based, not gossamers spun out of the store-house of my own fancy. On to these questions then and my answers to them, for you to ponder and reflect on.

The First Question

22. I formulate the first question as under :

"Is Faith, then, the prerogative only of the learned? Have those who are of limited intellectual capacity no access to Faith?"

23. In this context, please consider :

(*a*) Those who pose this question, wrongly assume that Faith is a possession that one either has or does not have; that it is either there or not there.

(*b*) They forget that Faith, and its opposite doubt/unbelief, are present in all men (Prophets excluded) in varying degrees in relation to both quality and magnitude. What is more, even in a single individual Faith is a dynamic element, increasing or decreasing proportionate to variations in three parameters :

(1) Knowledge or Understanding.

(2) Acts of obedience.

(3) Divine Grace (which is, more often than not, though not always, a product of the first two factors).

(*c*) It is clear that, the other factors remaining constant (in both quality and magnitude), an increase in Knowledge or Understanding will lead to a corresponding increase in Faith. What is more, this Understanding has a direct bearing on the quality (and even the quantity) of the acts of obedience performed in the external world.

(*d*) Understanding, then, is the primary source of Faith—illuminating (adding meaning and significance) to our acts of obedience, and preparing our individual receptacles for the receipt (acceptance) of Divine Grace.

24. The conclusions, then, are clear :

(*a*) Faith is a quality open to all, the learned and the ignorant both. None is barred from Faith.

(*b*) But, in quality and magnitude, the faith of the ignorant man is not the same as that of the man of Knowledge (who combines understanding with acts of obedience). And more often than not, it is men of the second category who become the recipients of Divine Grace.

(*c*) As we ascend the ladder of Knowledge (Understanding plus Acts of Obedience), we ascend the ladder of Faith. By degrees we ascend, through shades of decreasing darkness till we reach a rung that merits the name of Light; and thence we continue to ascend, through shades of increasing light in an endless climb to the top which is the exclusive station of the prophets. Not equal is the faith of the ignorant man standing in the darkness of the bottom rung of the ladder and the Prophet standing in the full blaze of the top rung. Those who find themselves in the lower half of the ladder (below the rung of Light) have their faith veiled by varying layers of darkness; those who find themselves in the upper half of the ladder (above the rung of "Light") attain a faith that is veiled by varying layers of light. None but the Prophet reaches the blaze at the top; but not equal is the faith of those who stand in the lower half, thinking they have Faith; and those who stand in the upper half, weeping that they have not Faith enough. Not equal is the faith of the confident fool and the frightened seer.

(*d*) I believe, yes, I believe ! But is my faith the same as that of Abū Bakr, 'Umar, 'Uthmān, 'Ali? I believe; yes, I believe! But is my faith the same as that of Ṭalḥa, Az-Ẓubair, Abd ar-Raḥmān bin Auf, S'ad bin Abu Waqqāṣ, Said bin Zaid, Abū Ubaida bin al-Jarrah, Zaid bin Thābit, Ubayy bin Ka'b, Muadh bin Jabal? I believe; yes, I believe! But is my faith the same as that of Abū Hanifah, Al-Shāfi'i, Mālik, Aḥmad Ibn Hanbal, Sufyān al-Thawri? I believe; yes, I believe! But is my faith the same as that of Al-Ghazzali, Ibn Taimiyyah, Shah Waliullah, Shaikh Ahmad of Sirhind, 'Umar Ibn Abd al-'Aziz ; Bukhāri, Muslim, Abū Dāwud, Tirmidhi, Ibn Mājah; or even a Maududi or a Frithjof Schuon?

(*e*) What are talking about, my friends? Faith is indeed open to all; but not equal is the faith of all. In proportion as we know (Knowledge = Understanding + Acts of Obedience), so shall we believe. Knowledge and Faith are inextricably inter-linked. "Blind Faith" is a contradiction in terms.

25. In this context of the role of the Intellect in the acquisition of Knowledge, and the role of Knowledge in the acquisition of Faith, permit me to read out to you some selected excerpts from Section VII of Imām Ghazzali's *Al-Kitāb al-Ilm* (which is Vol I of his 40 volume masterpiece entitled the *Ihya Ulum al-Din*) :

(*a*) "Intellect is the source and fountainhead"...(p. 221).

(*b*) "The first thing that God created was the intellect . . ."(p. 222).

(*c*) " Thereupon the Prophet said: 'What kind of intellect hath that man?'. . . " (p. 223).

(*d*) "Man doth not gain anything like a worthy intellect . . .". "For everything there is a support. . ." (*Ibid.*)

(*e*) "For everything there is an instrument and a tool. . ." (p. 225).

(*f*) 'Ā'isha asked: 'O Apostle of God! wherein do people excel . . ." (p. 224).

(*g*) "In other words, every human being is created and born a believer. . ." (p. 230). "These facts are evident . . . the relation between insight and sight is evident." (p. 231).

26. So much for the nature, quality and quantum of Faith as it varies from man to man on the Scale of Knowledge :[5] from the Zero of Ignorance at one end to the human infinity of Prophetic insight at the other end of the scale.

The Second Question

27. We turn now to the next question that vexes the mind :

"If my faith is proportionate to the intellect that God has

---

(5) On praiseworthy and objectionable branches of knowledge, see: Ghazzali, *The Book of Knowledge*, as under :

(*a*) Knowledge that is Farḍ 'Ayn (pp. 30-36).

(*b*) Knowledge that is Farḍ Kifaya (pp. 36-79).

(*c*) Limits of praiseworthy knowledge and degrees of acquisition (pp. 98-107).

(*d*) Debate and Disputation (pp. 110-117).

(*e*) Envy, Pride, Rancour, Back-biting, Self-Justification, Peeping-Tommery, Deception, Contentiousness, Hypocrisy and allied vices (pp. 118-123).

(*f*) Characteristics of learned men (pp. 124, 125).

(*g*) The Good Student (pp. 126-144); The Good Teacher (pp. 144-153).

(*h*) *The truly learned and the teachers of falsehood* (pp. 154-220): General (154-165); No disparity between word and action (165-170); Seeking useful knowledge (170-173); Austerity (173-179); Shunning authority/powers temporal (179-183); Deliberation, Circumspection (183-188); Seeking the substance (188-191); Increasing Faith (192-200); Lowliness (200, 201); Five qualities en-bloc (204, 205); Practical-religion orientation (205-208); Insight (209-212); Shunning innovation (212-219); Seclusion and Solitude (219, 220).

given me, is it my fault that I remain I and Ghazzali becomes Ghazzali? How am I to compensate for this handicap that is God-given; how am I to compete with Ghazzali? This is, from the word "go", unequal combat; and the issue is foreclosed. Why should faith and salvation be more Ghazzali's than mine, when the creator of the difference is not me?"

28. The answer to that question is simply this:

(*a*) Indeed, my potential for faith is proportionate to the intellectual potential that God has given me. Indeed, I cannot grow beyond my potential; I cannot be more than myself. Precisely for this reason, I do not have to compete with Ghazzali.

(*b*) But, I certainly have to compete with myself, Actualisation competing with Potentiality, till I am all that I can be with regard to both Knowledge and Faith. If in me, Actualisation = Potentiality, I am through. More I cannot become; and more the Lord does not demand of me.

(*c*) Let me illustrate the point through a hypothetical example. Allāh alone knows what potential He gave Ghazzali and how much of it Ghazzali actualised. For purposes of illustration, let us assume that Allāh gave Ghazzali 1,000 units of potential of which he actualised 995. Let us assume that Allāh has given me 10 units of potential and I actualise 10 by the day I die—that day stretched to the farthest end of the moment that I die.

(*d*) If this be the comparative situation on the Day of Judgement when Ghazzali and I stand before the Lord, I am through with my 10/10, while Ghazzali with his 995/1000 must stand back before the Lord to render account of the 5 units of unactualised potential.

(*e*) There you have a hypothetical illustration of a Divine Law that the Qur'ān proclaims at numerous places in its text. The judgement of the Lord proceeds on the basis of ratio and proportion, not in terms of the absolute (Ghazzali's massive 995, my tottering 10). "On no soul doth God lay a burden greater than it can bear; each gets what it earns . . ." And since "no burden-bearer can bear the burden of another", "ranged in tiers as we are (in terms of potential) one above the other", it remains for me to actualise my potential and for Ghazzali to actualize his. In matters of Faith and salvation in the Hereafter (as in all other matters of life), there is no competition between the one and the other of us; each competes with himelf : a life-long struggle within the individual soul betwen the two poles of Potentiality and Actualisation, till the two do coincide.

29. This is my answer to that second vexing question, within the limits of my present understanding of the Qur'ān. And Allāh knows best !

The Third Question

30. But even if we were to assume these two questions as having been answered with an acceptable measure of immediate satisfaction, another painful question rears its head. I say: "Fine, so far so good! But how am I to know what my potential is ? So often I say to myself : this is my limit ; more I cannot. This far I have come; farther I cannot go. Am I right in my assessment of myself ? How am I to know ? Tell me, tell me— so that I do not uselessly strive trying to attain what lies beyond me !"

31. The answer to that question, within the bounds of my present understanding, seems to be this :

(*a*) Indeed, we have no means, this side of the Hereafter, of knowing exactly what our potential is beyond the general notion that having been born as human beings we have the potential for humanity. To this extent we are circumscribed : that we cannot become jinns or angels, any more than a plant can grow into a human being or the egg of a fish develop into a bird that glides through the air.

(*b*) Our General Potential is known; but as individual members of the species to which we belong, we also have a Specific Potential. What this potential is we may guess, though none but God knows. Each one of us is circumscribed by this (to us) unknown Specific Potential and none can grow beyond himself, any more than a banana-sapling can grow into an oak or a Kikar seed into a Poplar, a Cedar or a Cypress.

(*c*) Such being the nature of our limited Specific Potential and our human ignorance of its actual dimensions, the only sensible course open to us is to stop worrying about what we shall grow into and instead concentrate on just growing : as purposefully, as firmly, as beautifully as we possibly can. Just as it is the business of every banana-sapling to strive to grow into the finest fruit-laden banana tree anywhere around in the countryside, regardless of what the oak, the poplar, the cedar and the cypress are doing or not doing—so also, it is incumbent on each one of us to actualise his Specific Potential regardless of its poverty or otherwise in relation to others.

(*d*) In this single-minded drive towards the actualisation of our Specific Potential, we need to bear in mind that antecedent to actualisation we have no means of judging what lies dormant in our God-given potential. Not only do we not know what we are : banana-sapling, cedar or poplar seed ; we do not even know how fruitful big, strong or beautiful we can be. Not only the nature but also the limits of our Specific Potential remain unknown to us. As we keep actualizing our potential in serial time, the unalterable past defines the quantum of potential so far actualised but even this does not provide us with adequate data for any reliable evaluation of how much could have been actualised. The totality of our Specific Potential being unknown and even the unalterable past eluding evaluation in terms of Potential and Actualisation, we are in no position to determine what remains hidden in the womb of the future : how much of our Specific Potential still remains to be actualised, and how much of this that remains will be actualised.

(*e*) For every individual, the Term for the actualisation of his Specific Potential is the life-span granted to him by the Lord. The Potential is circumscribed, as also the Term; but within these limits, which are there regardless of our inability to define or de-limit their boundaries, we are free to become what we will : our actualisation falling drastically short of potential ; or getting very close to it; or in the case of the blessed, victorious few, actualsiation equalling or over-lapping potential. There is, of course, none who can go beyond his potential.

(*f*) This, to my mind, is the true meaning of that popularly misunderstood word: *Kismet. Kismet* is not a pre-ordained course of events in the life of an individual with their corresponding notes of a sealed, unalterable measure of success or failure; nor is man a helpless projectionist unreeling in serial time a life-film processed in the pre-eternal laboratory of the Lord. *Kismet* is indeed a Divine definition of limits with regard to both Potential and its allotted Term for actualisation. *Kismet* limits what we can be; it does not determine what we will be (within the limits of what we can be).

(*g*) It is another matter that in the transcendental knowledge of the Lord—an omniscience that does not suffer from our serial fragmentation of time into Past, Present and Future—our lives are indeed a closed book, all "recorded in a clear register". He knows not only what our Potential (*Kismet*) is, but also how and how much of it we will actualize. This is an aspect of His Omniscience, His transcendental knowledge; but there is no compulsion imposed on how and what we make of our potential. It is as if the Lord sent us into the bazaar of life : some with 10 paisas, some with 100, others with more or less. To all He also gave guidance on how to spend this amount. And so we entered the bazaar of life, each with his specific sum, free to spend and buy as we will—in accordance or contrary to His instructions, as we will. But at sun-down, when the bazaar is closed, we return to render account : each of the sum granted to each.[6] And this account-taking is for our benefit, not His; for He knew at sun-rise what sun-set would bring. But we did not. On that Day of Final Accounting we shall clearly know what our Potential was and what we made of it. On that day our knowledge of ourselves will equal His; on that day we shall be to ourselves the closed book that we have always been to Him.

(*h*) This, then, is the state of affairs that we find ourselves in. This side of the Hereafter, we have no means of knowing what our Potential is and what the Term fixed for its actualisation. We only know that within the perimeters of this *Kismet* we are free to make of

---

(6) Mian Muhammad of Mirpur (Kharri Sharif), *Saiful Maluk*. Consider the following couplet :

"Loey loey bhar laiy kuriey, jay tu bhanda bharna;
Sham pai bin Sham Muhammad, ghar jandi nay darna."

In this context, also consider the story of "Marshal Layautey's tree", *Great Books of the Western World*, Volume 1.

ourselves what we will. The maximum radius of our circle is fixed; the question posed to us, with decision left to us, is whether we will or will not stretch our compass to the full.

(*j*) For practical purposes, the dilemma of Potential vs. Actualisation is resolved (even in the face of our ignorance of the nature and limits of our Specific Potential) when, from the cradle to the grave, we stoutly refuse to yield to the assertion: "This is my limit; this is my ceiling. Farther I cannot go; higher I cannot rise." Indeed, such an assertion would be logically false on two decisive counts :

(1) Not knowing the limits of our potential, we cannot at any stage assert that we have reached our limits.

(2) Since the Term for the actualisation of Specific Potential is the total life-span granted to an individual, it would obviously be premature to assert the end as having been attained prior to the expiry of the Term fixed for the purpose.

(*k*) In the conduct of life, then, this side of the Hereafter, we may presume with fair assurance that we are actualizing our Potential, only (and only) when we are engaged in an unbroken, uninterrupted, continuous, unflagging, relentless drive towards perfection till death overtakes us in the process.[7] When the

---

(7) Mian Muhammad of Mirpur, *Saiful Maluk*. Consider the following couplet:

"Mali da kum pani dena, bhar bhar mashkan pavey;
Malik da kum phal phul laona,
Lavey ya na lavey!"

In this context, read that beautiful parable on striving towards perfection: Richard Bach, *Jonathan Livingstone Seagull*. It is a book well under 100 pages, almost one quarter of them being photographs capturing the saga of striving towards perfection.

individual cord of life, so stretched, snaps at last at the moment of death, our individual soul can with peace pray :

> "Lord! This is the Term you granted me. Within this term, I have stretched myself as far and as much as I knew how—as truthfully, as resolutely, as beautifully as I knew how. Lord! If aught yet remains of Potential unactualised, forgive me this failure to measure up to the Design that you designed for me. Lo! This is the *Kismet* that I have fashioned for myself; and whatever its worth, I lay this now with trembling hands a humble offering placed at Thy feet. Accept, O Lord, this life-time of striving in Your way; wipe out its flaws; blot out its iniquities! Lift me up, clasp me to Your bosom; cover me with Your grace and mercy! Lo, Thou art the Oft-Returning, the Most Forgiving, the Most Merciful, Lord of Bounties Unbounded! Lo! Thou art able to do all things! Accept, O Lord, accept . . . [8]

32. This much each one of us may do with regard to Potential and Actualisation; whoever does less has only himself to blame. What is our responsibility we cannot palm off to God; what is our failure we cannot ascribe to *Kismet*.

In a Nut-Shell: Six points

33. This discourse, Gentlemen, has dragged itself out longer

(8) Consider the following lines from Tagore, *Gitanjali* :

"Like a rain-cloud of July hung low with its burden of unshed showers, let all my mind bend down at Thy door in one salutation to Thee.

Let all my songs gather together their diverse strains into a single current and flow to a sea of silence in one salutation to Thee.

Like a flock of homesick cranes, flying night and day back to their mountain nest, let all my life take its voyage to its eternal home in one salutation to Thee."

than. I intended it to be. What I wanted to say, in a nut-shell, was this:

(*a*) That "Blind Faith" is a contradiction in terms; that Knowledge is necessary for the acquisition of Faith; that the clearer our Understanding, the firmer will our Faith be; that in proportion as understand, so shall we believe.

(*b*) That Knowledge has two components :

(1) Rational understanding of the *Din* (the revealed way of life).

(2) Devoted performance of the prescribed acts of obedience (regardless of the shadow-lands in our understanding of them at any given stage).

(*c*) That we ascend the ladder of Faith, as we ascend the ladder of Knowledge—through shades of decreasing darkness and increasing light.

(*d*) That Faith is indeed open to all, but not equal is the faith of all. Not equal is the faith of those who stand on the lower rungs of the ladder thinking they have faith and those who stand on the upper rungs weeping that they do not have faith enough. Not equal is the faith of the confident fool and the frightened seer.

(*e*) That in matters of faith and salvation in the Hereafter (as indeed in every other aspect of our life) there is no competition between the one and the other of us. Each competes with himself : a life-long struggle within the individual soul between the two poles of Potentitality and Actualisation, till the two do coincide.

(*f*) That as individual members of the human race each one of us has a divinely circumscribed Specific Potential, with a pre-ordained or fixed Term (the life-span allotted to each individual) for its actualisation; that this side of the Hereafter, we have no means of knowing either the nature or the limits of this potential; that the best that we can do is to engage ourselves in an unbroken, uninterrupted, continuous, relentless drive towards perfection till death overtakes us in the process; that if aught should yet remain of Potential unactualised, we can only cry out to the Lord seeking forgiveness; that having tried, we may peacefully leave the rest to the Lord of Bounties Unbounded.

Concluding Remarks

34. These, then, were the salient features of this grossly inadequate discourse on "Reason, Knowledge and Faith". I say again, that these personal perceptions lie within the perimeters of my painfully limited understanding of the Qur'ān as of today. Logically, I claim for these views neither completeness nor infallibility—either for myself or for you. In this great voyage of discovery towards the shores of the Faith that we all seek, we remain essentially alone, each his own mariner. And as we sail the high seas, acting as we should, the rest in prayer :

(*a*) "I seek refuge in Allāh from this : that I should be counted among the ignorant."

(*b*) "My Lord ! Leave me not alone to myself (forsake me not). Lo! Thou art the best of Protective Guardians."

(*c*) "My Lord! Expand my breast. Ease for me this task undertaken...
My Lord! Increase me in knowledge."

(*d*) "My Lord !
Let my entry be through the Gate of Truth and Honour;
And (likewise) let my exit be through the Gate of Truth and Honour;
And grant Thou me, from Thy presence,
A power to aid me."

(*e*) "Our Lord !

Cause not our hearts to deviate,
Once Thou hast guided us aright;
And grant us mercy from Thy presence.
Lo! Thou, only Thou art,
The Giver Unlimited."

(*f*) "Our Lord !
Perfect for us our light;
And grant us forgiveness.
Lo ! Thou art able to do all things."

(*g*) "There is no god but Thou;
Exalted be Thy Person;
Lo! I am of those that have transgressed Thy limits."

(*h*) "Lord ! Forgive and have mercy.
Lo! Thou art the Best of the Merciful."

(*j*) "Lord ! Thou knowest what I conceal and what I openly show; and there is naught on earth or in the heavens that is hidden from Allāh. Our Lord! We have transgressed against our souls; and if Thou forgive us not and have mercy, without doubt we are of those condemned."

(*k*) "Our Lord !
Condemn us not if we forget,
Or miss the mark.
Our Lord !
Lay not on us a burden such as Thou didst lay on those before us!
Our Lord!
Lay not on us a burden greater than we can bear !
Pardon us; absolve us; and have mercy on us !
Thou, our Protector,
And give us victory over those that reject Thee."

(*l*) "Our Lord !
Accept from us this act (of prayer and service performed),

Lo ! Thou art the All-Hearing, All-Knowing !
Our Lord!
Make of us Muslims (a people bowing to Thy Will),
And of our progeny a people Muslim (bowing to Thy Will).
And show us our ways to prayer and sacrifice;
And turn to us (in forgiveness);
Lo! Thou art the Oft-Forgiving, the Most Merciful!"

SELECTED BIBLIOGRAPHY

1. Marmaduke Pickthall, *The Meaning of the Glorious Qur'ān: Text and Explanatory Translation.* Accurate Printers, Urdu Bazar, Post Box, 1338, Lahore-2.
2. Abdullah Yusaf Ali, *The Holy Qur'ān: Text, Translation and Commentary.* Sheikh Muhammad Ashraf, Kashmiri Bazar, Lahore.
3. Abul Ala Maududi, *Tafheemul Qur'ān* (*The Meaning of the Qur'ān*). Translation by Chaudhry Mohammad Akbar. Islamic Publications, Lahore.
4. *The Holy Bible* (*Containing the Old and New Testaments*). British and Foreign Bible Society, London, 1611 (Eyre and Spottiswoode Ltd).
5. G. A. Parvez, *Islam : A Challenge to Religion.* Idara-e-Islam, Gulberg, Lahore.
6. *Great Books of the Western World,* Encyclopaedia Britannica Inc, Chicago (Private Library Edition).
7. Abu Bakr Kalabadhi, *Doctrine of the Sufis.* Translation by A. J. Arberry. Sheikh Muhammad Ashraf, Kashmiri Bazar, Lahore.
8. Bertrand Russell, *History of Western Philosophy.* George Allen and Unwin Ltd, London).
9. Al-Ghazzali, *al-Kitāb al-Ilm* (*Vol. 1 of Ihya Ulum al-Din*). Translation (*The Book of Knowledge*) by Nabih Amin Faris. Sheikh Muhammad Ashraf, Kashmiri Bazar, Lahore.
10. Mian Muhammad of Mirpur (Kharri Sharif), *Saiful Maluk.* As recited to me by Lt.-Col. Muhammad Aslam (Arty) and Lt.-Col. Mazhar-ul-Haq (Baluch) !
11. Richard Bach, *Jonathan Livingstone Seagull.*
12. Rabindra Nath Tagore, *Gitanjali.* Translation (into English) by Tagore. Macmillan and Co. Ltd, Calcutta.
13. Muhammad Iqbal, *The Reconstruction of Religious Thought in Islam.* Sheikh Muhammad Ashraf, Kashmiri Bazar, Lahore.

TAQWA (GOD-CONSCIOUSNESS)

The First Pre-Requisite

1. "This is the Book whereof (and wherein) there is no doubt, a guidance for the God-fearing (those who ward off evil).."[1] (*Quran*, 2 : 2)

2. The first step on the way to becoming a Muslim is to read and understand the Quran, to obtain Guidance from the Quran for the shaping of one's inner life and conduct in the external world. And the first requirement, the most fundamental

---

(1) The term Muttaqi is variously translated: by *Abul Ala Maududi*, as "the God-fearing"; by *Marmaduke Pickthall*, as "those who ward off (evil)"; by *Abdullah Yusuf Ali*, as "those who fear Allah". Its connotation includes piety, righteous conduct, keeping one's duty towards God. Whatever the specific translation in a specific context, the spring from which Taqwa springs is that universal God-consciousness to which a reference was made in the talk on *The Religious Impulse* (*p.* 5, *para* 10). The intensity of this consciousness determines the intensity of our fear and love of God, our resolve and capacity to ward off evil, to practise virtue, to guard our duty towards God, to abide by His commandments. "God-consciousness", so it seems to me, is the most comprehensive English term for the many nuances of meaning implied in the term Taqwa. I have proceeded from the standard translations, keeping strictly on the rails of the Quran, and eventually arrived at this definition of Taqwa: "God-consciousness, which maturing into God-awareness, progressively spills over as God-oriented action in the external world." (*Synopsis, para* 1). This definition, I think captures not only the spirit of Taqwa but also the process by which it develops, both in the inner world of man as also in his external conduct. I have recently come across an English translation of the Quran by *Abdul Hamid Siddiqui* (translation still in progress) in which he renders the word "Muttaqi" directly as "the God-conscious".

pre-requisite, for those who want to obtain guidance from the Quran is Taqwa: the fear of God, which the writer of the Proverbs in the Old Testament calls the "beginning of wisdom".[2]

The Quality of Fear Implied in Taqwa

3. To obtain guidance from the Quran, we must approach it in the spirit of the Muttaqi—a man whose mind and soul are suffused with Taqwa: the fear of God. This "fear" is not a paralysing dread in the negative sense of the term; it is not the sort of fear that causes man to run away from the object of his fear. On the contrary, Taqwa binds man to God. It is the fear of offending Him or doing anything that will forfeit His good pleasure. It is a state of mind with an intense desire to discriminate between good and evil, and then to practise virtue. Taqwa, the fear of God, implies not merely the rejection of evil but also the hugging of the good. It is refraining from evil (the consequence of which is the displeasure of God), as a stepping stone to the performance of good deeds (the consequence of which is the pleasure of God). It is the "fear" of the righteous, the one fear that drives away all other fears. It is the fear of the man who hears deep within him the call of the Lord: "Fear them not but fear Me, so that I may complete My grace upon you, and that ye may be guided aright." (*Quran*, 2 : 150). It is the fear of the man who, having heard that call, goes on to seek His grace and His guidance—through study,

---

(2) *The Holy Bible.* The Proverbs:

(*a*) "The fear of the Lord is the beginning of knowledge; but fools despise wisdom and instruction." (1 : 7).

(*b*) "The fear of the Lord is to hate evil : pride and arrogancy and the evil way; and the forward mouth do I hate." (8 : 13) "I love them that love me; and those that seek Me early shall find Me." (8 : 17).

(*c*) "The fear of the Lord is the beginning of wisdom; and the knowledge of the holy is understanding." (8 : 10).

understanding of and reflection on His book, and conduct in accordance with its tenets. The Muttaqi is a man restlessly in search of the truth; a man intensely anxious to distinguish right from wrong, to discriminate between good and evil; a man with an innate propensity to run away from sin towards virtue, the moment discrimination is granted to him. For such a man, the Muttaqi (the man of Taqwa), there is guidance in the Quran.[3] Driven by the fear of the displeasure of God (the consequence of evil conduct) and drawn by the prospect of gaining His pleasure (the consequence of good conduct), the Muttaqi turns his countenance full square towards God; and his one fear leads him eventually to total fearlessness: "Nay, whosoever surrendereth his purpose to Allah while doing good, his reward is with His Lord; and there shall no fear come upon them, neither shall they grieve". (*Quran*, 2 : 112). The Muttaqi, fearing God and sincerely seeking guidance, finds guidance in the Quran; and having found it follows it; so that the whole

---

(3) Consider the following verses from the Quran :

(*a*) "O, Believers!
If you are God-fearing, He will provide you with a criterion.
And cleanse you of your evils, and forgive your sins.
Lo, Allah is bountiful in His favours."
(Taqwa—Criterion—Guidance : true knowledge and right understanding to distinguish between truth and falsehood, good and evil, right and wrong. A criterion that will serve as a "signal at every turning, every crossing, every up and down and show them the right way (the way of God) and warn them of the false ways (the ways of Satan)".
See: Maududi, *Tafheemul Quran* (*The Meaning of the Quran*), Vol. 4, p. 135, Editorial Note 24.

(*b*) "True believers are only those whose hearts tremble with awe, whenever Allah is mentioned to them; whose faith increases when the revelations of Allah are recited to them; who put their trust in their Lord, who establish *Salat* and spend in Our way out of what We have given them". (8 : 2-3)
(Taqwa → Iman → Increasing Iman → Acts of Islam).
See: *Ibid.*, Vol. 4, p. 125, Editorial Note 2.

process eventually leads him to the conquest of fear: "... But verily there cometh for you from Me a guidance; and whoso followeth My guidance, there shall no fear come upon them and neither shall they grieve". (2 : 38).

The Quality of Love Implied in Taqwa

4. We have seen that Taqwa (the fear of God) is the first pre-requisite for Hidayat (Guidance), and this guidance is a pre-requisite for Iman (Faith) on our way eventually to Islam (the surrender of our will to the will of God). Till now, we have examined only one facet of the meaning of Taqwa, calling it the "fear of God", the fear that causes us to ward off evil. Look at the other side of Taqwa, the positive side, the desire to draw near to God, and progressively nearer, through the continuous performance of good deeds. "To be righteous merely for the hope of reward for one's self or for fear of punishment may be good at a certain elementary stage of spiritual progress when higher motives are yet unintelligible. But as the light of Islam illumines the soul more and more, it is seen that virtue is its own reward and evil its own punishment: for the one accords with the will of God, and the other is contrary to it—and therefore also contrary to the pure nature of man as made by God ... (1) "God's handiwork according to the pattern on which He has made mankind; no change let there be in the work wrought by God: so that is the standard religion." (*Quran*, 30 : 30)... (2) "Surely We created man of the best stature; then We reduced him to the lowest of the low; save those who believe and do good works, and theirs is a reward unfailing." (*Quran*, 65 : 4-6)... The 'fear of God' is the beginning of wisdom; but is not fear in the ordinary sense of the term, for on the righteous 'there shall be no fear, neither shall they grieve' (*Quran*, 2 : 38): The fear of God is not a passive oppression by an outside feeling, but an active assertion of our own will not to offend our Lord and Cherisher. The fear is lest we lose His good pleasure. It is on our will that our future

depends under the grace and mercy of God. We must strive to reach His grace. Our strength is small, but He will accept the submission of our will (Islam), and His grace will search us out; and our progress will proceed according to the Law which God in His wisdom has established."[4]

5. Taqwa, then, is a quality of fear that propels us towards God and not away from Him. The Quran admonishes: "O Ye who believe! Fear God as He should be feared..." (*Quran*, 3 : 102).[5] This fear is not the abject fear of the coward, nor is it the dread of the child or the ignorant when confronted with the unknown; it is not even the fear of the competent adult whose developed faculties enable him to devise ways and means of protection but "the reverence which is akin to love, for it fears to do anything which is not pleasing to the object of love". In his commentary on the Quranic verse that I have just quoted, Abdullah Yusuf Ali refers to these four kinds of fear and observes: "The first is unworthy of man; the second is necessary for one spiritually immature; the third is a manly precaution against evil as long as it is unconquered; and the fourth is the seed-bed of righteousness. Those mature in faith cultivate the fourth; at earlier stages, the third or the second may be necessary: they are fear, but *Not* the fear of God. The first is a feeling of which anyone should be ashamed.[6]

6. Taqwa, then, is that fear which is a concomitant of love; the product of that desire *Not* to offend the Beloved; "with it dawns the consciousness of God's loving care for all His creatures".[7] This fear, which is a product of love, makes us amenable to Divine guidance, exhorts us Here ("today") to make provision for the Hereafter ("tomorrow"): "O ye who

---

(4) Abdullah Yusuf Ali, *The Holy Quran : Text, Translation and Commentary*. Vol. 3, Appendix 2, p. 1465, para 5.

(5) On "fearing God as He should be feared", also see: *Nahjul Balagha*, p. 176.

(6) Abdullah Yusuf Ali, *op. cit.*, Vol. 3, p. 149, Note 427.

(7) *Ibid.*, Vol. 3, p. 1769, Note 6234.

believe! Fear God; and let every soul look to what (provision) he has sent forth for the morrow. Yea, fear God: for God is well-acquainted with (all) that ye do." (*Quran*, 59 : 18, 19).

Taqwa to Iman to Islam

7. Taqwa, which is essentially God-consciousness with its dual aspects of the love and fear of God is, as we have observed, the beginning of wisdom. It is the first sign of God turning towards the man who has turned towards him. Taqwa prepares the individual human receptacle for the acceptance, storage, preservation, assimilation and absorption of Divine guidance. It is the first cleansing of the human spirit, the first ablution of the soul, the first awakening in man on his long journey towards God—through the progressive acquisition and perfection of his Iman (faith) and Islam (subservience to God). Taqwa—the self-restraint, the righteousness, the piety, the warding off of evil through the performance of good deeds: all proceeding from the love and fear of God—this Taqwa is the spiritual foundation of the mansion of peace that every Muslim, on his way to becoming a Muslim, firmly lays. As the superstructure of Iman and Islam rise on the foundations of Taqwa, God becomes a co-worker with, a helper of the man striving to be a Muslim. Divine guidance orients human search, adds impetus to human effort and strengthens the original foundation of Taqwa. The Quran declares : "But to those who receive guidance (and it is the Muttaqi who receives guidance), He increases (the light of) Guidance and bestows on them Taqwa (piety and restraint from evil)." (*Quran*, 47 : 17).

Tangible Character Traits of the Muttaqi

8. We have so far, with the aid of the Quran, made an attempt to acquire some understanding of the inner content of Taqwa—the love and fear of God. But what are the external manifestations of the inner presence of Taqwa? How is a man to know, what concrete evidence can he cite to himself, in his

effort to evaluate the quantum and the quality of Taqwa residing in his inmost soul? What are the hall-marks, the tangible character and conduct traits of the Muttaqi,—the God-fearing man? The answer is to be found in the almost innumerable references to this issue in the Quran, some directly and some indirectly; but since I have been exhausted by my attempt to piece them all together for a comprehensive and integrated presentation of the whole, I shall restrict myself to citing just one striking passage from the Quran. What is piety, what is righteousness, who is the Muttaqi? The Quran declares: "It is not righteousness that ye turn your faces towards East or West, but righteous is he who... And those who... Such are the people of truth (the sincere), the God-fearing." (2 : 177).

9. The Muttaqi, then, is a man whose heart enshrines an unwavering faith in God and His decrees; a faith that finds expression *Not* in a deadening formalism and the perfunctory performance of rituals, but a deep love for all mankind; a love that finds its expression in an ever-expanding circle of Charity, Generosity, Magnanimity; a faith that is captured by and leads to Truthfulness and Sincerity; a character that abides by the covenants it makes, a staunch witness to Justice; a spirit regular in Prayer, constantly renewing its contact with God; a man imbued with *Sabr*—calm, cool, collected, patiently persevering, firm and steadfast in pain, in suffering, in adversity and through all periods of panic and disaster. This is only a partial definition of the Muttaqi and the quality of Taqwa, for we have focussed the light of only verse on this issue and that too without elaboration. But even this little is enough for the while and for many subsequent hours and days of deliberation, reflection, self-evaluation and renewed effort on our way to the acquisition of Taqwa.

Role of Fear in the Acquisition of Faith

10. We shall shortly proceed to a very brief review of the quality of Taqwa as exemplified in the character and conduct

of the Prophet; but before we do that, I should like to do what I can to remove one popular misconception about the element of "fear" in the acquisition of "faith". Many of us are profoundly disturbed and some "intellectuals" among us draw away in revulsion from the many vivid descriptions in the Quran of the dire consequences of living a life contrary to the laws of God. Why talk of God's inexorable grip of those who girt themselves around with sin; who not instead talk only of His love, His mercy, His compassion? To begin with, we ought to be clear that these passages about Hell and punishment reveal a reality which actually exists; and no amount of wishful thinking, in the name of modern psychology harnessed to the manipulation of the human mind, can alter its objective status. These passages were not devised by a human mind to terrorize, coerce and trick mankind into a fearful submission; but to simply state, through vivid divine revelation, the consequences of wrong-doing; of Kufr, of injustice, tyranny, persecution; lust, avarice, rage and greed; hypocrisy, slander, pride, envy, malice; severing the ties that bind mankind together and spreading confusion over God's good earth. These are bad things and their consequences are bad; we cannot erase them from the structure of reality by merely refusing to look at them or think of them. We cannot wish them out of existence; but we can ward them off and blot them out by action—righteous action in conformity with the laws of God. For those of us who so act in the way of God, there are just as many passages in the Quran which state in equally vivid terms the joyous consequences of God-oriented good action : of faith and charity; of justice, love, truthfulness and sincerity; of generosity, magnanimity, prayer and piety; of combativeness in the face of evil and steadfastness in times of adversity; of modesty, humility, austerity, simplicity; of a life dedicated to the service of God and all God's creation.

11. The passages in the Quran that speak of Hell are no less real than the passages that speak of Paradise. Together

they represent the two sides of the consequences of human action—good and bad. There is nothing emotional about all this; but a factual exposition based on divine revelation. This is how God's law operates: we cannot run away from the consequences of the evil that we do; and we are not denied the fruits of the good that we perform. Given guidance and discrimination, and given the free will to choose whichever of the two ways we wish to choose, we remain responsible for what we do. For good or bad, we are the architects of our own destiny; we are the makers of our own hell and heaven.

12. I said that there is nothing emotional or sentimental about the Quranic exposition of the agonies of Hell and the joys of Paradise. To the best of my understanding, there is even no motive behind these descriptions—to either coerce or lure man into belief and righteous action. In matters of faith, there can be and there is no compulsion. The Quran exposes Reality as it is: a warning and a call for all, a guidance for those who accept it, a reminder for those who pay heed. We are free to accept or reject its call; free to feel or not to feel the emotion of fear when confronted by some of its passages; and equally free to feel or not to feel the emotion of joy when confronted by their anti-theses. Those of us who consider the "fear" passages in the Quran as bad psychology for the purposes of moving men to faith, need only recognize that they are the very ones who either feel no fear (in which case they have no logical cause for complaint) or they wish to close their eyes and run away from the reality. In either case, they err. The Muttaqi, fearing God, fears no evil—he faces it, he wards it off and moves on to righteous action. His action insulates him from and makes him independent not only of evil but also its consequences—pain, suffering, bitter remorse, black despair, hopelessness and abject fear. The one fear of the Muttaqi, his fear of God, emancipates him from all other fears. He enters the fold of the righteous, the men of God-oriented action, and rejoices over the Lord's own assurance: ". . . there shall come no fear upon

them, neither they shall grieve". Satan and his minions, the forces of evil, have no power over the good--so long as they remain good, doing good.

The Prophet : The Perfect Muttaqi

13. The Prophet, that most fearless of all men, was a man intensely afraid of God—the Perfect Muttaqi. He heard the call : "Fear them not, but fear Me !" (*Quran*, 2 : 150); and he never forgot that message. Here was a man who knew that he was the Chosen of God; taught by Him and shown by Him His signs; sanctified by Him, purified by Him and given wisdom; cast in the noblest mould, His finest creation and the seal of His prophets; His most dearly beloved, the foremost of His friends and helpers, assured of Paradise. Yet, in all history you cannot cite one man more intensely afraid of God—a man absorbed in prayer in its innumerable forms, and continually seeking His forgiveness, His mercy, His grace. Here was a man whose hair had gone prematurely grey because of his fear of the Lord when reciting such passages as Ha Mim al-Dukhan (*Quran*, 44 : 43-49); a man who could not hold back his tears (some of it out of fear and some of it out of joy) when he took his stand on the prayer mat; a man whose companions heard a gurgling sound rising from deep within him as he prayed; a man whose supplications breathe a spirit of Taqwa which no Muslim before or after him has matched, but all emulate.

14. Here was a man who, fearing God, feared none else; a man God-oriented, seeking His pleasure and avoiding His displeasure, in all he did from the moment he stepped out of bed to greet each new day to the moment he turned in to sleep. And even in that death of each day's life, he rose to pray (several times, for several hours long), secure in the refuge that he found with God, pouring out his prayers with an intense love of his Master, a deep consciousness of His unbounded favours, an unfaltering faith in His might and power, an unshakable confidence in His grace and mercy, with a

deep sense of humility, fearing God as he should be feared. Here was a man in total bondage to God; His foremost, most complete slave and bondsman—who having been granted the protection of his Master, needed and sought no other protection. Here before us is the paragon of Taqwa; and if we are too small, too rushed, too absorbed in the pettinesses of our daily existence to capture its full meaning and significance as exemplified by this man, we can at least, once in a while, find some little time to read, absorb and translate into action the spirit that breathes through his prayers. If you wish to understand what Taqwa is and absorb some of it into the stream of your blood as it courses through your veins, I know of no instrument more powerful and effective, after the Quran, than these prayers of the Prophet.[8]

15. How shall I capture for you, or even for myself, the spirit of Taqwa as exemplified in the character and conduct of this man : his truthfulness, his sincerity, his trustworthiness; his humility at all times; his faithfulness to every covenant made; his charity, seen and unseen, open and secret; his combativeness in the face of every evil; his generosity, his magnanimity, his grateful rush to prayer when victory and success came crowding in; his courage, his fortitude, his patience and steadfastness in times of sorrow, pain, defeat, failure, adversity and panic; his calm forbearance, his unyielding faith ; his firm rejection of Satan and his minions; his love of mankind and all God's creation; his overflowing compassion for and his resolute rush to the aid and succour of the weak, the oppressed, the poor, the forsaken, the destitute, the weary and the forlorn; the unguided and even the misguided? How am I to capture for you, or even for myself, all this and more of the spirit of Taqwa, the fear and love of God, as it blossomed forth in the character and conduct of this the greatest, the most sublime, the most perfect Muttaqi in the entire realm of God's vast creation? Here was a human

(8.) *Masnun Duaen* (*The Prayers of the Prophet*).

receptacle washed clean, a breast enlarged and a spirit expanded by Taqwa—a vessel prepared to receive God's guidance; and into it He poured His grace, His mercy, all the attributes that characterise the Perfect Man, cast in His image and true to the last detail of that first pre-eternal covenant between God and Man. I do not have the competence, and lacking the competence, thank God, not the courage either to present before you even a partial analysis or even description of the element of Taqwa in the life of the Prophet. That being the truth, the best that I can do is to urge you, for a beginning, to read, absorb and translate into action whenever you can, the spirit of Taqwa as it continually and variously expresses itself for examination in two important works:

(1) *Mishkat al-Masabih.* Translation by Dr. James Robson. Published by S. M. Ashraf, Kashmiri Bazar, Lahore.

(2) *Ibn Ishaq, Seerat Rasool-Allah* (*Life of Muhammad*). Translation by Guillaume, Oxford University Press of Pakistan.

16. Once you have read these two works, alongside your continuous study of the Quran, you will know for yourself what fresh directions to strike out in : may be, you will go on to Bukhari, Muslim, Al-Shafii, Malik, Ahmad Bin Hanbal, Abu Hanifah, Sufyan Al-Thawri, Ghazzali, Ibn Taimiyyah, Shaikh Ahmad of Sirhind, Shah Waliullah and others. May be : Frithjof Schuon, Maudoodi, Iqbal, Rumi, Attar, Hujwiri and the many others that they introduce you to. But all the while, keep your touch with the Quran : on your lips, in your heart, and in the actions that your limbs perform.

Intermediate Recapitulation and Elaboration

17. We were talking about Taqwa : God-consciousness, which maturing into God-awareness, leading on to God-oriented action in the external world. Not just knowing Him to be but also feeling Him to be closer to himself than his jugular

vein, the Muttaqi is a man being pursued by God—all too ready to be captured and to surrender. He feels within himself the dragnet of God drawing around him; he feels within himself the feeling that Francis Thompson must have felt when he wrote those famous lines in his celebrated poem "The Hounds of Heaven" : I fled him down the arches. . . "[9]

18. Such a man, knowing that he cannot run away from God, turns to Him, yields to Him and becomes a receptacle ready to receive His guidance. Over-awed, over-powered, aware of his helplessness in a cosmos that will grant him no peace except by conduct in accordance with His will, the Muttaqi is a man driven to God : "Thee (alone) we worship; and Thy aid (alone) we seek!" And when we seek that aid—sincerely, with humility, aware of how all the false gods that he turned to before have failed him, aware also of his newly-won freedom now that he has rejected them and is no longer a hostage in their hands[10] —now when he seeks that aid of Him, and Him alone : that aid is forthcoming, in the form of a

---

9. "I fled Him, down the nights and down the days;
I fled Him, down the arches of the years;
I fled Him, down the labyrinthine ways
Of my own mind;
And in the midst of tears, I hid from him,
And under running laughter.
Up-vistaed hopes I sped,
And shot, precipitated;
Adown titanic glooms of chasmed fears,
From those strong Feet that followed, followed after.
But with unhurrying chase,
And unperturbed pace,
Deliberate speed, majestic instancy,
They bear - and a Voice beat
More instant than the Feet—
All things betray thee, who betrayest Me."
(Francis Thompson, *Hounds of Heaven*).

10. *Quran*, 36 : 74, 75.

Guidance whereof (and wherein) there is no doubt. The Muttaqi's restless wandering leads him to the threshold of the one, true Divine guidance; his cry, seeking God, resounds over the expanse of the heavens and the earth and the Lord Himself responds to that cry :

> "And when My servants ask thee (O, Muhammad)
> Concerning Me,
> Lo! I am nigh (unto thee and them).
> I hear the cry of every crier,
> When he crieth unto Me.
> Let them also, then (with a will),
> Listen to My call (the Quran) and believe in Me;
> So that they may be guided aright." (*Quran*, 2: 186)

19. Taqwa, which is the first pre-requisite for a human receptacle washed, cleaned, purified and made ready for the acceptance of Divine guidance, is—as I have said several times before—God-consciousness, God-awareness leading to God-oriented action. Taqwa, we have seen, consists of two parts : the fear of God, leading to the avoidance of sin; and the love of God, leading to the pursuit of virtue. These two aspects inter-twine, each reinforcing the other; and it is very difficult to tell which of these has precedence over the other for the practical purposes of the acquisition of Taqwa. From one point of view, the avoidance of evil is a general pre-condition for the performance of good; from another point of view, the finest mode of conquering a particular evil (e.g. lust, rage, greed, envy, arrogance) is to deliberately cultivate through a series of conscious acts its opposite virtue (e.g. abstinence, tolerance, generosity, gratefulness, humility). It is to this latter mode that William James, the most perceptive of modern psychologists, refers when he talks of "the expulsive power of the opposite emotion". [11]

20. Be that as it may in the realm of action, no perception

---

11. *Great Books of the Western World*, Vol. 53.

and conception of what is good is possible without an awareness of what is evil. This awareness precedes action and unfolds itself in two stages : what Ghazzali calls "Deliverance from Error" (*Al-Munqidh min al-Dalal*) and "The Beginning of Guidance" (*Bidayat al-Hidayat*). For an understanding of what Taqwa is and how to cultivate it, I would strongly recommend that you read these two books also—two books which were in the nature of preliminary, introductory works preceding his masterpiece : the *Ihya Ulum al-Din* (Revival of the Religious Sciences)—a single work in 40 volumes, arranged in four quarters, each of ten volumes. The First Quarter (ten volumes) deals with "Acts of worship" ; the Second Quarter (ten volvmes) deals with the "Usages of life"; the Third Quarter (ten volumes) deals with the "Destructive Matters of life"; and the Fourth Quarter (ten volumes) deals with "the Saving Matters of life".[12] Directly relevant to our understanding and practice of Taqwa are the last two quarters :

(*a*) The Third Quarter, which examines such "destructive matters of life" as : lust and gluttony; idle chatter, lying and malicious slander; anger, rancour and envy; inordinate love of the world and its fleeting pleasures; wealth and avarice; pride, conceit and vanity.

(*b*) And the Fourth Quarter, which examines such "saving matters of life" as : repentance; patient perserverance and gratitude; fear and hope; simplicity and austerity; seeking refuge in and placing one's trust in God; a yearning for Him and constant recollection of Him; contentment; truthfulness and sincerity; self-examination and self-evaluation. Strik-

---

12. See: Ghazzali, *Al-Kitab al-Ilm* (The Book of Knowledge), Chapter 1. Nabih Amin Faris' English translation of the *Ihya Ulum al-Din* (being published by Sheikh Muhammad Ashraf of Lahore) has so far reached only the Sixth Volume.

ingly, the last two volumes of this quarter are devoted to "meditation" and "death".

I fear we do not have the time here to go into these details of the two facets of Taqwa: the withdrawal (the clean break) from evil and the resolute pursuit of virtue. Unhappily, we must stop here; a little more of this I hope to cover when I come to my subsequent talk on the "Basic Attributes of the Muslim".

More Models of Taqwa : The Companions

21. An important key to our understanding of Taqwa put to practice is to study the character and conduct of the great Muttaqeen. I have already made a brief reference to the Prophet. After him, study the lives of his companions, such towering, God-fearing men as : Abu Bakr, Umar, Uthman, Ali, Talha, Az-Zubair, Abd Ar-Rehman B. Auf, Sad B. Abu Waqqas, Said B. Zaid, Abu Ubaida B. Al-Jarrah, Zaid B. Thabit, Ubay B. Kaab and Mu-adh B. Jabal.[13] Each of these lives variously reflect the many facets of Taqwa and of these men the Prophet said : "My companions are like the stars; so whichever of them you copy, you will be guided."

22. I should have liked to have quoted at least one striking instance of the element of Taqwa as exemplified in the lives of each of these men; but since we do not have the time here and now I'll leave this and more for you to discover on your own. But talk of the fearlessness of the man who fears God, one anecdote about Umar haunts my mind : "Sa'd b. Abu Waqqas narrates that Umar Ibn al-Khattab asked permission from God's messenger to enter when there were with him some women of Quraish who were talking volubly to him with loud voices. They got up when 'Umar asked permission and hastened to veil themselves; and when Umar entered, God's messenger was laughing. So, he said: 'God keep you smiling, messenger of God!' The Prophet replied: 'I was astonished at these women who are with me, for when they heard your voice they hastened to veil them-

13. See : *Mishkat al-Masabih,* Vol. 4, pp. 1316-1359.

selves.' Umar then said: 'Enemies of yourselves, do you stand in awe of me and do not stand in awe of God's messenger?' They replied: 'Yes, you are churlish and harsher.' God's messenger then said: 'Never mind, son of al-Khattab; I swear by Him in whose hand my soul is that the Devil has never met you walking on a mountain-road without going to another one than yours."[14] Can you see, gentlemen, as I see : Umar walking on a lonely, mountain road; and Satan, with all his minions, their tails tucked in between their legs, slinking away to other tracks and alleys, keeping a safe distance and eyeing from behind bushes this man, who fearing God, struck terror into their hearts? Such is the man of Taqwa, the Muttaqi, whose fear of God not only insulates him and emancipates him from evil but whose rejection and warding off of evil, causes evil itself to run away from him. The Muttaqi puts evil to flight; and his power comes from the fear of God and the conduct that this fear inspires. The forces of evil have no authority, no hold over the God-fearing (the righteous); all false fears and the sources from which they spring are themselves afraid of the man who fears God. The Muttaqi who has perfected his Taqwa is not only a man who is himself fearless ("there shall no fear come upon them, neither shall they grieve"); but also a man who having heard, absorbed and actualised the call of the Lord "Fear them not, but fear me", strikes terror into the hearts of those who reject Him, rebel against Him, fear Him not and act contrary to His injunctions. The Muttaqi is a vessel and also an instrument, filled and forged by the fear of God.

More Models : The Imams, The Great Sufis

23. We were talking about understanding the spirit of Taqwa through a study of the character and conduct of the great Muttaqeen. A brief reference has already been made to

14. See : *Mishkat al-Masabih,* Vol. 4, p. 1325.

the Prophet and his immediate companions. Let your mind range over the pages of subsequent history, and you will come across such exemplars of Taqwa as: Al-Shafii, Malik, Abu Hanifah, Ahmad Ibn Hanbal and Sufyan Al-Thawri. I made my first acquaintance with them in Ghazzali's *Kitab al-Ilm* (pp. 59-72), the first of the 40 volumes of his *Ihya Ulum al-Din*; and I remain thirsty for more. Find your way to them, through whichever way you will, and may God guide you in your quest! Drink at the fountain of their knowledge and wisdom, seek their companionship and watch their conduct —if you would know what Taqwa is. The knowledge and the wisdom of these great savants of Islam both staggering as they are, it is their conduct as men of Taqwa about which I should like to say a few introductory words:

(*a*) *Take Al-Shafii*: a man who read the Quran, with concentration, from cover to cover, each day during the 30 (or 29) days of Ramadan. And throughout his life, he divided each night into three parts: one-third devoted to study, one-third reserved for prayer, and one-third for sleep. During his nocturnal devotions —I wish to remind you, a full third of the total hours of darkness each day—he seldom managed to recite more than 50 verses of the Quran, so intense was his concentration on and his absorption in what he recited. And at the end of each verse, he would beseech God for mercy on himself and all believers. Consider this man's self-control: "Never have I been satisfied these 16 years," he once said, "because a full stomach fattens the body, hardens the heart, dulls the intellect, fosters sleep, and renders a man lazy in worship." How this man guarded his tongue, his ears and every limb from every frivolity, every obscenity and every act that would be displeasing to God is something that each one of us must discover for himself. As for the fear of God lodged in his inmost being, it is narrated that Al-Harith Ibn-Labid was once reciting some verses from the Quran to him. When he came to the lines "On that day they shall not speak, nor shall it be permitted them to make excuses" (*Quran*, 77 : 35, 36), Al-Shafii's colour changed, his face become a blanched white, his body began to tremble and he fell into a swoon. When he regained consciousness, his face moistened with tears and beads of sweat, he was heard repeating: "I seek refuge with God against the den of liars and the scoffing of the thoughtless! O Lord, to Thee the hearts of the gnostics (*Arifin*) have submitted themselves and before Thy throne the heads of those who yearn for Thee are bowed low! O Lord, bestow Thy bounty upon me, and crown me with Thy intelligence. Through the grace of Thy countenance, forgive me my short-comings." . . . On the attribute of steadfastness (*Tamkin*), that luminous hall-mark of the Muttaqi, Al-Shafii once said: "Steadfastness is the grade attained by the prophets, and there is no steadfastness except after trial (*Mihnah*). When a prophet is tried and endures, he manifests the quality of patience (*Sabr*); and when he manifests the quality of patience, he proves his steadfastness (*Tamkin*). Hast thou not seen how God hath tried Abraham and then established him in steadfastness; and hath done the same with Moses, Job and Solomon to whom He had also given a position of dominion and power? Steadfastness is the most excellent grade." . . . And talk of such other hall-marks of the Muttaqi as his love and compassion for his fellow-beings, his humility, his dispassionate search of the truth, his emancipation from all pride, conceit and envy—consider what Al-Shafii was once said about teaching and learning. But before I quote to you what he said, I should like to remind you what Ahmad Ibn

Hanbal once said about this man to his son: "O my son, Al-Shafii was like the sun to the world and like health to men; think, then, is there anything that could replace either of these two things?" He also used to say: "There is not a single man who has touched a pen with his hand that has not been indebted to Al-Shafii." Such a man of profound learning was Al-Shafii and this man once said: "Never have I debated with anyone and wished that he should fall into error; nor ever talked to any person and did not desire that he may be divinely favoured, guided and helped, and that he may enjoy the care and keeping of God. Never have I spoken to anybody and paid the least attention to whether God would reveal the truth through my words or through his; nor ever met a person to whom I had related the truth and the proof thereof and he had accepted it, without respecting him and believing in his sincerity; on the other hand, no one has ever disputed the truth before me and accepted not its proof, without falling from the place which he had held in my regard and without my rejecting him." So many of us try to learn and so many of us try to teach; but here is the way of the Muttaqi to knowledge: both learning and teaching.

(*b*) *Look at Malik also*: his sincerity, his truthfulness, his fear of God preventing him from passing any judgement beyond the span of his understanding. Al-Shafii said that when the learned men are enumerated, Malik would be the most outstanding; and yet, of this very man Al-Shafii narrates: "I (once) saw Malik being queried about 48 problems, to 32 of which he replied: 'I do not know'." Such is the truthfulness of the men of Taqwa. Study the life of Malik also, for some great lessons in the love of God and His Prophet, some great lessons in piety, charity, magannimity and generosity;

the rejection of wealth, avarice, pomp and pride—the many other facts of Taqwa to which we have made repeated references.

(*c*) *A very brief reference to Imam Abu-Hanifah, Ahmad Bin Hanbal and Sufyan Al-Thawri.* Besides being men who dedicated a life-time to the pursuit and practice of the kind of knowledge that availeth man in the Hereafter, these men were also models of Taqwa in the total integration of their personalities—with one or the other ingredient acquiring special prominence. According to Ibn Al-Mubarak, the two outstanding characteristics of *Imam Abu Hanifah* were "manliness and much prayer"—two of the leading elements of Taqwa as defined by the Quran. Read about his firm rejection of the snares of earthly authority, his contempt of wealth and secular power, his absorption in God through long periods of silent contemplation. Like Al-Jonaid of Baghdad after him, for forty consecutive years he performed his Fajr prayers on the basis of his Maghrib ablutions (having spent the whole night in continual Salat and Zikr). He performed the pilgrimage to the House of God 55 times; saw himself in the presence of God in his sleep a hundred times—so deeply soaked in God was he to the roots of his unconscious. This is the God-awareness that I was referring to as the very foundation of Taqwa. *Ahmad Bin Hanbal and Sufyan Al-Thawri* also were models of God-oriented action, men living and working Here in accordance with the tenets of God, their eyes fixed on the Hereafter. Study the lives, conduct and works of these men, my friends, for a deeper understanding and absorption of the spirit of Taqwa.

24. The story of Islam presents us with *many more models of Taqwa*, if only we would care to probe into it, shake off this spiritual indolence which makes us vulnerable to the lure, the

glitter, the eventually destructive tug of false heroes. Have we, in our search for an understanding of those qualities that constitute Taqwa (fear and love of God leading to faith, charity, prayer, courage, steadfastness, truthfulness, sincerity, generosity and magnanimity, piety, humility, gratitude, above all—a sense of bondage to Him and none else)—have we in our search for that understanding, looked into the lives, the character and conduct of *such men as* : Hasan of Basra, Malik Ibn Dinar, Habib Al-Ajami, Rabea Al-Basri, Al-Fozail Ibn Iyaz, Ibrahim Ibn Adham, Bishr Ibn Al-Harith, Dhol Nun Al-Mesri, Bayazid of Bostam, Shaqiq of Balkh, Dawud Al-Tai, Hatem Al-Asamm, Maruf Al-Karkhi, Yahya Ibn Moadh, Abu Hafs Al-Haddad Al-Jonaid of Baghdad, Abul-Husain Al-Nuri, Abu Said Al-Kharraz, Ibn Ata, Somnun, Al-Termidhi, Khair Al-Nassaj, Al-Shibli and several others? If I were to attempt to illustrate, through even one anecdote about each of these men, the manner and mode in which they imbibed, cultivated and put to concrete expression the spirit of Taqwa—it would take us the better part of the day. Since we do not have the time here and now for such an understanding, the best that I can do is to recommend—humbly, out of the very limited fund of my own study—that you read four books which I have read with such joy, wonder, a sense of expansion and elevation, a feeling of being washed and swept clean as I cannot communicate, try as much as I might. These four books I urge you to read, not olny to understand the spirit of Taqwa but a whole world of thought, action, character and conduct connected with it. These four books are:

(*a*) Farid Al-Din Attar, *Tadhkirat Al-Auliya.*
(*b*) Ali Al-Hujwiri, *Kashf Al-Mahjub.*
(*c*) Abu Bakr Al-Kalabadhi, *Kitab al-Taaruf li-Madhab Ahl al-Tasawwuf.*
(*d*) A. J. Arberry, *Sufism*: *An Account of the Mystics of Islam.*

Taqwa: Integrating Knowledge and Action

25. The hour grows long, Gentlemen, and I must round off

this talk—as soon as I can. To truly understand what Taqwa is, two things are necessary: Knowledge and Action. I have tried to stress the importance of both; and here towards the end, I wish to stress (for you and for myself) that there is *No* short cut to either.

26. Knowledge without action is vanity; and action without knowledge can lead to collossal blunders. The sole purpose of knowledge is to lead us to righteous conduct and vigorous action in the way of God; and in this context, remember the Prophet's prayer : "I take refuge with Thee, O Lord, from the knowledge that profiteth naught." As our understanding of Taqwa progresses, we must at each stage, after due reflection, put to practice what we have so far learnt. Seeking knowledge without action is like planting a tree that will bear thorns, *Not* fruit. Such knowledge is not only empty, idle pursuit; it will destroy within us even that dubious peace which is the questionable gift of the ignorant, and lead us to one of the most heinous of all crimes: hypocrisy. And that is a trait that any man with the slightest fear of God in him must perpetually guard against. Indeed, we must seek knowledge; for it is obligatory on us; because we cannot act rightly without knowledge. But even as we seek knowledge, of Taqwa or whatever, we would do well to constantly remember that well-known anecdote about Ibrahim Ibn Adham. One day, taking a stroll all by himself, he came upon a large stone with the inscription on it: "Turn me over and read!" He walked across, turned the stone over and this is what he read written on the other side of it: "O Ibrahim! Thou dost not practise what thou (already) knowest; why then dost thou seek to know what thou knowest not?"[15]

27. I cannot over-emphasize the importance of the fact that it is the acts of Taqwa that breed Taqwa in the heart of man;

(15.) Attar, *Tadhkirat al-Auliya*. Translation, Chapter on Ibrahim Ibn Adham.

but then I cannot over-emphasize the importance of knowledge either as a prelude to correct action. This is a vast subject, and we must close this discourse—in the context of Taqwa—with a recollection of what Hatim Al-Asamm once said : "I have chosen four things to know, and have discarded all knowledge in the world besides." "What are they?" he was asked. He answered :

(*a*) "I know that my daily bread is apportioned me, and will neither be increased nor diminished; consequently, I have ceased to seek to augment it."

(*b*) "Secondly, I know that I owe to God a debt which no other person can pay instead of me; therefore I am occupied with paying it."

(*c*) "Thirdly, I know there is one pursuing me (i.e. Death); accordingly, I have prepared myself to meet it."

(*d*) "Fourthly, I know that God is observing me; and so, I am ashamed to do what I ought not."[16]

28. There, my friends, you have as near complete a definition of Taqwa as I have been able to find (outside the Quran)—covering both its aspects of knowledge and action. Note the careful formulation of Hatim Al-Asamm's words : Knowledge precedes action; and no piece of knowledge is formulated without a corresponding formulation of action. And if you were to study a little of William James, that great psychologist to whom I earlier made a reference, you would know that while knowledge precedes action, action clarifies, fortifies, reinforces the knowledge from which that action sprang. Such then must be the way to our comprehension and absorption of Taqwa: Taqwa, which I earlier broadly defined as God-consciousness, which maturing into God-awareness, leads on to God-oriented action in the external world. It is the urge to avoid God's displeasure in all that we think and do; it is the determination to purge all our thoughts and deeds of the last trace of contamination abominable to God. It is also the urge to seek

(16) Hujwiri, *Kashf al-Mahjub*. Translation, p. 13.

God's pleasure in all that we undertake, so that we may lay every moment of our life (thought, feeling and action) as a sacred offering before Him, and Him alone. That man has captured, assimilated, absorbed and actualised the spirit of Taqwa who can truthfully declare what the Quran asks him to declare :

"Say : My prayer and sacrifice,
And my life and my death
Are all for Allah, Lord of all the worlds.
I ascribe no partners unto Him,
And this I have been commanded;
And I am the first of those
Who surrender their will to His."

(*Quran*, 6: 162).

Concluding Remarks

29. We have ranged, as far and as wide as a single, short talk would permit in our quest of the meaning of Taqwa. Since we have been able to determine the essence of Taqwa as a state of mind and a pattern of conduct that seek to avoid His displeasure and win His approval, we may close this talk with a selection of verses from the Quran which describe the people whom Allah dislikes and the people whom Allah loves:

(*a*) *Whom Allah Dislikes*

(1) And Allah guideth not the forward folk.
(2) And Allah loveth not those who make mischief.
(3) And Allah guideth not wrong-doing folk (those who commit excesses).
(4) And Allah guideth not the disbelieving folk.
(5) Surely Allah loveth not any treacherous ingrate.
(6) Surely He loveth not the proud.
(7) Be not prodigal; surely He loveth not the prodigal.
(8) Surely Allah guideth not him who is a liar, an ingrate.
(9) Whoso ascribeth unto Allah associates, of a

certainty he had wandered far away (from the right path).

(*b*) *Whom Allah Loves*

(1) And do good; surely Allah loveth those who do good.

(2) Surely Allah loveth those who turn unto Him in repentance and he loveth those who keep themselves clean.

(3) He who fulfilleth his pledge and wardeth off evil, (let him know) that surely Allah loveth those who ward off (evil).

(4) And Allah loveth the steadfast.

(5) Surely Allah loveth the equitable (those who hold firmly to justice).

(6) And (know that) surely Allah is with those who ward off evil.

(7) Surely the mercy of Allah is nigh unto the good.

(8) Allah wasteth not the reward of the good.

(9) As for those who strive towards Us, of a certainty we guide them to Our paths, and of a certainty Allah is with the good.

(10) Surely Allah loveth those who put their trust in Him.

30. There you have a partial selection from the Quran, throwing light on the essence of Taqwa. If you still want me to summarize, I can only cry out in anguish : who dare summarize the Quran? Turn to it, and read it for yourself, my friends—for the understanding that you seek. Read it, recite it with concentration, with a spirit of enquiry soaked in the fear of God—as Al-Shafii and the many other illustrious men before us have done; and pray that this striving of ours to establish contact with what Frithjof Schuon calls "the spiritual essence behind the husk of the literal meaning of the words" may eventually reveal the Quran to us even as it was revealed to the Prophet. The Taqwa that we bring to our study of the Quran

will be reinforced, expanded and deepened by our study of the Quran. Taqwa drives us to the Quran, even as thirst drives the thirsty to the fountain; and increasing thirst, deepening Taqwa will guide us to "a Guidance about which (and in which) there is no doubt" and so lead us through Iman to the Islam that is our goal. And as we embark on that joyous journey, calling ourselves men who strive to be Muslims, we may pray even as the Quran teaches us to pray :

"O Lord! Let my entry be through the gate of Truth and Honour; And (likewise) let my exit be through the gate of Truth and Honour; And grant Thou me, from Thy presence, a power to aid me!"

SELECTED BIBLIOGRAPHY

1. Marmaduke Pickthall, *The Meaning of the Glorious Quran: Text and Explanatory Translation.* Taj Company Ltd., Lahore.
2. Abul Ala Maududi, *Tafeehmul Quran* (*The Meaning of the Quran*). Translation by Chaudhry Muhammad Akbar, Islamic Publications, Lahore. Translation not yet completed.
3. Abdullah Yusuf Ali, *The Holy Quran: Text, Translation and Commentary.* Sheikh Muhammad Ashraf, Kashmiri Bazar, Lahore.
4. Abul Kalam Azad, *Tarjumanul Quran.* English translation by Syed Abdul Latif, Sind Sagar Academy, Lahore.
5. Abdul Hamid Siddiqui, *The Holy Quran: English Translation and Explanatory Notes.* Islamic Book Centre, Lahore.
6. *Mishkat al-Masabih,* English translation by Dr. James Robson. Sheikh Muhammad Ashraf, Kashmiri Bazar, Lahore.
7. *Nahjul Balagha* (*Sermons, Letters, Sayings of Hazrat Ali*), English translation by Muhammad Askari Jafery. Khorasan Islamic Centre, Karachi.
8. Farid Al-Din Attar, *Tadkhirat Al-Auliya.* English translation ("Muslim Saints and Mystics") by A. J. Arberry, Routledge and Kegan Paul Ltd., London.
9. Ali Al-Hujwiri, *Kashf Al-Mahjub.* English translation by R. A. Nicholson, Luzac and Co., London.
10. Abu Bakr Kalabadhi, *Kitab al-Taarrof li-Madhab Ahl al-Tasawwuf.* Eng-

lish translation ("Doctrine of the Sufis") by A. J. Arberry. Sheikh Muhammad Ashraf, Kashmiri Bazar, Lahore.

11. Al-Ghazzali, *Al-Kitab Al-Ilm.* English translation ("The Book of Knowledge") by Nabih Amin Faris. Sheikh Muhammad Ashraf, Kashmiri Bazar, Lahore.

12. Al-Ghazzali, *Al Munqidh min al-Dalal* ("*Deliverance from Error*") and *Bidayat al-Hidayat* ("*Beginning of Guidance*"). English translation ("*The Faith and Practice of Al-Ghazzali*") by Montgomery Watt. Sheikh Muhammad Ashraf, Kashmiri Bazar, Lahore.

13. A. J. Arberry, *Sufism : An Account of the Mystics of Islam.* George Allen and Unwin Ltd., London.

14. *Masnun Duaen* (*Prayers of the Prophet*). Sheikh Muhammad Ashraf, Kashmiri Bazar, Lahore.

15. *Al-Hizb al-Azam* (*Collection of Quranic Prayers*). Sheikh Muhammad Ashraf, Kashmiri Bazar, Lahore.

16. *Great Books of the Western World.* Encyclopaedia Britannica Inc, London-Chicago-Toronto-New York.

17. *The Holy Bible* (*Containing the Old and New Testaments*), British and Foreign Bible Society, Eyre and Spottiswoode Ltd., London, 1611.

TAQWA : SYNOPSIS

Definition and Implications

1. In its widest, most comprehensive sense, Taqwa may be defined as : God-consciousness, which maturing into God-awareness, spills over as God-oriented action in the external world.

2. The two major components of Taqwa, as is evident from this definition which emerges from our study of the Quran, are :

   a. God-consciousness, God-awareness.

   b. God-oriented action.

3. In its initial stages, in its embryonic, rudimentary form Taqwa is God-consciousness. This consciousness of the existence of God (a supreme, omniscient, omnipresent, omnipotent Being) is inherent in the mind of man as a consequence of the breath breathed into man by the Lord. Taqwa, as God-consciousness, is present in all men, except for those who choose of their own free will to stifle, strangle or snuff out this consciousness. When men deliberately so choose to efface or wipe out this natural consciousness of God from the tablet of their minds, they become what we call Atheists : men for whom God has died, men for whom God does not exist. Such men are few; and they are unnatural because they have persuaded themselves to

forget or to twist, warp, mutilate and eventually expel that consciousness of God which is naturally present in all men as a consequence of the breath that God breathed into the breast of mankind. (59 : 18, 19).

4. Those who go on to nourish this seed of God-consciousness implanted and inherent in them, gradually develop and transform this Consciousness into Awareness. In them, Taqwa graduates from God-consciousness to God-awareness : a progressively clearer grasp, with both mind and spirit, of His essence and His attributes.

5. As God-consciousness gradually matures into God-awareness, this movement in the inner world of man actuates God-oriented action in the external world : actions, in quality and magnitude, corresponding to the inner perception in the mind and spirit of man. These actions spring from that awareness; and that awareness is further clarified (rendered more vivid and firm) by the performance of these actions.

6. Taqwa, then, in its totality, capturing the process by which it grows from an embryonic consciousness of God into an enlightened awareness of God and leads on to God-oriented action, is a direction of the human soul towards its Origin : a progression, and a propulsion of the human spirit towards God. Taqwa is : God-consciousness, which maturing into God-awareness, spills over as God-oriented action in the external world.

Taqwa →Guidance →Iman →Islam

7. Let us now take a look at Taqwa, in relation to Hidayat (Guidance), Iman (Faith) and the culmination of all these in Islam (Iman concretised, through the submission and surrender of our total being to the will of the Lord).

8. The first step, my friends, on our way to becoming Muslims is to read and understand the Quran; and the first pre-requisite for understanding the Quran is Taqwa.

9. Open the book, my friends; and see how it proceeds. At the beginning, it teaches man to articulate his cry for Divine Guidance (1 : 5); and then proclaims : "This is the book in which (and of which) there is no doubt, a guidance for the Muttaqeen..." (2 : 2)

10. To understand the Quran, we must approach it in the spirit of the Muttaqi; to obtain Guidance from the Quran, we must bring to it Taqwa: that universal God-consciousness which the Quran takes hold of; and as we study it with understanding, gradually transforms this God-consciousness into a God-awareness that leads to God-oriented action. Indeed, the Quran is a warning for all; a reminder for those who pay heed; but it is a criterion and guidance for only those who bring to their search for understanding the spirit of Taqwa. (8 : 29). And the Taqwa that we bring to our study

of the Quran, increases with our study of the Quran. (47 : 17). The Quran is thus the means, open to all who wish to avail of it, for the transfiguration of the God-consciousness inherent in the universal nature of man into that awareness of God which alone leads to sustained God-oriented action the external world.

The Inner Content of Taqwa

11. Let us examine the nature of this Consciousness and awareness: the first component of Taqwa.

12. With reference to this inner content, Taqwa has two facets (like the two faces of a single coin): the Fear of God and the Love of God. Together, they constitute the inner content of Taqwa: Fear predominating in the stage of Consciousness, and Love predominating in the stage of Awareness; although at no stage is Taqwa fear alone or love alone. In fact, in its perfected state, Taqwa is a total fusion of these two components of the Fear and the Love of God, each stretched to its Nth degree, attaining an equilibrium and a unity that defies further dichotomy.

13. For the purposes of rational understanding, however, let us consider these two elements of the Fear and the Love of God : each separately, and then in relation to each other, for an understanding of that Taqwa which they together constitute.

14. *Taqwa as Fear of God.* Taqwa is indeed Fear of God; but it is not fear in the ordinary sense of the term. What sort of a fear is it?.

a. Not the abject fear, not the paralysing terror, not the life-draining dread and horror of the lamb before the tiger, the fear of primitive man before his primitive concept of God.

b. Not the helpless fear of the child either, unable to comprehend and therefore unable to coordinate his responses to the object of his fear.

c. Not even the fear of the intellectually mature adult whose reason, coupled with past experience, provides him with tentative answers for a rational confrontation with the object of his fear.

15. No, Sir! Taqwa, the Fear of God, is none of these. These are fear alright, but *not* the fear of God, *not* Taqwa. Taqwa is that quality of fear which is best expressed as Reverence, a sense of awe and wonder before the majesty of the Lord; a majesty that the spirit of man gazes on and recognises as his very own Source and Origin; a majesty that calls to his Awareness and causes him to fall prostrate before the Lord in boundless gratitudes and limitless surrender, crying out:

"Thee (and Thee alone) we worship;
Of Thee (and Thee alone) we seek aid!" (1 : 4)

It is this quality of fear that is Taqwa: this joyous bondage of the slave to his Sole Master; these trembling limbs, these flowing tears, this mind and spirit inundated by the light and the power of the Lord of the Throne of Honour, the Lord of Glory Supreme. It is this fear that is Taqwa: this awe, this wonder, this reverence, this falling prostrate before the Lord in one eternal bow as an expression of man's boundless gratitude and limitless surrender—the only mode by which the created returns to its Creator.

16. And when the Muttaqi is so prostrated before the Lord, he hears the words of the Lord well up from deep within him :

a. "Verily, there cometh to you from Me a guidance, and whosoever followeth this guidance : there shall no fear come upon them and neither shall they grieve." (2 : 38).

b. "Nay! whosoever turneth his countenance full square towards Allah, while doing good: there shall no fear come upon them and neither shall they grieve." (2 : 112).

c. ". . . Therefore, fear them not, but fear Me; so that I may complete my bounties upon you and that you may be guided aright." (2 : 150).

17. And so the Muttaqi rises, seeking guidance and finding it in the Quran, and having found it, follows it: regardless of temporal consequences, regardless of the ebb and the tide in the flux of fortune in serial time. His one fear of Allah drives away all other fears; his one fear of Allah emancipates him, insulates him, liberates him, lifts him above and helps him transcend all other fears :

"Woh aik Sajda jise tu gran samajhta hai
Deti hai tujhe hazzar Sajdoon se najaat . . . "

On the lips of the Muttaqi, in his heart, flowing through his veins, suffusing his mind and spirit, ringing in his ears is the call of the Lord : "Fear them not but fear Me; so that I may complete my bounties upon you and that you may be guided aright." (2 : 150).

18. This is Taqwa, my friends : the fear of God and none but Him; the fear that drives man to bow before Him and none but Him; the fear that propels man towards God and not away from Him; the fear that binds man to God and breaks all other chains; the fear that is the highest freedom from fear, the Fear of the Righteous on whom "there no shall fear come and neither shall they grieve". This is Taqwa, my friends : the fear of the Muttaqi; the man who fearing God is restlessly in search of the Truth, a man with an intense desire to discriminate between Good and Evil (between Right and Wrong, between Truth and Falsehood, Beauty and Ugliness, Light and Darkness, Knowledge and Ignorance, Faith and Bigotry, Peace and

Conflict). And when this restless urge within him drives him to threshold of the one true guidance, the Muttaqi cries out with joy:

- *a.* "This is the Book whereof (and wherein) there is no doubt, a guidance for the God-fearing." (2 : 2)
- *b.* "Say : the guidance of Allah is the (only true) guidance; and we are commanded to accept, submit and surrender ourselves to the Lord of all the worlds."

19. See, my friends, what Taqwa (this Fear of God) has done : driven us to the one true guidance, given us the Criterion to distinguish Truth from Falsehood (Right from Wrong, Good from Evil), sparked in us the first spark of Iman and lo! opened before us the Deen (the way) of Islam (the surrender of our will to the will of the Lord of all the worlds)...

20. *Taqwa as Love of God.* Just as the Fear of God drives us to the Lord, so does Love of God draw us to the Lord. Driven by Fear and drawn by Love, the Muttaqi, is on the double on his way towards the Lord. Pushed by Fear and pulled by Love, the Muttaqi runs to his Lord ; and lo ! for every step that he takes towards Him, the Lord comes racing towards him, a hundred steps for every faltering step that he takes towards Him.

21. In the beginning, the engine of Fear in the rear pushes more than the engine of Love pulls in the front. But as the train gathers speed, Love pulls more than Fear pushes. Soon, a momentum is reached and lo! the Muttaqi full steam ahead on his way to the Lord : pushed and driven by Fear, pulled and drawn by Love—both with equal vigour.

22. The Fear of God is the dragnet of the Lord, the Divine cordon closing in on the Muttaqi; and the Love of God is the tug of the Lord which causes the Muttaqi to joyously rush into the net of the Lord. Glad to be pursued and all too ready to surrender; chased by the Lord and running towards the Chaser; haunted, obsessed, over-whelmed and over-powered by the Lord, glad to yield, glad to submit, glad to surrender: this is that other face of the coin of Taqwa, called the Love of God.

23. Such, in brief, is the nature of Taqwa with its co-existent, concurrent, co-developing elements of Fear and Love of God. And so does God-Consciousness mature into God-Awareness, spilling over into God-oriented action in the external world

Taqwa in the External World

24. In the external world, the element of Fear in Taqwa manifests itself as the avoidance, the warding off and resistance of all that is evil, all that would incur the displeasure of God; and the element of Love in Taqwa manifests itself as the performance, the expansion and establishment of all that is good, all that helps win the pleasure of God. Taqwa is the fearful Avoidance of

Sin, and the joyous Cultivation of Virtue; a manifestation in the concrete world of action of the Muttaqi's hankering for His good pleasure and his abhorrence of all that would displease Him.

25. Well might the Muttaqi say these words (which I learnt in my childhood and which grow in meaning as I grow in years):

"For Him who loves me,
Who knows me true :
For the Cause that lacks assistance,
For the Wrong that needs resistance,
For the Future in the distance,
And the Good that I can do. . . "

26. Such is Taqwa : that God-consciousness, which maturing into God Awareness, leads on to God-oriented action in the external world.

TAQWA

Passages from the Quran

(Ref. Page 41)

This is the Scripture whereof there is no doubt, a guidance unto those who ward off (evil). (2 : 2)

٢- ذٰلِكَ الْكِتٰبُ لَا رَيْبَ ۛ فِيْهِ ۛ
هُدًى لِّلْمُتَّقِيْنَ ۝

(Ref. Page 42)

Fear them not, but fear Me, so that I may complete My grace upon you,and that ye may be guided. (2 : 150)

فَلَا تَخْشَوْهُمْ وَاخْشَوْنِيْ ۗ
وَلِاُتِمَّ نِعْمَتِيْ عَلَيْكُمْ وَلَعَلَّكُمْ تَهْتَدُوْنَ ۝

(Ref. Page 43)

Nay, but whosoever surrendereth his purpose to Allah while doing good, his reward is with his Lord ; and there shall no fear come upon them neither shall they grieve. (2 : 112)

١١٢- بَلٰى ۗ مَنْ اَسْلَمَ وَجْهَهٗ لِلّٰهِ
وَهُوَ مُحْسِنٌ فَلَهٗٓ اَجْرُهٗ عِنْدَ رَبِّهٖ ۠
وَلَا خَوْفٌ عَلَيْهِمْ وَلَا هُمْ يَحْزَنُوْنَ ۝

(Ref. Page 44)

We said : Go down, all of you, from hence ; but verily there cometh unto you from Me a guidance ; and whoso followeth My guidance, there shall no fear come upon them neither shall they grieve. (2 : 38)

٣٨- قُلْنَا اهْبِطُوْا مِنْهَا جَمِيْعًا ۚ
فَاِمَّا يَاْتِيَنَّكُمْ مِّنِّيْ هُدًى فَمَنْ تَبِعَ
هُدَايَ فَلَا خَوْفٌ عَلَيْهِمْ وَلَا هُمْ
يَحْزَنُوْنَ ۝

Surely We created man of the best stature.

٤- لَقَدْ خَلَقْنَا الْاِنْسَانَ فِيْٓ اَحْسَنِ تَقْوِيْمٍ ۝

Then We reduced him to the lowest of the low,

٥- ثُمَّ رَدَدْنٰهُ اَسْفَلَ سٰفِلِيْنَ ۝

Save those who believe and do good works, and theirs is a reward unfailing. (95 : 4-6)

٦- اِلَّا الَّذِيْنَ اٰمَنُوْا وَعَمِلُوا الصّٰلِحٰتِ
فَلَهُمْ اَجْرٌ غَيْرُ مَمْنُوْنٍ ۝

(Ref. Page 45)

O ye who believe ! Observe your duty to Allah with right observance, and die not save as those who have surrendered (unto Him). (3 : 102)

١٠٢- يٰٓأَيُّهَا الَّذِينَ ءَامَنُوا
اتَّقُوا اللَّهَ حَقَّ تُقَاتِهِۦ وَلَا تَمُوتُنَّ
إِلَّا وَأَنتُم مُّسْلِمُونَ ○

(Ref. Page 46)

O ye who believe ! Observe your duty to Allah. And let every soul look to that which it sendeth on before for the morrow. And observe your duty to Allah ! Lo ! Allah is Informed of what ye do. (59 : 18)

١٨- يٰٓأَيُّهَا الَّذِينَ ءَامَنُوا اتَّقُوا اللَّهَ
وَلْتَنظُرْ نَفْسٌ مَّا قَدَّمَتْ لِغَدٍ
وَاتَّقُوا اللَّهَ
إِنَّ اللَّهَ خَبِيرٌۢ بِمَا تَعْمَلُونَ ○

While as for those who walk aright, He addeth to their guidance, and giveth them their protection (against evil). (47 : 17)

١٧- وَالَّذِينَ اهْتَدَوْا
زَادَهُمْ هُدًى
وَءَاتَىٰهُمْ تَقْوَىٰهُمْ ○

(Ref. Page 47)

It is not righteousness that ye turn your faces to the East and the West ; but righteous is he who believeth in Allah and the Last Day and the Angels and the Scripture and the Prophets ; and giveth his wealth, for love of Him, to kinsfolk and to orphans and the needy and the wayfarer and to those who ask, and to set slaves free ; and observeth proper worship and payeth the poor-due. And those who keep their treaty when they make one, and the patient in tribulation and adversity and time of stress. Such are they who are sincere. Such are the Godfearing. (2 : 177)

١٧٧- لَّيْسَ الْبِرَّ أَن تُوَلُّوا وُجُوهَكُمْ
قِبَلَ الْمَشْرِقِ وَالْمَغْرِبِ
وَلَٰكِنَّ الْبِرَّ مَنْ ءَامَنَ بِاللَّهِ
وَالْيَوْمِ الْءَاخِرِ وَالْمَلَٰٓئِكَةِ وَالْكِتَٰبِ
وَالنَّبِيِّۦنَ
وَءَاتَى الْمَالَ عَلَىٰ حُبِّهِۦ ذَوِى الْقُرْبَىٰ
وَالْيَتَٰمَىٰ وَالْمَسَٰكِينَ
وَابْنَ السَّبِيلِ وَالسَّآئِلِينَ وَفِى الرِّقَابِ
وَأَقَامَ الصَّلَوٰةَ وَءَاتَى الزَّكَوٰةَ
وَالْمُوفُونَ بِعَهْدِهِمْ إِذَا عَٰهَدُوا
وَالصَّٰبِرِينَ فِى الْبَأْسَآءِ وَالضَّرَّآءِ وَحِينَ
الْبَأْسِ
أُولَٰٓئِكَ الَّذِينَ صَدَقُوا
وَأُولَٰٓئِكَ هُمُ الْمُتَّقُونَ ○

(Ref. Page 54)

And when My servants question thee concerning Me, then surely I am nigh. I answer the prayer of the suppliant when he crieth unto Me. So let them hear My call and let them trust in Me, in order that they may be led aright. (2 : 186)

١٨٦- وَإِذَا سَأَلَكَ عِبَادِي
عَنِّي فَإِنِّي قَرِيبٌ ۖ
أُجِيبُ دَعْوَةَ الدَّاعِ
إِذَا دَعَانِ ۖ
فَلْيَسْتَجِيبُوا لِي
وَلْيُؤْمِنُوا بِي لَعَلَّهُمْ يَرْشُدُونَ ○

(Ref. Page 65)

Say : Lo ! my worship and my sacrifice and my living and my dying are for Allah, Lord of the Worlds.

١٦٢- قُلْ إِنَّ صَلَاتِي وَنُسُكِي
وَمَحْيَايَ وَمَمَاتِي
لِلَّهِ رَبِّ الْعَالَمِينَ ○

He hath no partner. This am I commanded, and I am the first of those who surrender (unto Him). (6: 162-163)

١٦٣- لَا شَرِيكَ لَهُ ۖ
وَبِذَٰلِكَ أُمِرْتُ
وَأَنَا أَوَّلُ الْمُسْلِمِينَ ○

IMAN (Faith)

Introduction

1. In my earlier talk on Taqwa, I had indicated that for those of us who strive to be Muslims the stages of our journey are three. We proceed by stages : from Taqwa to Iman to Islam. Of the first stage of this journey, of Taqwa—that God-consciousness, God-awareness which is the first pre-requisite for and the beginning of Divine Guidance—I have already spoken. Today, we shall attempt to acquire some understanding of Iman (faith, belief) : both as a prelude to Islam and also as its foremost integral component, the fountain-head from which all genuine acts of Islam proceed.

2. Iman is a vast concept, with aspects too innumerable to cover in a single talk; and our inquiry will bring us no satisfaction, however limited and temporary, if we do not deliberately restrict the scope of our study. The primary thrust of my talk today, therefore, revolves round the following seven propositions :

(*a*) That Iman and Islam are not identical terms, though the two are inseparable.

(*b*) That a mere declaration of the fundamental articles of the faith ("There is no being worthy of worship other than Allah, and Muhammad is the Prophet of Allah") does not automatically make us Muslims (in terms of the Hereafter).

(*c*) That such a declaration, even when it is the product of a sincere and genuine acceptance in the heart, confers on us no more than the first pre-requisite for becoming a Momin (a man with Iman, a man of faith) and a Muslim (a man whose character and conduct accords with that faith).

(*d*) That such a Momin, who has taken only this first step, is still a long, long way from becoming a Muslim. Not only is his Iman incomplete without the acts of Islam; but what is more dangerous : even this little Iman, even this first spark for the lighting of the flame, may well die out if the acts of Islam in the external world be absent or wanting.

(*e*) Iman and Islam are indeed inseparable terms; but in the initial stages of the journey, the two are not identical. In the initial stages of the journey, a Momin is not automatically a Muslim. It is only in the final stage of perfection that the two unite : Iman, sealed by a life-time of the acts of Islam, fashions at last the true Momin; and a life-time of the acts of Islam, proceeding from and crowned by Iman, fashions at last the true Muslim. It is only at that final stage of perfection, that Iman and Islam become identical; when the Momin is also the Muslim complete, and the Muslim the Momin complete.

(*f*) That Iman is not a static but a dynamic condition of the human spirit; a variable element, increasing in depth and magnitude with the performance of every act of Islam and diminishing with the performance of every act of Un-Islam.

(*g*) That, in view of the above assertions, we ought to exercise the greatest care in evaluating the quality if our own Iman (faith), and the greatest caution before conferring on ourselves the distinction of being called Muslims. That, as a corollary, we must beware, beware of pronouncing judgements on the faith of others: the quality of their Iman, and the merit or otherwise of their acts of Islam—however isolated and fragmentary those acts may appear to us to be.

3. These, then, are the seven basic assertions round which

this talk revolves : by way of enquiry and examination, elucidation, elaboration and adequate proof.

Meaning of the Terms

4. To begin with, we must attempt to acquire a clear and precise understanding of the terms Iman and Islam.

(*a*) Literal Meaning

(1) Literally, Iman (belief) means Tasdiq (acceptance). This *acceptance* of the truth and the reality so intensely condensed in the formulation "There is no being worthy of worship other than Allah, and Muhammad is the Apostle of Allah" is a function of the human heart, and the tongue is merely an instrument for its external, audible expression. Note here, that the tongue is only one of the instruments for the expression of this inner acceptance; but, being audible, is of great public consequence (for the organisation of the Millat in the external world).

(2) Iman, then, is *inner acceptance* in the heart, followed by its verbal expression with the tongue. Islam, however, means *submission* and *surrender* (Taslim and Istislam) to the will of God, through "compliance" (Inqiyad) with His commandments as revealed through His Prophet : as contained in the Quran, and as actualised in the Prophet's Sunnah.

(3) It is obvious, then, that Islam is the more comprehensive term. Within the orbit of Islam lie the functions not only of the heart and the tongue, but of all the senses, all the limbs, the mind and the body : *the total being* of the man. On our way to becoming Muslims, Iman is a prelude to Islam and this prelude is itself an integral part of Islam—its foremost and noblest part.

(4) From this brief acquaintance with the literal meaning of the two terms, we may conclude that *acceptance*

(Iman) is *submission* (Islam) in part; but there may well be acts of *submission* (Islam) which are not necessarily tied to unconditional and total *acceptance* (of the fundamental articles of the faith : the two testimonies and all that proceed therefrom—belief in Allah, His angels, His books, His prophets and the Hereafter).

(5) It is possible that a man may perform several acts of Islam, without Iman. Within a limited span of time and with reference to specific actions, a man may be a Muslim without being a Momin, and of course, *vice versa*. And as I elaborate on this issue, think of such men and women as : Albert Schweitzer in the jungles of Africa, Florence Nightingale on the battlefields of Crimea, Father Damiens among the lepers of Molokai, Helen Keller bringing light and sound to the blind and the deaf, Maria Montessori, Augustine, Thomas Aquinas—and in a different way, yes, in a different way : Col Tran Van Tra . . . In our own times, we know of many individuals and communities who perform several acts of Islam (*e.g.* the rejection of usury, the prohibition of prostitution, drinking, gambling; the resisting of tyranny, prosecution, oppression, the exploitation of man by man; the institution of justice, charity, the care of the sick and the diseased, the widow, the orphan, the disabled, the dispossessed). These individuals and communities are literally Muslims when they so act (with reference to these actions and within the duration of time in which these actions unfold themselves), even though they may not be formally and legally within the fold of Islam for want of that *acceptance* (both inner and verbal) which we call Iman. Likewise, we know of many individuals and communities who profess to be Muslims, indeed are legally so because of their formal declaration of the faith; and

yet, their actions abound in acts of Un-Islam : acts of disobedience, flouting His commandments. When they act, (with reference to these actions and within the duration of time in which these actions unfold themselves), these individuals and communities are not Muslims (literally, Non-Muslims)—even if we were assured that their *inner acceptance* is genuine, sincere and their outward actions a manifestation of human weakness only. There then is the clear distinction between Iman and Islam, between the Momin and the Muslim. These two categories of individuals/communities to which I have referred represent :

(*a*) In the first case, Muslims whose Islam is incomplete for want of its foremost ingredient—which is Iman.

(*b*) In the second case, Momins whose Iman is incomplete for want of the acts of obedience (Islam) which that Iman makes obligatory.

Incomplete Muslims (of the first category) and incomplete Momins (of the second category)—I ask you : which pot dare call which kettle black? So far as we who belong to the second category are concerned, ringing in my ears are the words which the Lord flung at the Christians and the Jews of the Prophet's time, and may now be flung at us with equal justice :

"What, enjoin ye righteousness upon mankind, while ye yourselves forget (to practise it)? And ye are readers of the Book! Have ye then no sense?" (2 : 44)

So much, for now, of this aspect of Iman and Islam.

(6) Having considered the *literal* meaning of Iman and Islam, we may now go on to consider their technical meaning.

(*b*) **Technical Meaning**. In the Quran and the Hadith, these two terms—Iman and Islam—have been used as :
different (*i.e.* each having its own meaning, different from the other), as *related* terms (*i.e.* each being a part of the

other), and as "synonymous" terms (*i.e.* interchangeable terms, being identical in their connotation) :

(1) Look at the first usage : *Iman and Islam as "different" terms.* In this usage, Iman signifies belief in the fundamental tenets of the faith; and Islam signifies the actions, conduct and behaviour conforming to the commandments of God. The Quran repeatedly addresses "those who believe" and urges them to act in a particular fashion : *e.g.* to fear God as he should be feared; to establish regular prayer and charity; to be staunch witnesses to justice; to practise self-restraint and steadfastness; to be truthful, sincere and trustworthy; to enjoin good and forbid (ward off, resist) evil. In this usage, Iman (faith) is obviously a-priori to and distinct from Islam (acts of obedience in conformity with God's commandments). Having believed in the fundamental tenets of the faith, the Momin is then shown the way to Islam, the actions which will make him a Muslim. The Prophet was once asked what Iman was and he replied : "... that you should believe in God, His angels, His books, His apostles, the Last Day (resurrection and Divine judgement) and the decrees of God, both good and evil". Asked on the same occasion about what Islam was, he replied : "... that you should testify that there is no god but God and that Muhammad is God's messenger, that you should observe the prayer, pay the zakat, fast during Ramadan, and make the pilgrimage to the House if you have the means to go".[1] Note then, that according to this first usage :

(*a*) Iman signifies faith in things *unseen.* (2: 1-4) facts that cannot be either perceived or verified by the human senses during man's tenure on earth, facts that

1. *Mishkat* (*Vol. 1*), p. 5.

lie beyond the ken of the rational intellect in so far as they cannot be empirically established, facts that reason alone (unaided by the spirit) can neither logically formulate nor prove nor disprove, facts that we must "accept" on the authority of the Prophets[2] : such facts as the existence of a Single Supreme Being with all His divine attributes, His angels (powers), His revelations (for the guidance of mankind), the Hereafter (the resurrection of the dead, the calling to account before God for an exposition of the quality of our lives on earth), His judgement and our continued existence (in conformity with that judgement) in a state of ascending and unceasing bliss (Paradise) or a state of remorse, agony, despair, pain, anguish; a state of an eternal standing still with no prospect of moving forward; a state "with nothing to look back upon with pride; nothing to look forward to with hope"; a state of such dark darkness, filth and horror as only the Quran can describe; a state of continual death (Hell). Belief in these eschatological truths, on the authority of the divine revelation vouchsafed to the prophets (which the rational intellect cannot a-priori discover, but can certainly a-posteriori apprehend), this belief constitutes Iman (faith) : a state of mind, a condition

---

2. Connect with lecture on "Reason, Knowledge and Faith". Truths that cannot be empirically established but are not, on that score, contrary to reason. Truths that are :—

(*a*) Supra-rational but not ir-rational.

(*b*) In the direction that reason points; but cannot take us to all the way, to the end.

(*c*) Perceived by the "Leap of Faith", having been brought to the point of the leap through much reflection proceeding from a clear and adequate base of conscious reasoning.

(*d*) Perceived following a conscious, deliberate, knowing "leap"; not an un-conscious, blind, ignorant "leap".

(*e*) The ignorant leap leads to Bigotry; the knowing leap leads to Faith.

of the spirit suffused with an intense, throbbing, tingling inner *awareness* of these truths. This is Iman.

(*b*) Islam, on the other hand, signifies the actualisation or concretisation of this Iman in the external world through the performance of deeds in accordance with His commandments. The Prophet's definition of Islam, which I quoted earlier, pithily cited the *five pillars* and put a full stop after it. A little study of the Quran will reveal the significance, scope and inner content of these five commandments; a little study of the life of the Prophet, his companions and the great savants of Islam will unfold to our understanding something of the almost inexhaustible meaning—potential of these *five pillars*. I hope, some day later, to devote at last a talk to each; but for the while, I shall restrict myself to one major observation pertinent to all of these. These *five pillars* which constitute Islam are such vital instruments for the transformation of the Momin into the Muslim, completing both his Iman and his Islam, that these "instruments"—when truly performed and perfected, their effects overflowing and entering into every nook and cranny of our daily lives—in that state of perfection these instruments become an end in themselves. Only then, and *not* before. To observe these *five pillars* is certainly *not* a matter of ritual, even when we seek the aid of every formalistic device taught to us by the Prophet to capture their inner meaning and effect. Even those little things that some of us sneer at as *ritual* acquire a spiritual—psychological significance which deep reflection accompanying devoted practice over a prolonged period of time only gradually reveals (consider just two : (1) Wudu; (2) form of the Salat). I do not wish to say any more on this subject now. We were talking of Iman and Islam as *different* terms : Iman signifying that inner state of *acceptance* of certain divinely revealed truths (which we commonly call *faith*); and Islam signifying the performance of specific deeds in obedience to His commandments (which we may conveniently label as the *acts of faith*).

(2) Consider now the second usage : *Iman and Islam as "related" terms*, each being inseparable from the other. During our examination of the literal meaning of Islam we noted that Islam signifies total *submission* and *surrender* to the will of God : submission and surrender of the Qalb (mind and heart), the tongue, all the senses and every limb of man. In this surrender of the total being of man, which expresses itself through deeds in compliance with His commandments, the foremost act of obedience is the submission of the mind—its unconditional acceptance of the fundamental articles of the faith. Iman is thus a part of Islam, and its foremost part at that, as is also evident from the Prophet's definition of Islam cited earlier. On another occasion, asked what works were the best, the Prophet replied : *Islam*; asked what in Islam was the best, he replied : *Iman* (*Al-Nasai, Iman* : 1 : 11). Iman is thus the foremost of the integral parts of Islam; Islam is the whole which includes Iman as its noblest part. Islam is not complete without Iman. On the other hand, Iman, being a part of Islam, cannot be isolated (separated, plucked apart) from the whole to which it belongs. Iman acquires meaning and becomes real only in relation to the excellence achieved in the other parts which taken together constitute the whole of Islam. Iman and Islam are *related* terms, inextricably interlinked, inseparable, neither complete without the other in terms of reality—although, conceptually, Iman signifies only a part of Islam (*viz.* submission with the Qalb) whereas Islam signifies the whole,

submission in its totality (*viz.* with the Qalb, in word and in deed). This aspect of Iman and Islam as *related* terms, each inseparable from the other, comes into clear focus in the repeated references in the Quran to "those who believe and do good deeds." Only to such men, who combine Iman and Islam (each reinforcing the other), does Allah promise His guidance, His mercy, His grace and in the Hereafter a reward unceasing.

(3) Consider now the third usage : *Iman and Islam as "synonymous" terms—i.e.* terms that are interchangeable, both signifying the same thing. Consider just these two verses from the Quran :

(*a*) "And Moses said : O my people! If ye believe in Allah, then put your trust in Him—If (indeed) ye be Muslims." (10 : 84)

(*b*) "Then we brought forth such Momins as were there. But we found there only one house of Muslims (to be rescued)." (51 : 35-36)

There you have Iman and Islam used as *synonymous* terms, the Momin equated with the Muslim, and the Muslim equated with the Momin. The Prophet is on record as having said : "Islam is built upon five pillars" (*Bukhari, Iman* : 1); and asked about Iman, he referred to the same: the observance of the "five pillars." (*Bukhari, Iman:* 40)

5. Our enquiry into the three technical usages of the terms Iman and Islam (as *different*, *related* and *synonymous* terms) set against the back-drop of their literal meanings, should make the following points amply clear :

(*a*) That at *the initial stages* of our journey towards becoming Muslims, *not* Iman and Islam are identical but different terms. At the initial stages of the journey, a Momin is not automatically a Muslim. Beginners in both, imperfect in each—we are still far from the goal.

(*b*) As we proceed, somewhere in *the middle stages,* we realise that Iman and Islam are related terms : that each causes the other to grow. Every act of submission (Islam) fortifies faith (Iman); and every added assurance of faith (Iman) leads to further acts of submission (Islam). And so we proceed progressively nearer to the goal.

(*c*) *In the last, final stage* it dawns on us that Iman and Islam are indeed synonymous terms. Iman, perfected by a life-time of the acts of Islam, fashions at last the true Momin; and a life-time of the acts of Islam, suffused with the glow of a perfected Iman, fashions at last the true Muslim. At this final stage of perfection, an equilibrium is reached between Iman and Islam; the two fuse and become identical. The completed Momin becomes the Muslim complete; the completed Muslim becomes the Momin complete. There is now no distinction between the two.

Degrees of Iman

6. Having understood the meaning of the two terms Iman and Islam, we may now go on to examine the various degrees of Iman. This examination proceeds from what our previous enquiry has established to be the three components of Iman, *viz* : (1) *Inward acceptance* (Aqd-bil-Qalb) of the fundamental articles of the faith (2) *Verbal confession* (Shahadah-bil-Lisan) of the same; (3) *Works* according to and as is implicit in the five pillars of Islam. What are the implications for the Hereafter, for the various possible combinations of these three elements? In presenting this examination to you, I should in the main like to follow, as I have done in the past, Imam Ghazzali's fine exposition in the "Kitab Al-Qawaid Al-Aqaid" (Vol. II of Ghazzali's 40-volume master-piece : *Ihya Ulum al-Din*). Ghazzali

identifies six degrees of Iman through varying combinations of the three components of Islam :

(*a*) **First Degree.** Those who in their lives combine all the three elements (inward acceptance, verbal confession, works according to and as is implicit in the observance of the *five pillars*). Upon such there shall no fear come, neither will they grieve. Such will become the recipients of God's grace and mercy; and in the Hereafter theirs will be a reward unceasing.

(*b*) **Second Degree.** Those who have the first two elements (inward acceptance and verbal confession) but only a part of the third (some works of submission and some disobedience). Such are obviously incomplete Muslims, and as a consequence their Iman too is incomplete. Allah will not suffer the reward of their good works to perish (18 : 30); Allah will grant them the "wages" for the good they have done (9 : 120). But they will *not* get away with the evil that they have done; they will pay the price for it proportionate to what they have done. Most of us belong to this category (I hope and pray, to this category at least and not lower down), and we would do well to ponder over the following verses of the Quran :

> "And surely We are best aware of those most worthy to be burned therein (hell). Not one of you is there who shall not go down into it : this is a settled decree with thy Lord. Then shall We rescue those who kept away from (some) evil (at least), and leave the (total) evil-doers crouching there." (19 : 70-72)

If we belong to this second category of Momins, we pay the price for the evil done, till the reward of the little good that we did salvages us at last. Said the Apostle : "Whosoever hath in his heart even the weight of an atom of belief will be brought forth from hell-fire". Please note : not "escape" hell-fire but "be brought forth from hell-fire"—salvation at last, but not without paying the full price for the evil done. Talk of the full price to be paid for the evil done, the least that we who belong to this category can do is to avoid the *mortal sins* (Shirk—associating others in whatever is due to God; fornication and adultery; murder, plunder and theft; misappropriating the wealth of others; devouring usury; lie, slander and breach of trust; bearing false witness; believing in or practising magic; being a deserter from a war truly waged in the cause of Allah; drinking and gambling; deliberate neglect of the prescribed prayers; unlawful disobedience of parents; molestation or excommunication of legal Muslims because of specific acts of Un-Islam *i.e.* crass bigotry). These, gentlemen, are *mortal sins* and manisfestations of that most heinous of character traits : "hypocrisy".[2a] The wages of these sins are severe; several of them go so far as to temporarily push us out of the fold of Islam and no return is possible without purging our faith of the poison and the cruel deformities that these violent acts of Un-Islam introduce into our Iman. That purging of the faith is possible only through a sincere and sustained act of Taubah.[3] What we can wash away through our reinvigorated acts of renewed Islam is fine; as for the stains that may yet remain, we can only pray for His grace and His mercy. I shall close this discourse on the second category of Momins by referring you once more to those verses of the Quran which I cited earlier (19 : 70-72).

(*c*) **Third Degree.** Those who have the first two elements (inward acceptance and verbal confession) but none of the third (works according to and as is implicit in the *five pillars*). We viewed with fear the fate of such men as belong to the Second Degree; how much more fearful must we then be, if self-examination should reveal ourselves as belonging to this category; How

2-*a*. *Mishkat*, Vol. I, Book I, Chap. II, pp. 17-18.

3. See Altaf Gauhar, *Translations from the Quran*, pp. 142-145 and 153-169.

much longer and more cruel must be the pain, the agony, the remorse, the anguish, this dark darkness, filth and horror, this state of continuous death in hell that we must endure before our grossly imperfect, miniscule, "atomic" Iman salvages us at last ?

(*d*) **Fourth Degree.** Those who have the first element (inward acceptance) and the third (works according to and as is implicit in the five pillars), but do not have the second (verbal confession). Such men God will *not* condemn to eternal hell-fire; God will *not* suffer the reward of their good deeds to be lost. Their failure to make the *verbal confession* is at par with the failure of others to pray, fast or pay Zakat. The wages of this failure they must pay, but they are *not* doomed to eternal hell-fire. Iman is, above all, acceptance with the heart; the tongue is only then called upon to declare what the heart has already accepted. The heart does not become void of Iman, because of a person's failure to fulfil the duty of verbal confession. For this failure to actualize Element 2 (which, as I said before, is at par with specific failures within the orbit of Element 3; *cf.* Prophet's definition of Islam), the incomplete Muslims of this category must pay the appropriate price in hell before their inward acceptance (which may well be more than "the weight of an atom of belief") and their good deeds eventually salvage them ("bring them forth") from the horrors of eternal hell-fire. To my mind, this category of men, though belonging to the Fourth Degree, are *not* far removed from the Second. To my mind, they are higher up on the scale than those to whom Ghazzali assigns the Third Degree. But Allah knows best !

(*e*) **Fifth Degree.** Those who have the first element (inward acceptance), none of the second (verbal confession) and only some of the third (works according to and as is implicit in the five pillars). A grade below the Fourth Degree just mentioned, the men of this category too are, to my mind, not far removed from the Second. Once again, Allah knoweth best! Without formulating a new category, one thing, however, is amply clear : that mere verbal profession of the two testimonies of the faith (even when accompanied by a feeble inner acceptance and partial good works) is *no* sure guarantee against all hell-fire (19 : 70-72).

(*f*) **Sixth Degree**. Those in whom Element 1 (inward acceptance) is altogether absent, Element 2 (verbal confession) present, Element 3 (good works) partially present or altogether absent. Such men belie their hearts with their tongues; they declare the opposite of what they conceal; they are liars in the face of God, even though in the temporal world we must legally accept them as Muslims and have no business to either molest or excommunicate them. Hypocrites within the fold of Islam in this temporal world, they are far (far) removed from All the other five degrees of Iman. In the Hereafter, their abode is in the most violent, horrendous, lowest reaches of hell. I confess I do not know how God will reward them for the little good that they do; perhaps, in accordance with His natural laws, they will reap their little benefits in this world and face the Hereafter with empty hands. God preserve us all from slipping into this Sixth Degree, ominously reserved for that particular section of legal Muslims! And while talking of this category, I shudder to think how close how many of us are to totally extinguishing Element 1 in our hearts, while parading Element 2 in the hotels, bazaars, homes, conference rooms, clubs, schools, colleges, public and private places of Pakistan; in our politics, our economics, our social mores; in the

orientation, structure, character and conduct of our civil executive and the armed forces, the legislative, the judiciary; in the warped and twisted ways of worship at our burgeoning mazars—in the dark ignorance and the soulless emptiness of our noisy, verbal profession of Islam. In this context, we ought to reflect long over what Altaf Gauhar wrote in what appears to me to be a stirring story of a modern Pakistani Muslim's conversion to Islam : "Those (of us) who have been educated in the Western tradition need to study the Quran with particular care so that they may either discard the pretence of being Muslims or adopt their faith as a matter of conviction. The present state of *no-acceptance, no-rejection* makes our conduct ambivalent. Since all our actions are governed mainly by considerations of (earthly) competition and success, our formal attachment to Islam creates a dichotomy in our life. Whether this dichotomy exists or not, is a question which everyone has to answer for himself."[4]
This is a crucial question and it acquires a poignant urgency in view of the fact that for every community, as for every individual, there is *a fixed term* beyond the expiry of which there is no possibility of taking any remedial action. How close we are to the crossing of the rubicon should not be too difficult to see; and on the way to re-ordering our collective life in accordance with the tenets of Islam, the first most important step—so it seems to me—is to set our individual lives in order. So long as the individual lives in chaos, little can be done to transform the life of the community. Our salvation lies in an expanding number of God-oriented, God-fearing men who continually strive to become Muslims—so that, their own individual lives set in order, this expanding band of men may one day coa-

4. Altaf Gauhar, *Translations from the Quran*, p. 1.

lesce and eventually swamp the forces of collective disorder. Till that goal is reached, there is *no* salvation for us : either as individuals or as a community. In closing this discourse on the Sixth Degree of Iman, I wish to draw your attention, once again, to the fact that on *no* individual or community does the wrath of God descend with such violence as on the Hypocrite —nay, not even those guilty of Kufr.[5]

Iman : A Dynamic Condition of the Spirit

7. The hour grows late, and from this brief discourse on the various degrees of Iman, we must now proceed to a quick review of the sixth assertion that I made in my introduction to this talk : that Iman is not a static but a dynamic condition of the human spirit. It is a variable element, subject to appreciation and depreciation—increasing with every act of obedience, every good deed; and decreasing with every act of disobedience and sin.

8. We shall consider the dynamic nature of Iman under each of its three technical connotations—as a term different from, related to and synonymous with Islam :

(*a*) Iman : As "Different" From Islam

(1) In his usage, you would recollect, Iman signifies acceptance with the heart (Tasdiq-bil-Qalb). In the initial stages of our journey towards Islam, this Iman is a belief (Itiqad) based on the authority of others (Taqlid). At this stage, it does not yet enjoy what Ghazzali calls "the benefit of revelation and an open heart". At this stage, it is essentially acceptance—

---

5. *Cf.* Ghazzali, *The Foundations of the Articles of Faith*, pp. 105-116. In presenting the Degrees of Iman (para 6 above), I have retained the structure enunciated by Imam Ghazzali but there are substantial deviations with regard to both approach and coutent, particularly in my formulation and assessment of the Fourth and Fifth Degrees of Iman.

with, perhaps, only a modicum of understanding; a measure of understanding that, at best, only scratches the surface of Iman. This is the Iman, Ghazzali says, of the "common folk—in fact, in all except the elite".

(2) But once this Iman is lodged in the heart of man, it is subject to expansion and contraction, subject to increase and decrease, growing with the performance of good deeds and decaying with the performance of bad deeds (9 : 125; 48 : 4; 84: 16). To this truth Ali referred when he said: "Verily Iman will loom as a single white spot in the heart of man. If the man will do that which is good, the white spot will grow and spread until the whole heart becomes white. On the other hand, hypocrisy makes its first appearance as a black blotch in the heart of man. If the man will do that which is unlawful, the black blotch will grow and spread until the whole heart becomes black, and blackness becomes his second nature".[6]

(3) This aspect of the inter-action between the inner state of man and his external actions, each influencing the other, is the subject of a powerful exposition by one of the greatest of the psychologists of the 20th Century: William James. What James today empirically proves in many volumes is asserted by the Quran in a single sentence : "Nay, but their own works have got mastery over their hearts". (84 : 16). How a speck of Iman in the heart may lead man to acts of Islam in the external world, and how those acts in turn may expand that speck in the heart, and so proceed in an almost endless chain reaction is perceptively explained by Ghazzali. In his words : "In fact the person who believes that the orphan offers him the

6. *Nahjul Balagha* (*Sayings, Sermons, Letters of Hazrat Ali*).

opportunity to reveal the quality of mercy, will act according to this belief and show kindness towards the orphan. This action will assure him of the existence of mercy within him and this assurance will fortify (increase, expand, deepen, cause to grow) the already existent quality of mercy in him . . . Similarly, if the person who believes in modesty will, in accordance with his belief, humble himself before another person, he will sense the quality of modesty (within him). The same is true of all qualities of the heart : all bodily actions proceed from them, and then the very influence of these actions react upon them, thereby confirming (their existence) and increasing (their strength)".[7] The modern psychologist attempts to sum up this truth, when he says : our actions spring from our beliefs and those actions, in turn, modify our beliefs.

(4) Every act of obedience (Islam) or disobedience (Kufr) in the external world of His commandments makes a corresponding impact on the inner state in the heart of man. Just as every act of Islam (submission in the external world) causes Iman (acceptance in the heart of man) to grow; likewise, every act of Kufr (disobedience in the external world) breeds Kufr (non-acceptance, denial, rejection) in the heart of man. The heart of man is the life-long battle-ground between the contending forces of Iman and Kufr. When we perform acts of Islam in the external world, in the heart the forces of Iman advance and Kufr retreats; when we perform acts of Kufr in the external world, in the heart the forces of Iman retreat and Kufr advances. Between the two is the "no-man's

7. Al-Ghazzali, *Bidayat al-Hidayah*. Translation by Montgomery Watt ("The Faith and Practice of Al-Ghazzali").

land in which the heart of man cries out : "I do not know; what shall I do?" And so the battle in the heart wages, influenced by actions in the external world, with either Iman or Kufr gaining ground.

(6) From this understanding of Iman as a dynamic condition of the human spirit, the importance of Islam and its two important aspects (in relation to Iman) should be clear. On the one hand, *the presence of acts of Kufr* in the external world will rapidly vanquish whatever the forces that there be of Iman in the heart. On the other hand, *the absence of the acts of Islam* in the external world will cause Iman in the heart to atrophy for want of exercise and nourishment. *Prolonged neglect of Islam,* will cause even that last spark in this dwindling flame of Iman in the heart to be eventually extinguished. The conclusion, then, is clear : for the successful shaping of this dynamic condition of the human spirit, we must not only : (1) avoid and resist acts of Kufr in the external world (which is only the defensive aspect of the battle); but also (2) perform the positive acts of Islam (which is the offensive launched for the eventual destruction of Kufr).

(6) So much, gentlemen, for our inquiry into Iman as a dynamic condition of the human spirit—from the view-point of Iman as a term *different* from Islam, Iman signifying "acceptance in the heart" and Islam signifying "acts of obedience in the external world".

(*b*) Iman : As "Related" to Islam

(1) From the stand-point of Iman as a term related to Islam, the dynamic nature of Iman is even easier to logically comprehend. If we should formulate this stand-point as Iman being a composite of both : (1) acceptance in the heart and (2) works of obedience

in the external world, then it is logically evident that any increase or decrease in any one of its components would correspondingly increase or decrease the whole to which it belongs. Since works of obedience in the external world are variable (with regard to both quantity and quality), this *Variable Integral Component* of Iman makes Iman itself a *Dynamic* entity : in quality growing proportionately with good deeds and decaying with bad deeds, in magnitude increasing with the number of good deeds done and decreasing with the number of bad deeds. We may also formulate this stand-point as Iman being an *Integral* part of Islam. Even from this sub-standpoint, Iman reveals itself as a dynamic entity, for no whole (in this case, Islam) can grow or expand without a corresponding growth or expansion (a quantitative and/or qualitative change) in its integral components. Regardless of whichever of the two sub-standpoints we take in our view of Iman as a term related to Islam, the conclusion is the same : Iman is a *dynamic* condition of the human spirit, changing qualitatively and quantitatively in accordance with the nature (good or bad) and the number of deeds (more or less) done in the external world.

(2) In this context, I might draw your attention once more to the repeated joint references in the Quran to "those who believe and do good deeds", whenever it talks of a "reward unceasing" or designates those on whom "there shall no fear come, neither shall they grieve."

(3) So much for Iman as a *dynamic* condition of the human spirit, viewed from either of the two sub-standpoints of Iman as a term *related* to Islam.

(*c*) Iman : As "Synonymous" With Islam

(1) From the view-point of Iman and Islam as synonymous terms—a viewpoint which defines the Momin as the Muslim complete, and the Muslim as the Momin complete—Iman comes to signify that perfected states of certain and total acceptance (Yaqin) which Ghazzali identifies as the product of "revelation and an open heart".[8]

(2) Iman at this final stage of perfection is obviously (conceptually, at least) no longer subject to increase and decrease. This is the Iman of the Prophet: the complete Momin, the complete Muslim—with no distinction between the two, so that Allah confers on him his highest title: "My slave, My bondsman"!

Iman: Assessment and Evaluation

9. Having spoken about the meaning of Iman, its various degrees and Iman as a dynamic condition of the human spirit, I should like to devote this last part of the talk to the seventh assertion that I made earlier on in my Introduction *viz.* that we ought to exercise the greatest care in assessing or evaluating the quality of our own Iman, and the greatest caution before conferring on ourselves the distinction of being called Momins or Muslims. That, as a corollary, we must beware, beware of pronouncing judgements on the quality of the Iman and the Islam of others.

10. Before I list for you the compelling reasons for the exercise of this care and caution, I should like to cite to you a few examples of our illustrious fore-fathers and their approach to this problem :

(*a*) Al-Hasan Al-Basri was once asked : "Art thou a believer (Momin)?" He replied : " If it be the will of Allah!"

---

8. See, Ghazzali : (*a*) *Book of Knowledge*, pp. 46-49 and 192-200 and (*b*) *The Foundations of the Articles of Faith*, pp. 116-121.

(*b*) Ibrahim Ibn Adham once said : "Whenever you are asked, 'Are you a Momin?', say : "There is no god but Allah!"

(*c*) Al-Qamah (Ibn Qays) was asked : "Are you a Momin?" He replied : "I fervently hope so. If it be the will of Allah!"

(*d*) Sufyan Al-Thawri said : "We believe in Allah, His angels, His books, His apostles. But we do not know what we are in the sight of God."

11. Note the fervent hope, the shuddering fear, the care and caution, the hesitation, the reluctance almost with which these eminent men of faith assert their Iman; and how glib we are, shouting from roof-tops, declaring to all and sundry, even without being questioned, that we are Momins and Muslims. How thoughtless we are, how ignorant of what we assert; what vanity, what glib righteousness, what outrageous hypocrisy!

12. Even if we should be among those fortunate few who sincerely and strenuously strive to be Muslims, we have no business to confer on ourselves titles that must await the judgement of God, titles which we have no means of knowing whether we deserve them or not till after a life-time of continuous effort. Indeed, there are many compelling reasons for the exercise of the greatest caution and care, before we make even a guarded assertion about our being Momins and Muslims. With the little that we have learnt, during my earlier talk and this one, about Taqwa, Iman and Islam—even with that little at the back of our minds, it should not be too difficult to identify the compelling reasons for the utmost caution and care in asserting or even silently evaluating the quality of our Iman :

(*a*) Firstly, we have seen that Iman is a dynamic condition of the human spirit (dependent on deeds). I can never be sure of its present status; what is more, I cannot tell which way it will grow tomorrow and in the coming days. Today, I believe—fine! But will I continue to grow in faith the rest of my days towards the goal of perfection, or will I back-slide : my faith shrivelling instead of expanding, darkness creeping in where once there was some light? That's why the man striving to be a Momin continually prays : "Our Lord, perfect for us our light.." (*Quran*).. "My Lord, expand my breast and ease my task for me.." (*Quran*)..I am not sure of what I am today (besides a gnawing awareness of my imperfection), I do not know what I'll be tomorrow; above all, will I be among the believers the day I die? That is why the man who strives a life-time to perfect his Iman, prays along with every act of Islam : "Our Lord! Cause not our hearts to deviate.." (*Quran*).. "You are my Protector..cause me to die as a Muslim.." (*Quran*).. Just as the day (dawn to sunset) is the set period for the fulfilment of the fast, so is a life-time (adolescence to death) the set period for the fulfilment of Iman. To declare it as valid before its conclusion is obviously premature. It is over the end that the God-fearing have wept. It is not merely our entry into life as a Momin but also our exit from it as a Momin, that is important. Consider these two statements by two of Islam's great savants :

(1) "If I had known a certain person for 50 years and then even though so frail a thing as a pole should hide him from my sight before his death, I could not be sure that he died a true believer."

(2) "If I were given the choice between martyrdom at the outer gate of the house and death as a true Momin at the door of an inner room, I would choose the latter because I do not know what might occur to me and divert my heart from true belief on my way (from the

door of the inner room) to the outer gate of the house."

That is why the Momin, performing acts of Islam, continually prays : "O Lord! Let my entry be..and, likewise, my exit.." (*Quran*). Even that most perfect of all Momins, the last Prophet of Islam, prayed : "O, God! I seek refuge with Thee against the evil of things which I have done and the things which I have left undone." One of the companions asked : "Art thou (also) afraid, O Apostle of Allah?" and the Apostle replied : "What could make me feel secure, when the heart lies between the two fingers of the Merciful, and He doeth with them what He willeth." What, the Prophet is not secure, the Prophet is not sure and we dare, we dare assert our Iman with such glib thoughtlessness? Nay, "the final issue of all things is with God" (*Quran*, 22 : 42); and the maximum that we may say, if indeed we do so, is : Yea! I strive to be a Momin; I strive to be a Muslim.

(*b*) This "doubt" arising from an awareness of the imperfection of our Iman does no constitute un-belief. It is fully justified because in this temporal world we have no means of ascertaining the grade or degree of Iman attained by us. The Quran declares : "Allah will raise you who believe, and those to whom knowledge is given to lofty grades (plural)." (58 : 12). It also declares : "There are varying ranks before God." (3 : 157). Whatever that order of arraignment in terms of individual excellence within the fold of Islam, one mortal danger to which *all* of us who legally belong to the fold of Islam are exposed is hypocrisy (Munafiqat). In this context, please consider :

(1) The Prophet once said : "Four things, if they obtain in a person, make him an utter *Hypocrite*, no matter how much he prays, and fasts, and claims that he is a *Believer*: he who lies, when he speaks; breaks a

promise when he pledges his word; betrays a confidence when he is trusted; and deviates from justice when he enters a controversy." (*Bukhari*, *Iman* : 24). When a man striving to be a Momin says : "There is no being worthy of worship but Thou; exalted be Thy Person! (Forgive me, for) Verily I am of those who have transgressed Thy limits!"—he is not being overly modest but merely stating the truth. And knowing the truth about ourselves as we all do, who is there among us who dare confer on himself that highest compliment which any man may hope and strive for (but none will ever fully attain) : being called a Momin. Even if, within a given moment, we should feel such a surging assurance of Iman as to compel us to cry out, we would do well to cry aloud only the words of the testimony ("There is no god but Allah; (and) Muhammad is His Apostle") or recite some appropriate verse from the Quran; but never, never assert : "Lo, I am a Momin!" "Hast thou marked those who hold themselves to be righteous?" asks the Quran (62 : 33) and warns : "Assert not your own purity." (4 : 52). A wise man was once asked : "What is detestable truth?" He answered : "A man's praise of himself (even if what he says is true)."[9]

(2) To assert our Iman before others, knowing the truth about ourselves, is to be guilty of *Hypocrisy* : that most dreadful of all diseases of the heart. Ghazzali quotes Ibn Abi Mulaykah as having once said : "I have known 130 (according to another version 150) of the companions of the Prophet, all of whom feared Hypocrisy." Even 'Umar Ibn Al-Khattab once ran to Hudayfah, that knower of the secrets that

9. Ghazzali, *Ibid.*, Section 4.

men conceal in their breasts, ran to Hudayfah, seeking his assurance that 'Umar Ibn Al-Khattab was not a hypocrite! What, 'Umar Ibn Al-Khattab—and here we are parading our Iman and Islam, flinging our faith in the face of all and sundry! Al-Hasan Al-Basri was once told : "There are some who say that they do not fear hypocrisy." The reaction of that man of faith was spontaneous : "By God, I would rather be sure that I am free of hypocrisy than have all the world's contents of gold." And of all the myriad kinds of hypocrisy—all of which exhibit in the external world an appearance contrary to the reality concealed; a pleasant facade, a pleasing veneer, a shining exterior unmatched by a corresponding quality within—of all the many kinds of hypocrisy the easiest, the commonest, the most dangerous belong to the category of *disagreements between the tongue and the heart.* It is the fear of even a trace of hypocrisy that holds the Momin back from asserting that he is a Momin. All he knows is that he strives to be one, and continually seeks God's aid to that end. Conceit and self-satisfaction with his Iman are not the characteristics of a man who strives to be a Momin.

(3) Finally, when a Momin *is* questioned about whether he is a Momin and answers : "I fervently hope so. If it be the will of God!"—that second statement of his is not an expression of doubt or infirmity of resolve but a factual acknowledgement of the truth that nothing happens without His consent; He is the Ultimate Doer, His is the ultimate decree (48 : 27). "If it be the will of God" is a supplication—an expression of desire, not of doubt; a plea for God's aid for the crowning of human effort, not

a cover-plan for inaction, nor (far worse) a premeditated excuse for *not* wanting to do something. Indeed, we cannot be Momins without His acceptance of us as Momins; but we grossly err when we choose to, deliberately or otherwise, overlook His laws: He guides those who want to be guided and strive for such guidance; and He leads astray those who want to go astray and act accordingly. Divine dispensation follows human conduct; and is not antecedent to it (except in the knowledge of God, who knows what lies behind us and what lies ahead of us—a knowledge that does not interfere with the actual conduct of man who, having been granted free will, may take whichever path he chooses. Pre-destination is thus an aspect of His foreknowledge; it is not pre-ordainment—not a judgement passed antecedent to evidence, not a life sealed antecedent to its actual course). So, when the Momin (with reference to his Iman) says, "If it be the will of God", it is indicative not of passive resignation but a plea for added strength in his striving, a prayer for His aid, grace and mercy in accordance with His laws. The Momin says : "O Lord! I strive to be a Momin; make me one!" Beyond that limited assertion and that limitless prayer evident in every act throughout a life-time of the acts of Islam, no Momin ventures.

13. It is only correct that we should alternate between fear and hope, while striving to fortify our Iman through continuous acts of Islam. It is only natural that we should entertain some doubt about the validity of our Iman and the acceptance by God of our deeds of righteousness. And when there is so much doubt about my own self (whom I live with every moment and know so well), how much the more cautious must I be while evaluating the quality and quantum of another

man's Iman and Islam. In fact, such judgement is not for me to pronounce (except when called upon to do so for legal reasons within the frame-work of an Islamic state). Such judgement, in relation to the Hereafter, is the exclusive prerogative of God—Who alone knows the secrets in the hearts of men and Whose vision is all-embracing, unerring with the knowledge of "all that lies in front of them and behind them". It seems to me also necessary to bear in mind that the un-believer or dis-believer of today may be the believer of tomorrow—and *vice versa*. God protect us all! If I have once believed, I can only seek to fortify that faith with the acts of faith, while praying continuously : "Our Lord! Cause not our hearts to deviate.." "My Lord! Let my entry be..and (likewise) my exit..".. "Thou art my Protector..cause me die a Muslim.." "Our Lord! Perfect our light for us.." And the day I die, I pray I'll have this prayer also in my heart and on my lips, till my lips cease to move: "Our Lord! Accept this (sacrifice) from us..".

Conclusion

14. This, gentlemen, brings me to the end of this restricted talk on Iman : its meaning, its degrees, its dynamic nature and the care and caution that all of us must exert in evaluating its quality and quantum in ourselves. I can think of no conclusion more apt than to close this talk with that prayer which every Momin prays as the last part of that last meaningful act which he performs before descending into "the death of each day's life" :

> "*Allahumma Inna Nastainuka,*
> (Our Lord, of Thee (and Thee alone) we seek aid.
> *Wa Nastaghfiruka,*
> (And of Thee we seek forgiveness)
> *Wa Nu Minu Bika,*
> (And in Thee we repose faith)
> *Wa Natawakkalu Alaika,*

(And in Thee we place our trust)
Wa Nusnee Alaikal Khair,
(And to Thee race all good things)
Wa Nashkuruka,
(And we proclaim our gratitude to Thee)
Wala Nakfuruka
(And we are not ungrateful towards Thee)
Wa Nakhlau Wa Natruku Main-Yafjurka.
(And we abandon and sever connection with those that disobey Thee)
Allahumma Iyyaka Nabudu,
(Our Lord, Thee (and Thee alone) we serve)
Walaka Nusalli, Wa Nasjudu,
(And to Thee alone we orient ourselves, and before Thee alone we bow down)
Wa Ilaika Nasaa, Wa Nahfidu,
(And towards Thee we race, and in Thee we seek refuge)
Wa Narjuu Rahmataka,
(And cover us with Thy mercy).
Wa Nakhsha Azaabaka,
(And save us from the torments of Thy wrath).
Inna Azaabaka Bil Kuffari Mulhiq."
(Verily, Thy wrath is only for those who reject and rebel against Thee)

SELECTED BIBLIOGRAPHY

1. Marmaduke Pickthall, *The Meaning of the Glorious Quran : Text and Explanatory Translation.* Accurate Printers, P. O. Box 1338, Lahore.
2. Abul Ala Maududi, *Tafheemul Quran* (*The Meaning of the Quran*). Islamic Publications, Lahore.
3. Abdullah Yusuf Ali, *The Holy Quran : Text, Translation and Commentary.* Sheikh Muhammad Ashraf, Kashmiri Bazar, Lahore.
4. Altaf Gauhar, *Translations from the Quran.* Idara Tarjumanul Quran, Ichhra, Lahore.

5. *Mishkat al-Masabih,* Translation by Dr. James Robson. Sheikh Muhammad Ashraf, Kashmiri Bazar, Lahore.

6. *Nahjul Balagha* (*Sayings, Sermons and Letters of Hazrat Ali*) Translation by Mohammad Askari Jafery. Khorasan Islamic Centre, Karachi.

7. Al-Ghazzali, *Al-Kitab al-Qawaid al-Aqaid* (*Vol. II of the Ihya Ulum al-Din*). Translation by Nabih Amin Faris ("The Foundations of the Articles of Faith"). Sheikh Muhammad Ashraf, Kashmiri Bazar, Lahore.

8. Al-Ghazzali, *Al-Kitab al-Ilm* (*The Book of Knowledge*). Translation by Nabih Amin Faris. Sheikh Muhammad Ashraf, Kashmiri Bazar, Lahore.

9. *Al-Hizb al-Azam* (*Prayers from the Quran*). Sheikh Muhammad Ashraf, Kashmiri Bazar, Lahore.

10. Abul Ala Maududi, *Fundamentals of Islam.* Islamic Publications, Lahore.

IMAN (FAITH)

Passages from the Quran

(Ref. Page [illegible])

Enjoin [illegible] righteousness upon mankind while ye yourselves forget (to practise it)? And ye are readers of the Scripture ! Have ye then no sense ? (2 : 44)

۴۴- اَتَاْمُرُوْنَ النَّاسَ بِالْبِرِّ وَ تَنْسَوْنَ
اَنْفُسَكُمْ وَاَنْتُمْ تَتْلُوْنَ الْكِتٰبَ ؕ
اَفَلَا تَعْقِلُوْنَ ۝

(Ref. Page 84)

And Moses said : O my people ! If ye have believed in Allah then put trust in Him, if ye have indeed surrendered (unto Him). (10 : 84)

۸۴- وَقَالَ مُوْسٰى يٰقَوْمِ اِنْ كُنْتُمْ اٰمَنْتُمْ
بِاللّٰهِ فَعَلَيْهِ
تَوَكَّلُوْٓا اِنْ كُنْتُمْ مُّسْلِمِيْنَ ۝

Then We brought forth such believers as were there.

But We found there but one house of those surrendered (to Allah). (51 : 35-36)

۳۵- فَاَخْرَجْنَا
مَنْ كَانَ فِيْهَا مِنَ الْمُؤْمِنِيْنَ ۝
۳۶- فَمَا وَجَدْنَا فِيْهَا
غَيْرَ بَيْتٍ مِّنَ الْمُسْلِمِيْنَ ۝

(Ref. Page 86)

And surely We are Best Aware of those most worthy to be burned therein.

There is not one of you but shall approach it. That is a fixed ordinance of thy Lord. Then We shall rescue those who kept from evil, and leave the evil-doers crouching there. (19 : 70-72)

۷۰- ثُمَّ لَنَحْنُ اَعْلَمُ بِالَّذِيْنَ
هُمْ اَوْلٰى بِهَا صِلِيًّا ۝
۷۱- وَاِنْ مِّنْكُمْ اِلَّا وَارِدُهَا ۚ
كَانَ عَلٰى رَبِّكَ حَتْمًا مَّقْضِيًّا ۝
۷۲- ثُمَّ نُنَجِّى الَّذِيْنَ اتَّقَوْا
وَّنَذَرُ الظّٰلِمِيْنَ فِيْهَا جِثِيًّا ۝

THE BASIC ATTRIBUTES OF A MUSLIM

Introduction

1. In talking to you today, Gentlemen, about the basic attributes of a Muslim, I proceed on the fundamental assumption that we belong to that category of men who *want* to be Muslims. Given this *inclination* in the heart, this sincere *desire* to *become* Muslims, the next step on the long road to the *actualisation* of Islam in our lives is to *understand* what Islam is and what *being a Muslim* implies. As that understanding in the mind and the heart *dawns* and *expands*, we enter the realm of *conscious action* for the *concretisation* of what we have inwardly perceived. In this progression of Islam from a *stirring within* to the *seeking of knowledge* to *conscious action*, the role of the first two elements is of crucial significance to the third. The quality of our Islam in the external world is directly dependant on the quality of our *inner perception* (intellectual, emotional, spiritual) of it ; although it goes without saying that *Islam* culminates in *action* and does *not* stop at *knowledge*.

2. This talk of mine which seeks to serve the *second* element (the *acquisition of knowledge* about Islam) *will not* lead to the *third* (*conscious action* corresponding to the knowledge acquired) if the *first* element (the *desire to become Muslims*) is absent, insincere or so weak as to be condemned to premature death. If we *want* to be Muslims, it must be a *desire* and a *longing*, not a mere *wish*. It must begin as a violent *agitation* in the mind and continue as a life-long *craving* in the heart. Above all, it must be *sincere*. We have no business to be *legal* Muslims only, for *pragmatic* reasons formulated by a *dishonest* exercise of the *intellect* ; we have no business to *call* ourselves *Muslims* as a matter of *social convenience*, *hereditary habit* or *outright intellectual unconcern and indolence*. We must be Muslims, or whatever else we please, as a consequence of *personal reflection* and *conscious choice*. We have no

business to *loiter around* the outer gates of Islam ; we must either *enter* the mansion or clear out of the way of others whose vision we clog or whose entry we actually obstruct. To this imperative need of our times *Altaf Gauhar* refers when in the Preface to his *Translations from the Quran* (p. 1) he writes :

> "Those who have been educated in the western tradition need to study the Quran with particular care so that they may either discard the pretence of being Muslims or adopt their faith as a matter of conviction. The present state of 'no-acceptance, no-rejection' makes our conduct ambivalent. Since all our actions are governed mainly by considerations of (worldly) competition and success, our formal attachment to Islam creates a dichotomy in our life. Whether this dichotomy exists or not (in our individual and collective lives) is a question which everyone has to answer for himself."

3. This talk of mine proceeds on the assumption that our answer to that crucial question is : "No ! We do *not* wish to be guilty of 'no-acceptance, no-rejection'. We genuinely *want* to *become* Muslims ; and to that end, as the second essential step, we *want to know* what Islam is and what *being* a Muslim *implies*. Like my earlier talks an *Taqwa* and *Iman*, this one too is designed to meet that *need*—as much for *myself* as for *you*. This is only a beginning, and a very partial one at that within the constricted limits of my present understanding; but I am glad to have made a beginning and the *joy* of it is only heightened (with a restless admixture of fear and hope) as I catch a glimpse of the *long, long* way that I have yet to cover.

4. In framing this talk on the Basic Attributes of the Muslim, I have also proceeded on the assumption that we already know that *Islam* is not just another *Madhhab* with its own peculiar array of dogma, ritual and incantations but a *complete way af life* affecting every aspect of a man's character and conduct during his tenure on earth. The purpose of this

way of life is to mould and develop the human spirit, in both its inner constitution and its external conduct, in such a manner as to successfully survive the shock of death and lead it on to a higher state of existence in the Hereafter. The all-pervading feature of this *way* is acceptance of and submission, surrender, subservience to the will of God through compliance with His commandments—as revealed to His prophets since the beginning of man on earth, a *Din* (basic tenets of the faith) *confirmed* and a *Shariah* (laws, canons, axioms of conduct) *perfected* through the agency of the last of His prophets and preserved without error or alteration (and *no* possibility of decay) in the *Quran*.

5. In approaching my talk today on the Basic Attributes of the Muslim, I proceed on the assumption that we have no doubt about the definition of *Islam* and a *Muslim*. With what we covered in our earlier enquiries into *Taqwa*, *Iman* and *Islam* at the back of our minds, let us recapitulate that a *Muslim* is, by definition, "a being in total subservience to the Will of God", His slave, His bondsman; a creature not in conflict but in harmony with God, a being whose finiteness is *in tune* with the Infinite; a being—if you like the metaphor—*absorbing*, *pulsating* and *radiating* on the same "frequency" as God's.

6. We need to remember also that *Islam* is not the name of any *particular* religion but a "state of being" (mind, body and spirit) and a "way of life" which incorporates "the unalloyed kern and core of *all* religions revealed to man". Even when considered as a "religion" in the conventional sense, it is a *generic* term and not a *brand-name*. It is not a *religious Trade-mark* for the identification of any particular community, in much the same way as we talk of "*Old Spice*" shaving lotion to distinguish it from other shaving lotions. No, Sir ! When we talk of *Islam*, we refer, as it where, to *vitamin* "*C*"—*not* to 'Ascorbon' (by Dumex) or 'Celin' (by Glaxo) or 'Surbex' (by Abbott). No, Sir! Islam is not a *brand-name* for *yet another* religion; but a *generic term* referring to the unalloyed kern and core of *all* religions

revealed to Man : a ringing, final *re-affirmation* of *the universal truth, the way of life* (Al-Din) for *all mankind.* Some may choose to call themselves *Christians* following Christ, *Buddhists* following the Lord Buddha or Zoroastrians following Zoroaster[1]—but we, if we knew what we are talking about, we would refuse to be called *Mohammedans.* Instead, we would declare what the Quran asks us to declare :

> "Say (O Muslims) :
> We believe in Allah and that which is revealed unto us ; and that which was revealed unto Abraham, and Ishmael, and Isaac and Jacob, and the tribes; and that which Moses and Jesus received; and that which the prophets received from their Lord. We make no distinction between any of them, and unto Him we have surrendered."
>
> (Quran, 2 : 136).

7. We would do well then to remember that *Islam* was preached not by just *one* prophet, but by *all* prophets *all* over the world ever since the beginning of Man ; and those who accept the last of them, by this very acceptance put a seal on their acceptance of *all* of them. And because *Islam* is a *universal* and not a *particular* "way", we find that *Muslims* (*not* in the *temporal-legal* sense but in relation to the Hereafter)—are *not* confined to any particular community, country, race or even creed, and the many man-made distinctions that today cruelly divide man from man. *Islam* is the true faith and way of *mankind,* and no single community has a monopoly of it. *Incomplete Muslims* are scattered all over the earth; and the *complete Muslim,* now that there are no more prophets to come, we *cannot* find even within those communities who *legally label* themselves as "Muslims".

8. This is a very important point to remember, gentlemen : that a mere *verbal declaration* of the fundamental articles of the faith does *not* automatically make us *Muslims*; and the absence

1. Maududi, *Towards Understanding Islam.*

of such a declaration does *not* (in terms of the *Hereafter*) *altogether* exclude those guilty of it from the fold of Islam. We touched on this vital issue during our earlier enquiry into the degrees of *Iman*; and we would do well to recall to mind the extreme care, caution, fear, reluctance almost with which our illustrious forefathers asserted their own *Iman* and *Islam*. Cautious in our approach to ourselves, we need to be even more cautious in our approach to others. We have no business (*except* for *legal* reasons within the frame-work of an *Islamic* state) to pronounce judgements on the *Islam* of others. And even when compelled to do so, we would do well to remember that soaring above our *temporal-legal* judgements (which may be right *or* wrong) is the *unerring* judgement of God in the Hereafter. He alone Who has *complete knowledge* can pass the *final* verdict; and common-sense dictates that we refrain from arrogating to ourselves that which is the exclusive privilege of God.

9. These introductory remarks, Gentlemen, I thought were essential as a prelude to our enquiry into the Basic Attributes of a Muslim—attributes culled from Quranic references to the *Muttaqi* (the God fearing), the *Momin* (the man of faith), the *Rashid* (the rightly guided), the *Salih* (the upright, the doer of good), the *Munsif* (the upholder of justice), the *Siddiq* (the sincere, the truthful), the *Mohsin* (the doer of *Ihsan*), the *Adil* (the just, the stayer within the limits prescribed by Allah), the *Mutawakkil* (the one who places his trust in God), the *Alim* (the man of knowledge), the *Sadiq* (the man of charity, magnanimity, generosity), the *Mukhlis* (the sincere), the *Mutatahhir* (the clean, the pure) and so on : all fusing into that *integrated composite* called "*the Muslim*" (the man in *total subservience*—mind, body, spirit—the *total being in total subservience to God*).

10. In attempting a compilation of these "basic attributes" of the *Muslim*, I have been puzzled : in the first stage, by the *selection* to be made; and in the second stage, by my attempt to formulate what you might call a *priority list*. On both counts, I have been baffled. After much thought, it seemed to

me prudent to relegate this attempt at *logical systematisation* to the status of what you would call a "secondary thrust" or an "auxiliary effort"; and instead *concentrate* on the broad essentials as they naturally strike the mind and effortlessly pierce through the heart of a sincere reader of the Quran. These "basic attributes" of the *Muslim* are so closely inter-linked, each with so profound an impact on the other, that their logical consideration in part *cannot* be divorced from a continuous and unstraying vision of the *whole* to which these parts belong. The entire process of *becoming a Muslim* revolves round a continuous and snow-balling effort to absorb and actualize these individual attributes each carried to the limit of its perfection, while progressively *integrating* whatever is achieved in *one* with *all* that has been achieved in the *others*. It is this *progressive integration* heading for the *whole*, in both the inner constitution of the human spirit and its external conduct, that characterises *him* who *strives* to be a *Muslim*.

11. Before we consider these attributes *one by one*, let us look at them *as a package*. The basic attributes of a Muslim, as revealed by the repeated references to them in the Quran, are :

(*a*) God-consciousness, God-awareness (*Taqwa*).

(*b*) Trust in and Reliance on God (*Tawakkul al-Allah*).

(*c*) Purity (*Taharat*) : Eradication of the "Grave Diseases of the Heart" (Pride, Arrogance, Vanity; Envy, Jealousy, Malice, Rancour; Greed, Avarice; Love of Worldly Wealth, Property, Status, Pomp and Power; Anger and Rage; Lust and Sensuality; Hypocrisy; the Sins of the Tongue).

(*d*) Truthfulness (*Sidq*) and Sincerity (*Ikhlas*).

(*e*) Justice (*Adl*).

(*f*) Patient Perseverance and Steadfastness (*Sabr*).

(*g*) Prayer and Charity (cultivating a sense of wonder and a grateful heart).

(*h*) Modesty and Humility.
(*i*) A Universal Outlook and the Pursuit of Knowledge.
(*j*) Striving in Allah's Way.

BASIC ATTRIBUTES

God-Consciousness, God-Awareness (*Taqwa*)

12. Of all the basic attributes of the *Muslim*, the most fundamental, to my mind, is *Taqwa*: that God-consciousness, that God-awareness which guides him to and establishes him in God-oriented action. On *Taqwa* I have already devoted a full lecture. Here, within the context of this present talk, I shall restrict myself to a brief reference to how the individual may harness the words of the Quran to arouse, nourish, sustain, expand and deepen this God-consciousness inherent in the heart of man: a consciousness which wells up within us, as naturally as water gushes from a fountain. All it calls for is a progressively deeper boring, storage, preservation and purposeful channelisation ; till the waters of *Taqwa* inundate *every* tract (and *all* of it is *cultivable*) of our mind, heart and spirit; till we are soaked in God to the roots of our unconscious; till from deep within us there rises the joyous proclamation: "We take our colour from Allah (our baptism is of and by God) and who is better at colouring than Allah (and who can baptize better than Allah) ? And we are His worshippers." (2 : 138)

13. This God-consciousness, this God-awareness demands, in the first stage, a conscious application of the rational intellect for an understanding of His *Essence* and his *Attributes*, through an "analytical study" of the Quran. Having gone as far as this can take us, we must switch over to an attempt at "devotional perception" of those Quranic passages which describe His essence and His attributes. Both these modes should be put into operation concurrently, within the span of every 24 hours as the basic unit of time: analytical study being carried out at any convenient hour of the day *or* night, while reserving the early hours

of the dawn *and* the night when it is at its stillest for the devotional recitation (*with* understanding of the *literal* text) of those Quranic passages which simultaneously "describe" (for "rational" comprehension) and "reveal" (for "devotional" perception) His *essence* and His *attributes*.

14. *As for His essence*, we need to rationally perceive (to the outermost limit of such perception) and then devotionally absorb the facts : that He *exists*, is *one* (*the* Unity : not one in trinity ; not one of two ; without consort, without partners ; neither begetting, nor begotten : *One*), *Self-Subsisting*, *Eternal* (without beginning, "ancient (*Qadim*) from eternity (*Azali*)"), *Ever-lasting* (without end), *Transcendent* (beyond the confines of time and space), *Omnipresent* (present everywhere at the same time; with us wherever we are and closer to us than our jugular vein), *Omniscient* (all-knowing), *Supreme Will* and *Ultimate Ego*, *Beyond Vision and Comprehension, not comparable with any other being* : *Unique*.

15. *As for His Attributes*, we need to rationally perceive (to the outermost limit of such perception) and then devotionally absorb the facts that He is:—

(*a*) *The Creator* (2 : 29, 117 ; 6 : 73 ; 25 : 61);
The Originator and Evolver of all creation (27 : 64 ; 10 : 61);
Supreme Sovereign (3 : 180 ; 15 : 23 ; 19 : 40 ; 3 : 189 ; 4 : 126 ; 5 : 123 ; 67 : 1);
Ultimate Will, Doer of all He intends (85 : 16);
His is the command (6 : 57 ; 13 : 41 ; 16 : 1; 54 : 50; 16 : 90-91);
His the decision (3 : 109, 128; 42 : 53; 6 : 34; 18: 27; 6 : 115; 10: 109).

(*b*) *One* (2 : 163 ; 6 : 19 ; 16 : 22 ; 23 : 19-92 ; 37 : 1-5 ; 38 : 65-68 ; 112 : 1-4 ; 5 : 75 ; 16 : 51 ; 2 : 116; 6 : 100 ; 10 : 68 ; 19 : 35 ; 23 : 91 ; 6 : 100-101 ; 16 : 57 ; 37 : 149-157 ; 43 : 16-19 ; 6 : 22-24, 136, 163) ;

Alive (2: 255 ; 49 : 65) ;
Eternal (2 : 255 ; 22 : 111 ; 55 : 27 ; 28 : 88) ;
All-Seeing (3 : 163 ; 6 : 103) ;
All-Hearing (42 : 26-28 ; 2 : 186) ;
All-Knowing, Omniscient (2 : 284 ; 3 : 5 ; 29 : 6 : 3, 17; 13 : 8-10 ; 16 : 23 ; 31 : 34 ; 34 : 2 ; 64 : 4) ;
Omnipresent (43 : 84 ; 2 : 186 ; 34 : 50 ; 50 : 16 ; 56 : 85 ; 17 : 60 ; 57 : 4) ;
Omnipotent (2 : 284 ; 3 : 29; 6 : 12-13, 65 ; 10 : 55 ; 22 : 77-81 ; 53 : 42-54 ; 85 : 12-16 ; 51 : 58).

(*c*) *Lord of the Throne of Honour* (23 : 16) ;
Of Glory Supreme (9 : 129 ; 23 : 86 ; 40 : 51 ; 85 : 15) ;
Of the Mystery of Heaven and Earth (16 : 77) ;
Of Power (15 : 58) ;
Of the two Easts and Wests (55 : 17 ; 70 : 40 ; 73: 9);
Of the Dawn (113 : 1) ;
Of the Ascending Stairways (70 : 3) ;
Of Bounties Unbounded (3 : 174 ; 17 : 20-21 ; 96 : 3).

(*d*) *Cherisher* (1 : 2 ; 6 : 164) ;
Sustainer (7 : 54 ; 11 : 6-7 ; 13 : 16-17 ; 21 : 30-33 ; 66 ; 2-3 ; 29 : 60-62 ; 51 : 58) ;
Guardian (2 : 21-22 ; 39 : 14) ;
Protector (2 : 257 ; 3 : 150 ; 22 : 78 ; 6 : 71) ;
Helper (3 : 150 ; 4 : 45 ; 40 : 51 ; 110) ;
Supreme Refuge (113 : 114) .

(*e*) *The Most Beneficent* (52 : 28) ;
The Light of the Heavens and the Earth (24 : 35) ;
The Most Merciful (4 : 26 ; 5 : 77 ; 6 : 12, 54, 133 ; 9 : 117-118) ; 85 : 14 ; 35 : 2-3 ; 55 : 29 ; 7 : 151 ; 12 : 64, 92 ; 21 : 83 ; 23 : 109, 118) ;
Orphan's Shelter, Wanderer's Guide, Satisfier of thy needs (93) ;

Expander of thy Breast, Remover of thy Burden, Raiser of thy Esteem (94) ;
Remover of the Afflictions (6 : 17) ;
Deliverer from the dangers (6 : 63- 64) ;
Sender of Revelations (6 : 91) ;
Giver of light (6 : 122 ; 10 : 57 ; 9 : 32-33 ; 61 : 8 ; 24 : 35-36).

(*f*) *Most Forbearing* (2 : 225, 235, 263 ; 3 : 115 ; 5 : 104 ; 22 : 59 ; 64 : 17) ;
Most Forgiving (53 : 52 ; 4 : 25-26 ; 5 : 77 ; 15 : 49 ; 16 : 119 ; 39 : 53 ; 85 : 14) ;
Sender of Calm and Tranquillity (3 : 154 ; 9 : 26 ; 48 : 4, 18, 26, 10 : 25).

(*g*) *The Truth* (20 : 114) ;
Self-Subsisting (6 : 133 ; 3 : 2 ; 112 ; 31 : 26 ; 35 : 15) ;
Ultimate Reality (6 : 62 ; 31 : 30);
All-Wise (4 : 26 ; 6 : 18 ; 95 : 8);
Supreme Judge (21 : 47 ; 4 : 40 ; 95 : 8 ; 3 : 179 ; 24 : 39 ; 7 : 167 ; 13 : 6 ; 9 : 120-121 ; 11 : 115 ; 16 : 41-42);
Master Planner, Grand Architect (3 : 54 ; 13 : 42);
Disposer of all affairs (3 : 173 ; 72 : 9);
The Irresistible (6 : 18, 61).

(*h*) *Giver of life and death* (2 : 28 ; 6 : 122 ; 3 : 156 ; 6 : 95 ; 15 : 23 ; 39 : 42);
Tester (3 : 142 , 154, 166 ; 6 : 53 ; 29 : 2-5 ; 67 : 2);
Purger (3 : 141, 154);
He is the goal (53 : 42);
To Him is our return (96 : 8).

(*i*) *All creation speaks of Him* (23 : 12-13 ; 17 : 44 ; 24 : 41-46 ; 57 : 1) and
His are the most beautiful names (7 : 180 ; 17 : 110 ; 20 : 8 ; 59 : 24).

16. So much for a brief reference to his essence and His attributes, which words cannot fully capture, which the human *mind* may partially perceive and the human *heart* may largely absorb. The foremost hall-mark of the *Muslim*, to my mind, is the flame of God-consciousness which he lights within himself with the aid of these verses from the Quran; and then goes on to nourish it through God-oriented action, till the flame becomes a conflagration and God-consciousness matures into God-awareness : a state of body, mind and spirit *soaked* in God and *surrounded* by God ; a being throbbing with the awareness of His presence closer to him than his jugular vein : ashamed therefore to do what He forbids and joyously rushing to do that which would win His approval ; an awareness that reveals the Lord to His devotee as *the* One (the *Only One*):

(*a*) Whom he worships and in Whom he places his trust (1 : 4 ; 2 : 114, 152 ; 11 : 123 ; 67 : 29).

(*b*) Never forgotten (59 : 19); continuously sought with devotion (6 : 52 ; 18 : 28 ; 39 : 3-11 ; 40 : 14 ; 6 : 162); ceaselessly called on humbly, with fear and longing (7 : 55-56); celebrating his praises (1 : 1 ; 17 : 111 ; 30 : 17-19 ; 34 : 1 ; 37 : 180-182 ; 45 : 36-37 ; 55 : 78 ; 56 : 74, 96 ; 59 : 1 ; 61 : 1 ; 62 : 1 ; 64 : 1 ; 87 : 1) and striving in His way (9 : 95 ; 9 : 20-21, 88-89 ; 3 : 104-110) till the heart of the devotee becomes a niche for the light of the Heavens and the Earth (24 : 35-36).

17. This God-consciousness, this God-awareness, which is the fountain from which God-oriented action springs, is the foremost hall-mark of the Muslim. It is both the foundation and the pinnacle of his character and conduct; it is the beginning and the end, as also the sum total of a life which is consecrated to the service of God:—

"Say : My prayers and my sacrifice,
My life and my death,

Are all for Allah : Lord of all the worlds !
I ascribe no partners unto Him:
This I have been commanded;
And I am the first of those,
Who surrender their will to His."

18. This God-consciousness, this God-awareness does not come in a day. It is the product of a life-long search through striving in His way: through reflection and meditation in the inner world; and the concretisation of those inner perceptions through action in the external world. Permit me to bring this brief reference on *Taqwa* (God-consciouness, God-awareness), as the foremost attribute of the *Muslim* to a close with just three selected recitations from the Quran—passages which reveal the essence and the attributes of God to *him who strives to be a Muslim*:

(*a*) "Allah; There is no god save him, the Alive, the Eternal." (2 : 155).

(*b*) "All that is in the heavens and the earth glorifieth Allah; and He is the Mighty, the Wise." (57 : 1-6).

(*c*) "He is Allah, than Whom there is no other god, Knower of the invisible and the visible." (59 : 22-24).

Trust in and Reliance on God (*Tawakkul al-Allah*)

19. The second luminous hall-mark of the *Muslims* is his *Trust in* and *Reliance on God.* This is a product of "God-awareness" (*Taqwa*) and of "faith" (*Iman*) : awareness leading to, confirming, securing, broadening, deepening and eventually rendering inviolable his faith in Allah—his Creator, Cherisher, Sustainer, Guide, Guardian, Protector, Helper and Supreme Refuge.

20. Trust in and reliance on God implies *Dependence on Him Alone*, seeking aid (for whatever the need) of *none but Him*; absolute dependence on *Him*, and a glorious *in*-dependence of everybody and everything else. It is that state of the human spirit in which these words of the Quran well up from the inmost depths of its being :—

(*a*) "Thee (alone) we worship ;
Thee (alone) we ask for help." (1 : 4).

(*b*) "Say ; He is my Lord; there is no god save Him. In Him do I put my trust; and unto Him is my recourse." (13 : 40).

(*c*) "....(then) say : Allah sufficeth me. There is no god save Him. In Him have I put my trust, and He is Lord of the Tremendous Throne." (9 : 129).

(*d*) "And Allah is sufficient as a Friend,
And Allah is sufficient as a Helper." (4 : 45).

(*e*) "Say : I have been commanded to worship none but Allah,
And to ascribe no partners unto Him.
To Him do I cry out (for aid),
And to Him is my return."

(*f*) "Say : Allah sufficeth me :
He is the best of guardians,
The best of helpers."

21. It is that state of the human spirit which neither clutches at nor clings to temporal powers for protection, help or the satisfaction of its needs. It does not call on false gods for aid:—

(*a*) "O mankind! A similitude is coined, so pay heed to it! Lo! Those on whom ye call besides Allah (for aid and succour) will never create a fly though they combine together for the purpose. And if the fly took something away from them, they could not rescue it from it. So weak are (both) the seeker and the sought." (22 : 73).

(*b*) "....And when thou art resolved, then put thy trust in Allah. Lo! Allah loveth those who put their trust (in Him). If Allah is your Helper, none can overcome you; and if He withdraw His help from you, who is there who can help you? In Allah let believers put their trust." (3 : 159-160).

(*c*) "Knowest thou not that it is Allah unto Whom belongeth the sovereignty of heavens and earth; and ye have not, besides Allah, any friend or helper ? (2 : 107).

22. *Turst in and Reliance on God* implies not only the rejection of temporal authorities as the source of protection, aid and comfort; but also *not* clinging *to*, *nor* seeking strength *in* temporal power; *not* clutching at wealth; *not* fearfully saving for the temporal morrow; *not* forgetting God and clouding our vision of the Hereafter by soul-destroying material pursuits:—

> "And when they spy some merchandize or pastime, and break away to it and leave thee standing,
> Say :
>
> That which Allah hath is better than pastime and merchandize;
>
> And Allah is the Best of Providers." (62 : 11).

23. *Tawakkul al-Allah* implies striving in His way, seeking His pleasure in all that we do *regardless of temporal consequences*; concerned only with *acting as we should* (in accordance with His commandments), *not* hankering after the fruits of our action, *knowing* that effect will follow cause in accordance with His laws by His decree. *Tawakkul al-Allah* is that state of the human spirit which views every adversity, pain, suffering, sorrow, humiliation, defeat and failure as an occasion for *patient perseverance;* and every state of well-being, joy, peace, happiness, honour, victory and success as an occasion for *humble thanks-giving*— *both* seen as "*trials*" proceeding from God; *both* accepted as a challenge for the intensification of our God-oriented action; *both* leading to an increasing dependance on Him, a holding-fast to Him, a satisfaction with His decrees and continued striving in His way.

24. That man is on his way to becoming a *Muslim* whose

heart echoes and whose external conduct concretises the call of the Lord in sorrow and adversity:—

> "O ye who believe!
> Seek help in steadfastness and prayer.
> Lo! Allah is with those who patiently persevere.
> And say not of those slain in the way of Allah :
> '(They are) dead'.
> Nay, they live; only ye perceive not.
> And surely We shall try you with something:
> *Of fear* and *hunger*,
> And *loss of wealth* and *lives*,
> And (the) *fruits* (*of your labour*).
> But give glad tidings to the steadfast,
> Who when sorrow and adversity strike them,
> Say : 'Lo! We are Allah's,
> And unto Him we return'." (2: 153-156)

This is *Tawakkul al-Allah.*

25. That man is on his way to becoming a *Muslim* who takes to the prayer-mat when joy and success come crowding in, who sees in these an occasion for prayer and the seeking of forgiveness, *not* of vain and arrogant boasting:—

> "When Allah's succour and the triumph cometh,
> And thou seest mankind
> Entering the religion of Allah in legions ;
> Hymn thou, then, the praises of thy Lord,
> And seek forgiveness of Him.
> Lo! He is ever-ready to show mercy". (Q : 110).

This is *Tawakkul al-Allah.*

26. *Trust in and reliance on God* implies the cultivation of a grateful heart, an awareness of God as the Lord of bounties unbounded, a cheerful acceptance of whatever He decrees:—

> (*a*) "Say : Verily all bounties are in the hands of Allah.
> He granteth them to whomsoever He pleaseth.
> And He careth for all, knoweth all things.
> For His mercy, He chooseth whomsoever He pleaseth;

For Allah is the Lord of Bounties Unbounded,"
(3 : 73-74).

(*b*) "Say : O Allah,
Owner of all (power and) sovereignty!
Thou givest power unto whom Thou wilt;
And Thou withdrawest power from whom Thou wilt.
Thou exaltest whom Thou wilt;
And Thou abasest whom Thou wilt.
In thy hands is all good.
Lo ! Thou art able to do all things." (3 : 26).

This awareness of the munificence of an omnipotent Lord; this ready acceptance of whatever He decrees ; this cheerful submission to His authority; this unqualified surrender before His will; this state of the human spirit intensifying its striving in the way of God and holding fast to Him—alike in triumph and disaster; this deepening faith, this expanding trust; this unwavering, unfaltering pursuit of his commadments regardless of temporal consequences; this be-friending of God transcending the flux of temporal fortunes; this constancy of faith; this reliance; this forging of an unbreakable bond and bondage with Him : *this* is *Tawakkul al-Allah.* This is that state of the human spirit which hears, acts and joyously absorbs the assurance of the Lord when he calls: "So, establish worship, pay the poor due and hold fast to God. He is your protecting Friend : a blessed Patron and a blessed Helper." (22 : 78).

27. *Tawakkul al-Allah* is one of the main streams nourishing the character and conduct of the *Muslim* and from it flow many distributaries:—

(*a*) *Where there is trust in God, there is no room for false Gods* (7 : 194-198 ; 16 : 20-21 ; 21 : 22 , 24 ; 34 : 22-27 ; 41 : 47-48 ; 46 : 5-6 ; 71 : 23-24 ; 21 : 18 ; 51 : 8-11).

(*b*) *Where there is trust in God, there is no fear of men* (4 : 77); *No fear of evil* (3 : 175); *no fear at all* (2 : 38, 62,

112, 262, 274, 277 ; 5 : 72 ; 6 : 48 ; 7 : 35 10 : 62 ; 43 : 68 ; 46 : 13).

(*c*) *Where there is trust in God there can be no despair* (3 : 139 ; 3 : 146 ; 39 : 53).

(*d*) *Where there is trust in God, there is knowledge that with every hardship goeth ease.* (94 : 1-8).

(*e*) *Where there is trust in God, there is : striving in His way* (4 : 95 ; 9 : 20-21 ; 88-89) ; *firmness* (8 : 45); *obedience without losing heart* (8 : 46) ; *no weariness* (47 : 35); *the will to conquer odds* (8 : 65-66); *no seeking of exemption from danger* (9 : 43-45); *readiness to face persecution* (85 : 6-11) and *exile* (8 : 72, 74-75) *for His cause, rejoicing over the spiritual bargain made* (9 : 111 ; 61 : 10-11).

(*f*) *Where there is trust in God, there is no vain curiosity* (5 : 104-105) ; *no idle disputation* (29 : 46) ; *sincere love of truth* (57 : 19 ; 28 : 70-71, 90) *and staunch justice* (4 : 58, 65, 105, 135 ; 7 : 29 ; 16 : 90 ; 57 : 25); *faith revealed in and shining through good conduct* (61 : 23 ; 33 : 69-71 ; 48 : 29 ; 24 : 62-63 ; 49 : 12) *and gracious speech* (17 : 53-55).

(*g*) *Where there is trust in God, there is prayer* (14 : 31 ; 57 : 16 ; 1 : 1-7 ; 2 : 238-239 ; 3 : 8, 26-27, 147, 191-194 ; 4 : 43 ; 5 : 7 ; 11 : 114 ; 17 : 78-81 ; 23 : 118 ; 50 : 39-40 ; 52 : 48-49 ; 73 : 1-8, 29 ; 11 : 144 ; 17 : 78-79 ; 20 : 130 ; 30 : 17-18) *and charity* (2 : 110, 177, 195 215, 219, 254, 261-274 ; 3 : 134 ; 30 : 39 ; 57 : 18 ; 63 : 10 ; 64 : 16-17 ; 2 : 273 ; 9 : 60).

(*h*) *Where there is trust in God, there is His mercy, light, forgiveness, bounties unbounded* (57 : 28 ; 10 : 57).

These are some of the many *distributaries* emanating from the main stream of *Tawakkul al-Allah* ; and by that law of inter-action to which I referred in my talk on *Iman*, they are also the *tributaries* which follow into and feed the main stream of *Tawakkul al-Allah.* Between them there is a constant two-way flow : not one is nourished without nourishing the other; not one is impoverished without impoverishing the other. This is a vast, an intricate net-work; and the quality of the whole, taken in its totality, is the quality of the *Muslim.*

28. Within the time available to me, I cannot recite to you the many Quranic references noted in my script which illuminate our understanding of this basic attribute of the Muslim and show us the way to its acquisition; but permit me to recite to you at least two passages which throw into sharp and luminous relief all that *Tawakkul al-Allah* stands for: a boundless trust in the boundless bounties of God, a heart throbbing with gratitude, a spirit pleased with its Lord and the Lord pleased with it, a sipirit striving in His way and fulfilling its commitments, transcending the flux of temporal fortunes and so conquering both this world and the next. And even as I recite and you hear, we may wordlessly pray that the meaning of these verses may be revealed to us even as it was revealed to the Prophet; and may we actualise its call even as it was actualised by the Prophet. *Pray listen*:—

(*a*) "By the hours of the dawn,
And by the night when it is at its stillest :
Thy Lord hath not forsaken thee, nor doth He hate thee.

And verily, the latter portion will be better for thee than the former;

And verily, thy Lord will give unto thee so that thou will be content.

Did He not find thee an orphan and protect (thee)?
Did He not find thee wandering and guide (thee) ?
Did He not find thee destitute and enrich (thee) ?
Therefore : the orphan oppress not ;
Therefore : the beggar drive not away.

Therefore : of the bounty of thy Lord be thy discourse." (Q : 93).

(*b*) "Have We not caused thy bosom to expand ;
And eased thee of the burden,
Which weighed down thy back ;
And exalted thy fame.
But Lo ! With hardship goeth ease,
Lo ! With hardship goeth ease :
So when thou art relieved, still *Toil*
And *Strive* to please thy Lord." (Q : 94).

29. So much for *Tawakkul al-Allah* : "In Allah let believers put their trust" ; "In Allah let the trusting put their trust".[2]

Purity (*Taharat*)

30. The next fundamental attribute of the *Muslim* that I wish to touch on is *purity*. *Purification is of two kinds*: *Outward* and *Inward*. The two go together: *External cleansing* (of the body) being a means and an aid for the attainment of *inner cleanliness* (of mind, heart and spirit).[3]

31. *Taharat* is the *purfication of our thoughts, our feelings and our emotions* as a condition precedent to the *Actualisation of Islam* both in the inner constitution and the external conduct of man.

"The true *Hijrah* is the *flight from evil*," said the Prophet, "and the real *Jihad* is the *warfare against one's passions*." . The foremost goal of *Taharat* is the sweeping away, the explusion,

2. For some historical anecdotes exemplifying *Tawakkul al-Allah*, see *Tadhkirat al-Auliya*.
   (*a*) *Dhol Nun* : clutching at the saint, much weeping (p. 94).
   (*b*) *Habib al-Ajami* : the fur coat and Hasan (p. 36).
   (*c*) *Rabea al-Adawiya* : the thief and the chaddur (p. 43) ; prayers (p. 51) ; death (p. 51).
3. Hujwiri, *Kashf al-Mahjub*. Also see, *Tadhkirat al-Auliya*, p. 118 (anecdote about Bayazid and the dog).

the conquest and the ex-communication of all those *inner vices* in the mind and heart of man which clog, block and stand in the way of his spiritual progress. It is forcing the *exit* of those grave pollutants, those diseases of the human heart which *Ghazzali* called the "Destructive Matters of Life" (in the ten volumes of the *third quarter* of his 40 volume work : *Ihya Ulum al-Din*); so *that* the decks are cleared for the *entry* of those qualities of the mind, heart and spirit which draw us near and bind us to God : those "Saving Matters of Life," as *Ghazzali* called them (in the last ten volumes, *fourth quarter*, of his *Ihya Ulum al-Din*), which characterise the man nearing the completion of his *Islam*.

32. Through his study of, reflection on and practice of the Quran, *Ghazzali* :

(*a*) Identified these *Life-Annihilating, soul-destroying vices* as: Lust, Rage and Greed ; Rancour, Envy, Jealousy, Malice; Love of Worldly Wealth, Status, Pomp and Power; Lying, Slander, Abuse, Back-biting, Contentiousness, Idle Debate and Disputation ; Pride, Arrogance, Conceit and Vanity; and vying for the top place: *Hypocrisy*. (For a synopsis of his own, see : *Part II of his Bidayat al-Hidayah*, "The Beginning of Guidance", Tr. *Montgomery Watt*, "*The Faith and Practice of al-Ghazzali*," pp. 131-152).

(*b*) With these hounded to their hiding places in the heart of man, forced to combat, annihilated and swept away, room may now be made for such *Saving Graces of life* as: Repentance; Patient Perseverance; Gratitude; Truthfulness and Sincerity; Continence; Modesty and Humility; Gracious Speech; Moderation; Frugality ; Generosity and Magnanimity; Prayer, Charity, Self-Control and Justice; Combativeness in His Way, resisting the Wrong and Enforcing the Right ; the eventual acquisition of Serenity, Peace, Contentment, Equilibrium : *that total integration of the human personality in full accord with His commandments*, which is both the meaning and the goal of *Islam*.

33. The Quran declares : "... Lo ! Allah loveth those who turn (and Re-turn) to Him (with sincere repentance) and (cleanse and) *purify* themselves." (2 : 222). Like every other attribute of the Muslim, *purity* too is not acquired in a day, some months or even years. *Purification* is a life-long process, a continuous movement towards the goal till "the inevitable" comes to us.

34. On the *Process of Purification*, *Ali al-Hujwiri* observes : "Outward and inward purification must go together : *e.g.* when a man washes his hand, he must wash his heart clean of worldliness ; and when he puts water in his mouth, he must purify his mouth from mention of (anything) other than God ; and when he washes his face, he must turn away from all familiar objects and turn towards God ; and when he wipes his head, he must resign his affairs to God ; and when he washes his feet, he must not form the intention of taking his stand on anything except according to the command of God. Thus, he will be *doubly purified.* In all religious ordinances the external is combined with the internal ; *e.g.* in faith, the tongue's profession with the heart's belief." (*Kashf al-Mahjub, Tr. R. A. Nicholson*, p. 292). In saying all this, *Hujwiri* is making a brave (and yet a woefully incomplete) attempt to capture in his own words the spirit of the *Prophet's prayers* while performing the *wudu* (See : *Masnun Duaein, compilation by Maulana Anis Ahmad, translation by M. A. H. Siddiqui*, pp. 24-29).

35. What violent agitation this attempt at "double cleansing" can cause in the heart of a man who sincerely strives to be a *Muslim*, bringing forth the implications of the *wudu*, is clear from this historical anecdote that *Hujwiri* narrates :

> "One day *Shibli* purified himself. When he came to the door of the mosque, a voice whispered in his heart : 'Art

> thou so pure that thou enterest My house with this boldness?' *Shibli* turned back, but the Voice asked : 'Dost thou turn back from My door? Whither wilt thou go?' *Shibli* uttered a loud cry ; the Voice said : 'Dost thou revile Me?' *Shibli* stood silent ; the Voice said : 'Dost thou pretend to endure My affliction?' *Shibli* exclaimed : 'O Lord! Implore Thee to help me against Thyself'!"

Hujwiri goes on to add : "He who would serve God must purify himself outwardly with water and inwardly with repentance (*taubah*)." (*Kashf al-Mahjub*, p. 294).

36. The Quranic concept of *taubah* as a means of purification is again a subject by itself and we do not have the time here to go into it. For an understanding of its fundamentals, I would heartily recommend a study of the appropriate chapters in *Altaf Gauhar's "Translations from the Quran"* (pp. 140-169). Later, you may also wish to read Hujwiri's exposition (*Kashf al-Mahjub*, p. 294-299), followed by the historical anecdotes of some great conversions to Islam in *Farid al-Din Attar's "Tadhkirat al-Auliya"* (*Tr. A. J. Arberry, "Muslim Saints and Mystics"*): about *Hasan al-Basra* (pp. 21-22), *al-Fodhail Ibn Iyaz* (pp. 53-57), *Ibrâhim Ibn Adham* (pp. 63-66), *Bishr Ibn al-Harith* (pp. 81-82) and *Dhol Nun* (pp. 88-91)—to mention only a few. Your study along these lines, as a supplement to your own direct, personal enquiry into the Quran, will reveal to you the meaning and process of *taubah* as a means of *inner purification*. For the wrongs that we commit and the evil that we do (out of ignorance, inadvertently or because of sheer human weakness), we can always *stop* the moment the realisation of error dawns on us, *re-trace our steps* to the point where we started going wrong and there *re-turn* to the Way of and to God. This, in a sentence, is the essence of *taubah*: a means of purification open to all, except those who deliberately and consistently surround themselves with sin ; who wallow in filth and relish without restraint the evil that they do ; who have so blackened the "mirror of their heart" as to lose all power of discrimination ; men who have stifled to death the

voice of conscience in their hearts and banished God from their souls. He who strives to be a *Muslim* ensures that he comes nowhere near this point of no-return, so that he may still rejoice over the Lord's assurance of forgiveness and have Him respond to his cry when he cries out to Him :

(*a*) "O ye, My servants who have transgressed against your souls !
Despair not of the mercy of Allah.
Lo ! Allah forgiveth all sins ;
And verily, He is the Most Forgiving, the Most Merciful."

(*b*) "And when My servants ask thee (O Muhammad)
Concerning Me,
Lo ! I am nigh (unto thee and them).
I hear the cry of every crier, when he crieth unto Me.
Let them also then, (with a will), Listen to My call,
So that they may be guided aright."

37. The essence of *taubah* is a reaffirmation of *our* will to listen to *His* call (to obey His commandments). In this context, with particular reference to "coming nowhere near the *point of no return*," we would do well to keep a thousand leagues away from those acts which the Prophet classified as *grave* (*mortal*) *sins*. Consider the following sayings of the Prophet :

(*a*) "The major sins are associating other objects of worship with God, (unlawful) disobedience of parents,[4] murder and bearing false witness (deliberate perjury)."

(*Mishkat*, Vol I, p. 17).

(*b*) "Avoid the seven noxious things : associating anything with God, magic, killing one whom God has declared inviolate without a just cause, devouring usury, con-

---

4. See *Quran* : "Thy Lord hath ordained ....." (17 : 23).
Also : 29 : 14; 46 : 15-18. See : *Tadhkirat al-Auliya*, pp. 102-103(Mother, pitcher and door : the story of Bayazid of Bostam).

suming the property of an orphan, turning back when the army advances (*i.e.* becoming a deserter from a war waged in the way of God) and slandering chaste women who are believers but indiscreet." (*Ibid.*).

(*c*) "When one commits fornication, he is not a believer ; when one steals, he is not a believer ; when one resorts to plunder, he is not a believer ; when one drinks wine, he is not a believer ; and when one of you defrauds (another), he is not a believer. So, beware, beware!" (*Ibid.*).

38. We shall presently consider *at least some* of those *grave pollutants of the human heart* to which I made a reference earlier. As for the *process of purification* (which involves the performance of a series of God-oriented acts of obedience from day to day and year to year), those of you seeking a deeper insight would greatly enjoy reading and benefiting from *Ghazzali's* faithful, devoted, brilliant exposition of the theme :

(*a*) First, in part I of his "*Bidayat al-Hidayah*" (*Tr. Montgomery Watt*, "*The Faith and Practice of al-Ghazzali*", pp. 90-130).

(*b*) And then, for an even deeper foray : the *First Quarter* (10 volumes) on the "*Acts of Worship*" in his 40 volume master-piece : *The Ihya Ulum al-Din.*

39. And now, for a brief reference to a selected few of those *grave pollutants of the human heart*, the eradication of which is the first phase of the *Muslim's* march towards the attainment of *purity*. We shall consider them in packets :

(*a*) *Pride, Arrogance, Vanity.*

(*b*) *Envy, Jealousy, Malice, Rancour.*

(*c*) *Greed, Avarice : Love of Worldly Wealth, Property, Status, Pomp and Power.*

(*d*) *Anger and Rage.*

(*e*) *Hypocrisy.*

And even this brief review would be mutilated without a reference to those *sins of the tongue* which blacken the *heart* : *Lying; Slander and Abuse; Back-biting; Contentiousness, Idle debate and disputation; Self-praise; Cursing, Jesting, Ridiculing or Scoffing at people; Being loud-mouthed : noisy, empty or vain of speech.*

40. *Pride, Arrogance, Vanity.* These represent the foremost attributes of Iblis (2 : 34; 7 : 12-13) and whoever is tainted by these, whether an individual (28 : 39-40) or a community (41 : 15-16), is doomed to painful doom (4 : 172-73; 7 : 40; 16 : 29; 49 : 20). Allah loveth not the proud (16 : 22-23).

41. Consider the following sayings of the Prophet :

(*a*) "God Most High says : 'Pride is My cloak and majesty My lower garment. I shall cause him who vies with Me regarding any one of these to enter hell!'"
(*Muslim, Mishkat*, p. 1059).

(*b*) "He who has in his heart as much faith as a grain of mustard seed will not enter hell; and he who has in his heart as much pride as a grain of mustard seed will not enter paradise." (*Ibid.*, p. 1058).

(*c*) "There are three things which save and three which destroy. Those which *save* are : *Fear of God* in secret and in public; *Speaking the truth*, when pleased and displeased; and *moderation*, both when wealthy and poor. Those which *destroy* are : *Passion* followed; *Niggardliness* obeyed; and *Self-conceit*, which is the *worst of them.*"
(*Baihaqi, Ibid.*, p. 1061).

42. *Pride* and *Faith* cannot co-exist; where there is *pride* (and it derivatives : arrogance, vanity, self-conceit, smug self-satisfaction, self-praise, self-applause, egoism, egotism, a false sense of superiority) there can be no *faith*. *Pride* destroys faith: it is the first big leap towards *kufr;* it is what even that passionate sceptic, Bertrand Russell, recognised as "cosmic impiety".

43. *Pride* and *Arrogance* are among the most serious forms of *ignorance*. They stem from a false perspective of life, a failure of

the intellect and the spirit to grasp the ratio and the relationship between the *Here* and the *Hereafter*. They spring from an irrational reliance on worldly wealth and power, an unawareness of the evanescence of human life and its temporal acquisitions, a forgetfulness of death the leveller, a strange oblivion of the fact that one day "the inevitable" will come and "sceptre and crown must tumble down and in the dust be equal made, with the poor crooked scythe and spade." If this *pride* born of this unawareness, this forgetfulness, this oblivion, this heedlessness is not *ignorance*, what is? Consider what the Prophet once said :

(*a*) "I swear by God that this world, in comparison with the world to come, is just like one of you putting his finger into the sea. Let him consider what he brings out on it." (*Muslim, Mishkat*, Vol. III, p. 1070).

(*b*) "I swear by Him in Whose hand my soul is, this life is like a garment torn from end to end, held together by a single, slender thread; and even that thread is soon to be cut off." (*Ibid.*).

44. What fool would then be so foolish as to be *proud* ? And even as I say this, ringing in my ears are some lines that my father taught me when I was yet a school boy :

(*a*) "Tomorrow, and tomorrow, and tomorrow,
Creeps in this petty pace from day to day,
To the last syllable of recorded time ;
And all our yesterdays have lighted fools
The way to dusty death. Out, out, brief candle !
Life's but a walking shadow, a poor player
That struts and frets his hour upon the stage.
And then is heard no more : it is a tale
Told by an idiot, full of sound and fury,
Signifying nothing." (*Shakespeare*, "*Macbeth*")

(*b*) "I met a traveller from an antique land
Who said : Two vast and trunkless legs of stone
Stand in the desert. Near them, on the sand,

Half-sunk, a shattered visage lies, whose frown,
And wrinkled lip, and sneer of cold command,
Tell that its sculptor well those passions read
Which yet survive, stamped on these lifeless things...
And on the pedestal these words appear :
'My name is *Ozymandias*, King of Kings :
Look on my works, ye Mighty, and despair !'
Nothing besides remains. Round the decay of
That colossal wreck, boundless and bare,
The lone and level sands stretch far away."

(*Shelley*, "*Ozymandias*").

45. No, *Pride* has nothing to be proud of. It is among the most irrational and contemptible of human passions. Anyone who has read the Quran, reflected on what he has read and absorbed its guidance, will keep *pride* and *arrogance* a thousand leagues away from him. He will not forget that he was created of a drop of dirty fluid; that even in the prime of his youth he is vulnerable to the assault of the smallest microbe; that death comes suddenly, unawares, and will hound him out one day even if he should take refuge in lofty towers; that earthly wealth, power and authority are all fleeting acquisitions; that nothing avails except the good that one does *Here* for salvation in the *Hereafter*, the provision that one makes *today* for the long, long *morrow* to come; that there is no distinction between man and man, except the distinction that the Lord will one day make on the basis of the degrees of obedience rendered to Him by His servants. I shall close this brief reference to *pride* and arrogance with an advice from *Ghazzali* :

"The fruit of it (*pride*) in society is self-exaltation and self-advancement and the endeavour to be foremost...The arrogant man is he who, when he gives advice, mortifies; but, when he receives it, is rude. Everyone who considers himself better than one of the creatures of God Most High is arrogant. Indeed, you ought to realize that the good man is he who is good in God's sight in the mansion of eternity; and that is something unknown to man, postponed to the End. Your belief that you are better than others is sheer ignorance... *Arrogance* will not leave your heart except when you know that the great man is he who is great in the sight of God Most High. That is something which cannot be known until the end of life, and there is doubt about that (the end and whether it will be good or bad). So let fear of the end occupy you and keep you from making yourself out, despite the doubt about your end, to be above the servants of God Most High. Your certitude and faith at present do not exclude the possibility of your changing in the future; for God is the disposer of hearts : He guides whom He will and leads astray whom He will."

(*Bidayat al-Hidayah*, *Tr. Watt*, pp. 145-147)

46. *Envy*, *Jealousy*, *Malice*, *Rancour*. These are indeed grave diseases of the heart; they cut at the very roots of human happiness and spiritual progress. They poison us from inside with a consequence more deadly than their social ill-effects. Envy, jealousy, malice and rancour are symptoms of rank *ingratitude* towards *God* : ignorance again, blindness, oblivion, forgetfulness, failure to count our blessings, conscious only of what we *have not* and unconscious of what we *have*. *Envy* and *Jealousy* are forms of *niggardliness* towards others (17 : 29; 47 : 38) : they destroy faith, they neutralize our good deeds. The Prophet said :

(*a*) "By Him in Whose hand my soul is, a man *does not believe*, till he likes for his brother what he likes for himself." (*Mishkat*. Vol. III, p. 1033).

(*b*) "Avoid *envy*, for envy devours good deeds as fire devours fuel." (*Ibid.*, p. 1047)

47. The shunning of *envy* and *jealousy* is an aspect of that trust in and reliance on God which we considered earlier; an aspect of the way to peace, equilibrium, satisfaction with His decrees, contentment. The Quran forbids *envy*:—

"And covet not the things in which Allah hath made some of you excel others. Unto men a fortune from that which they have earned, and unto women a fortune from that which they have earned. (*Envy not one another*) but ask Allah of his bounty. Lo! Allah is ever-knower of all things." (4 : 32)

48. *Islam* has no place in a heart poisoned by *envy*, riddled with *rancour* and *malice*. *Islam* is too big to be accommodated *in* so small a heart. Envy, jealousy, malice and rancour corrode and pollute even that highest act which man is capable of: his worship of God. The Prophet said, "To harbour good thoughts is a part of well-conducted worship." (*Mishkat*, Vol. III, p. 1048)

49. Even from an exclusively worldly, pragmatic point of view the corrosive effects of envy, jealousy, rancour and malice are bad enough. You may wish to consider the following excerpts from *Bertrand Russell's* (*The Conquest of Happiness* pp. 52, 53, 54, 56-57 ; 86, 92, 106-7).

50. *Greed, Avarice* : *Love of worldly wealth, property, status, pomp and power.* These again are diseases which infect the hearts of those who know not whence they came and whither they will go or *why* they came at all. For them this life is an end in itself, a span of time between an accidental, unknown beginning and an equally accidental, pointless end. Into this vacuum step in *lust*, *greed* and *avarice* of all kinds : a mad pursuit of the earth's fleeting comforts; a frenzied orgy of wine, women and song; a nerve-wrecking, health-destroying, soul-annihilating, head-long rush for power, promotion, status, authority; a fear-ul amassing of wealth and property which the very process of acquisition turns into habit and transforms into an end : a mad, mad rush till it is stilled by the hand of death and all is sucked into the silence of the grave. The Quran warns:—

"Rivalry in worldly increase distracteth ye,
Until ye come to the graves.
Nay, but ye will come to know!

Nay, but ye will come to know!
Nay, would that ye knew (now)
With a sure knowledge! . . ." (102 : 1-5)

51. So you see : *Ignorance* again, rank ignorance. Where knowledge has reached its pinnacle, where it has become "sure", where *faith* has been attained through a full exertion of the intellect and the rational understanding—side by side with devotional practice—gearing the whole being of man to the service of God : in such a state of the human spirit there can be no love of the earth and its fleeting satisfactions; no lust, no greed, no avarice.[5] We who strive towards that goal, we who would become *Muslims*, would do well to read, ponder, reflect and act upon these observations and exhortations of the Prophet:

(*a*) *The Lure of the World*

(1) "Among the things I fear for you after I am gone are the beauty and adornment of the world which will be conferred on you. This wealth is green and sweet, and he who accepts it and applies it rightly finds it a good help; but he who accepts it wrongly is like one who eats without being satisfied, and it will be a witness against him on the Day of Resurrection."
(*Bukhari and Muslim Mishkat*; Vol. III, p. 1072).

(2) "I swear by God that it is not poverty I fear for you, but I fear that worldly goods may be given to you lavishly as they were to your predecessors, that you may vie with one another in desiring them as they did, and that they may destroy you as they destroyed them." (*Ibid.*)

5. For some anecdotes on "this world and seeking God", see *Tadhkirat al-Auliya* : Caravanserai (p. 64) ; seeking God (p. 63) ; water for ablution, not wealth (p. 78) ; the poor man's disdain of wealth (p. 85) ; seeking God, not the material world, not paradise (p. 94) ; the vision of God and knowing Him (p. 82) ; God-oriented even in death (pp. 98-99); the earthly provider is dead (p. 151) ; avaricious gazing on another's wealth (p. 131); Rabea' sprayers (p. 51); servant without desire (p. 75).

(3) "The world is accursed and what it contains is accursed, except remembrance of God and what He likes : a learned man or a learner."

(*Tirmidhi*, *Ibn Majah*; *Ibid*., p. 1075)

(4) "*Ibn Masud* noted that God's messenger slept on a reed mat and got up with the marks of it on his body so *Ibn Masud* said : 'Messenger of God, I wish you would order us to spread something out for you . . .' He replied: 'What have I to do with the world ? In relation to the world, I am just like a rider who shades himself under a tree, then goes off and leaves it'."

(*Ahmad*, *Tirmidhi*, *Ibn Majah; Ibid*, *p*. 1077).

(5) "Love of the world is the beginning of every sin." (*Baihaqi*; *Ibid*., p. 1081)

(6) "Be among the sons of the Hereafter and do not be among the sons of the world, for every mother is followed by her child."

(*Mishkat*, Vol. III, p. 1082).

(7) "*Malik* reported that *Luqman* said to his son: Son, what men are promised has been delayed for them, yet they are hastening to the Hereafter and passing away. You have put the world behind you since you were brought into existence, and have faced the Hereafter; and an abode *to* which you are going is nearer you than one *from* which you are going out."

(*Razin*, *Mishkat*, Vol. III, p. 1083)

(8) "*Ibn Masud* said that God's messenger recited 'Whomsoever God wishes to guide, he expands his breast for Islam,' (*Quran*, VI : 125) and then said: 'When the light enters the breast, it is enlarged.' He was asked if there is any sign of that by which it might be known and replied 'Yes; withdrawing from the abode of deception,

turning towards the abode of eternity, and preparation for death before it comes'."

(*Mishkat*, Vol. III, p. 1084).

(*b*) *Greed, Avarice, Wealth, Property*

(1) "Riches do not come from abundace of goods, but true riches are a contented mind."

(*Bukhari and Muslim; Ibid.*, p. 1074).

(2) "A man says: 'My property, my property!'; whereas the part of his property which is his consists of three things: what he eats and uses up, what he wears and makes threadbare, or what he gives away and so acquires. Everything else is left to others by him when he departs." (*Muslim*; *Ibid.*, p. 1073)

(3) "Three follow the dead, two returning and one remaining with him. His people, his property and his deeds follow him; but his people and property return, while his deeds remain."

(*Bukhari and Muslim* ; *Ibid.*)

(4) "Do not own an estate and so be pleased with the world." (*Tirmidhi*, *Baihaqi*)..."Cursed be the slave of the dinar; cursed be the slave of the dirham!" (*Tirmidhi*)... "Two hungry wolves let loose among sheep are not more destructive to them than a man's greed for property and self-esteem are to his religion." (*Tirmidhi*, *Darimi*).

(*Ibid.*, p. 1075)

(5) "Every building is a misfortune except what cannot, except what cannot (be done without)."

(*Abu Dawud; Ibid.*, p. 1076)

(6) "Guard against what is prohibited regarding buildings, for it is the foundation of ruin."

(*Baihaqi*; *Ibid.*, p. 1081)

(7) "The son of Adam has a right only to the

following : a house in which he lives, a garment with which he conceals his private parts, dry bread and water." (*Tirmidhi, Ibid.*, p. 1076)

(8) "In front of you is a difficult ascent which those who are heavily laden (with worldly wealth, goods and property) cannot get over."
(*Mishkat*, Vol. III, p. 1080)

(9) "...What is little and sufficient is better than what is abundant and causes negligence."
(*Abu Nuaim; Ibid.*, p. 1082)

(10) Offered by the Lord that the valley of Mecca be turned into gold for him, the Prophet cried out : "No, my Lord! But let me have enough to eat and be hungry on alternate days; then when I am hungry I shall make supplication to Thee and make mention of Thee, and when I have enough I shall praise and thank Thee." (*Ahmad, Tirmidhi; Ibid.*, p. 1077)

(*c*) *Power Pomp, Ostentation.*

(1) "God does not look at your forms and your possessions, but He looks at your hearts and deeds." (*Muslim*; *Ibid.*, p. 1103)

(2) "O God! Grant me life as a poor man; cause me to die a poor man, and resurrect me in the company of the poor."
(*Tirmidhi, Baihaqi, Ibn Majah; Ibid.*, p. 1087).

(3) "...What is lawful does not allow for extravagance." (*Sufyan Al-Thawri; Ibid.*, p. 1097)

52. *Anger and Rage.* These are cruel and corrosive passions, leading to injustice and injury to others. Where anger enters, reason flees and remorse follows. Anger and rage destroy peace within him who is angry. The poison spills over, resentment and discord spread. The very air that we breathe grows heavy

and the injury that we cause to others injures us even more in the end. "Anger spoils faith as aloes spoil honey", said the Prophet. Where anger rages, arrogance storms in. Consideration, prudence, moderation, modesty, humility, benevolence, and much else of all that is beautiful in the character and conduct of man are disfigured, mutilated and blighted by the ugliness of anger. Anger opens the way to oppression and in its wake follows heaviness of heart : a pall of gloom that spreads and settles over all that it touches long after the storm is over. Anger kills joy, stifles love, breeds bitterness, pollutes the spring of fellow-feeling and brotherhood at their very source.

53. When a man once asked the Prophet for some advice, he said repeatedly : "Do not be angry; do not be angry; do not be angry . . ." (*Bukhari, Mishkat;* Vol. III, p. Ch. 20). Restraining one's anger is a hall-mark of the *Muttaqi*, the *Momin*, the *Muslim*. The Quran urges the conquest of anger; and the Prophet is on record as having said: "The strong man is not the good wrestler; the strong man is he who controls himself when he is angry." (*Bukhari, Ibid.*). Anger is alien to the spirit of charity which the Quran repeatedly urges the *Momin* to cultivate; and the Prophet is on record as having said: "Do not be people without minds of your own saying that if others treat you well you will treat them well, and if they do wrong you will do wrong; but accustom yourselves to do good, and not to do wrong if they do evil." (*Tirmidhi, Mishkat*, Vol. III, p. 1063). And in the context of the conquest of anger, consider the wisdom, the eminent practicality, the beauty of the Prophet's advice:

(*a*) "Anger comes from the devil; the devil was created of fire; and fire is extinguished by water. So when one of you becomes angry, he should perform the ablution." (*Abu Dawud*; *Ibid.*, p. 1059)

(*b*) "When one of you becomes angry while standing, he should sit down. If the anger leaves him, well and good; otherwise he should lie down." (*Ahmad, Tirmidhi*; *Ibid.*)

54. Anger and rage are cancerous diseases to which the human heart is vulnerable and well may the *Muslim* ponder over what *Amenhotep IV* wrote (1360-1350 BC) in that magnificent treatise on the conduct of life which the Lamas of Lhasa preserved and propagated (since 732 AD) and an English archaeologist (going beyond the call of his duty) translated into English in 1749. Consider these lines from the chapter on "Anger":—

> "As the whirlwind in its fury teareth up trees, and deformeth the face of nature, or as an earthquake in its convulsions over-turneth whole cities; so the rage of an angry man throweth mischief around him.
>
> Danger and destruction wait on his hand.
>
> But consider and forget not thy own weakness; so shalt thou pardon the failings of others.
>
> Indulge not thyself in the passion of Anger; it is whetting a sword to wound thine own breast, or murder thy friend...
>
> Seest thou not that the angry man loseth his understanding?
>
> Whilst thou art yet in thy senses, let the wrath of another be a lesson to thyself.
>
> Do nothing in a passion. Why wilt thou put to sea in the violence of a storm ?
>
> If it be difficult to rule thine anger, it is wise to prevent it; avoid therefore all occasions of falling into wrath or guard thyself against them whenever they occur...
>
> Harbour not revenge in thy breast; it will torment thy heart and discolour its best inclination...
>
> A mild answer to an angry man, like water cast upon the fire, abateth its heat; and from an enemy he shall become thy friend.
>
> Consider how few things are worthy of anger, and thou wilt wonder that any but fools should be wroth.

In folly or weakness it always beginneth; but remember and be well-assured, it seldom concludeth without repentance.

On the heels of folly treadeth shame; at the back of anger standeth remorse."

("*Unto Thee I Grant*," *Rosicrucian Library* (*Vol. V*), *Supreme Grand Lodge of Amorc, San Jose, Calif* (*USA*); *pp.* 17-18)

55. So vile and violent then is the passion of *anger.* He who would be a *Muslim* must cleanse his heart of this disease and all its derivatives: rage, resentment, revenge, oppression, the uncharitable word, the uncharitable look; all that *anger* flows from: ignorance, arrogance, loss of self-control (self-mastery) and all that *anger* ends in: shame, remorse, heaviness of heart, the gloom that stifles joy, the discord that destroys peace. And the *Muslim* would do well to remember that this is a matter not of mere *temporal ethical propriety* but an issue of *total* concern embracing the Hereafter. The Prophet said : "Anger spoils *faith* as aloes spoil honey."

56. *Hypocrisy.* Of all the diseases that ravage the heart of man and pollute his spirit, stifling the breath that the Lord breathed into him, the vilest, the most dangerous and yet the easiest to succumb to is *hypocrisy.* The essence of *hypocrisy* is *deceit*: a shining *exterior*, a pleasant facade, a pleasing veneer that seeks to cloak and conceal the darkness and the ugliness *within. Disparity* between word and deed is its commonest form; but numerous are the ways in which it presents itself. *Hypocrisy* is the most perfidious form of *lying*: the swine in the garb of the saint; Ugliness in the garb of Beauty; Falsehood parading as Truth; Ignorance posing as Knowledge; Bigotry proclaiming itself as Faith; Darkness displaying its silver lining of Light; the spreaders of conflict and confusion heralding themselves as the harbingers of Peace and Harmony.

57. I know of no clearer description of the *hypocrite* than

that contained in the Quran:—

> "And of mankind are some who say : We believe in Allah and the Last Day, when they believe not.
> They presume to beguile none save themselves; but they perceive not.
>
> In their hearts is a disease, and Allah increaseth their disease. A painful doom is theirs because they lie.
> And when it is said unto them: Make not mischief in the earth, they say : We are peacemakers only.
> Are not they indeed the mischief-makers ? But they preceive not.
> And when it is said unto them : Believe as the people believe, they say: Shall we believe as the fools believe ?
>
> Are not they indeed the fools ? But they know not.
> And when they fall in with those who believe, they say :
>
> We believe; but when they go apart to their devils, they declare: Lo! we are with you; verily we did but mock.
>
> Allah (Himself) doth mock them, leaving them to wander blindly on in their contumacy.
> These are they who purchase error at the price of guidance, so their commerce doth not prosper, neither are they guided." (*Quran*, II: 8-16)

58. The supreme characteristics of the *Hypocrite* then are *Lie, Deceit, Dissimulation* and *Fraud.* He hunts with the hound and runs with the hare. The Quran identifies him as "swaying between this and that, belonging neither to these nor to those" (4 : 143) and the Prophet likens him to "a ewe which goes to and fro between two flocks, turning at one time to the one and at another time to the other". (*Muslim*; *Mishkat*, Vol. I, p. 18). Such conduct is the lowest form of the *negation of faith :* a way of life that *abandons* the clarity, constancy, consistency, the, firm-

ness of purpose and resolve that faith bestows, and *resorts instead* to the duplicity of a vile pragmatism and expediency. This chuckling cleverness, this low cunning, this smooth shiftiness of the *hypocrite* bring him some temporary gain ; but they eventually recoil on him, deceiving the deceiver and shattering his delusion of success. The hypocrites "beguile none save themselves", says the Quran ; their mockery rebounds on them, "leaving them to wander blindly on in their contumacy."

59. The *expediency of the hypocrite* springs from his *partial, incomplete* view of *Life*. His lack of perspective causes him to miss the vision of *life in its totality : the Here plus the Hereafter*. His myopic view causes him to concern himself only with *temporal existence* and this distorted pre-occupation with what in any case is the infinitely smaller part breeds cruel contradictions in his conduct. The *dichotomies* in which he wallows proceed from his failure to perceive the relationship and the ratio between the *Here* and the *Hereafter* which together constitute the *totality* of *life*. The Quran refers to the *hypocrites* as "a folk who understand not" (59 : 13), "a folk who have no sense" (59 : 14), who "comprehend not" (53 : 7), "know not" (53 : 8). At the root of *hypocrisy*, as at the root of the many other diseases of the heart examined above, is *ignorance* : an unawareness of the vileness of hypocrisy and its disastrous consequences for the Hereafter. The Quran declares :

(*a*) "Lo ! the hypocrites will be in the lowest deep of the fire, and thou (O Muhammad) wilt find no helper for them." (4 : 145)

(*b*) "Allah curseth them, and theirs is the lasting torment." (9 : 68)

(*c*) "Whether thou ask forgiveness for them or ask not forgiveness for them, Allah will not forgive them. Lo ! Allah guideth not the evil-living folk." (63 : 6)

60. *Hypocrisy* is the gravest disease of the heart to which the *Momin* is vulnerable, for his *Iman* shrivels and shrinks with every

failure to perform those acts of obedience which that *Iman* makes obligatory. To declare our allegiance to Allah and His Prophet, and then to discard the commandments of the Quran and the precepts of the Sunnah, is clearly worse than a frank confession of our inability to believe. To enjoin righteousness while we ourselves persist in evil ; to preach what we do not practise ; to present an exterior brighter than what we inwardly are ; to simulate a faith or love or loyalty or whatever else, more intense than we actually feel : *this* is *fraudulent* dealing with God, Prophet, self and fellow-human being. Truthfulness and sincerity (*Sidq* and *Ikhlas*) belong to the fundamental character-constituents of the *Muslim*, and *hypocrisy* is a cruel, callous negation of these. Where there is *hypocrisy*, there can be no *Taqwa* ; and where there is no *Taqwa*, there is no niche for *Iman*, no room for *Islam*. *Hypocrisy* is worse than *Kufr*.

61. He who strives to be a *Muslim* must be in a state of constant alert against *hypocrisy*, pouncing on it and obliterating it the moment it makes its appearance within him. This is a fungus and a cancer that cannot be ignored, a weed and a parasite that chokes *Iman*, an acid that corrodes, a poison that destroys. We live in difficult times ; and I wonder what times the Prophet was referring to when he said :

(*a*) "In the last times men will come forth who will fraudulently use religion for worldly ends and wear sheepskins in public to display meekness. Their tongues will be sweeter than sugar, but their hearts will be the hearts of wolves. God will say : 'Are they trying to deceive Me, or are they acting presumptuously towards Me ? I swear by Myself, I shall send trial upon those people which will leave the intelligent man among them confounded'."

(*Tirmidhi, Mishkat*; Vol. III, p. 1104).

(*b*) "I fear for my people polytheism and latent passion .. Yes, they will not worship sun, moon, a stone, or an idol, but they will act hypocritically and harbour latent passion. One of them will start the day fasting, but when one of his passions presents itself to him he will abandon his fast."

(*Ahmad, Baihaqi* ; *Ibid.*, p. 1106)

(*c*) "What I fear for this people is just every hypocrite who talks wisely and acts unjustly."

(*Baihaqi* ; *Ibid.*, p. 1107)

62. Consider also the following sayings of the Prophet about those who pose to be pious, who are righteous for worldly ends—to be seen, heard or be spoken of by men :

(*a*) "He who prays hypocritically has attributed a partner to God ; he who fasts hypocritically has attributed a partner to God ; and he who gives *Sadaqa* hypocritically has attributed a partner to God."

(*Ahmad ; Ibid.*, p. 1106)

(*b*) "When God assembles men on the Day of Resurrection 'for a day about which there is no doubt', a crier will call saying that if anyone has associated someone in a deed which he did for God's sake, he can seek his reward from (that) someone else than God, for God is One Who has least need of partners."

(*Ahmad ; Ibid.*, p. 1103)

63. Even "a little hypocrisy is *Shirk*"; and *Shirk* is the foremost of the cardinal sins identified by Islam. Consider the end of the hypocrite :

(*a*) "On the night when I was taken up to heaven, I passed by people whose lips were being cut by scissors of fire. I asked Gabriel who they were and he told me they were the preachers among my people who said what they did not do." (*Tirmidhi; Ibid.*, p. 1003)

(*b*) "You will find that the one who will be in the worst position on the Day of Resurrection will be the two-faced man who presents one face to some and another to others." (*Bukhari and Muslim; Ibid.*, p. 1006)

(*c*) "He who is two-faced in this world, will have two tongues of fire on the Day of Resurrection." (*Darimi; Ibid.*, p. 1010)

64. Having considered the nature of *Hypocrisy*, its vileness Here and its dire consequences for the Hereafter, we would do well to ponder over the major signs of hypocrisy and the major sins identified by Islam. The Prophet is on record as having said :

(*a*) "Four things, if they obtain in a person, make him an utter *hypocrite*, no matter how much he prays, and fasts, and claims that he is a *believer* : he who lies when he speaks ; breaks a promise when he pledges his word ; betrays a confidence when he is trusted ; and deviates from justice when he enters a controversy." (*Bukhari, Iman* : 24)

(*b*) "When one commits fornication, he is not a believer ; when one steals, he is not a believer; when one drinks wine, he is not a believer; when one takes plunder (on account of which men raise their eyes at him), he is not a believer; and when one of you defrauds (another), he is not a believer. So: beware, beware!" (*Bukhari and Muslim; Mishkat*, Vol. I, p. 17)

65. In a nut-shell, the *cardinal sins* identified by *Islam*—sins that temporarily push us out of the fold of Islam, sins that make us clear *Munafiqin* and draw on us the wrath of God (unless we make timely amends through a sincere and sustained act of *Taubah*)—these cardinal sins are : *Shirk* (associating others with whatever is due to God) ; fornication and adultery ; murder, plunder and theft ; misappropriating the wealth of others; devouring usury ; lie, slander and breach of trust ; bearing false witness ; believing in or practising magic ; being a deserter

from a war truly waged in the cause of Allah ; drinking ; gambling ; deliberate neglect of the prescribed prayers ; unlawful disobedience of parents ; excommunication or molestation of legal Muslims because of specific acts of un-Islam (*i.e.* crass *bigotry*). (*Mishkat;* Vol. I, pp. 17-19). These cardinal sins are clear manifestations of *hypocrisy ;* when we succumb to them, our actions violently belie the faith that we profess. He who strives to complete his Islam is constantly on the alert, guarding his heart and his actions against the encroachments of *hypocrisy.*

66. *The Sins of the Tongue.* This discourse on *Taharat* (purity) as one of the fundamental attributes of the *Muslim* would remain grossly incomplete without some reference, however brief, to those "sins of the tongue" of which every man striving to be a *Muslim* must steer clear of : lie, slander and abuse ; back-biting, contentiousness, idle debate and disputation ; self-praise ; cursing, jesting, ridiculing or scoffing at people ; being loud-mouthed and vain of speech. In this context, consider the following samplings from the Quran and the Hadith :

(*a*) *From the Quran.* 9 : 79 ; 24 : 23 ; 58 : 11-12.

(*b*) *From Hadith*

(1) "A man slips more by his tongue than by his foot."
(*Baihaqi; Mishkat,* Vol. III, p. 1009)

(2) " .. When a man gets up in the morning, all the limbs humble themselves before the tongue and say : Fear God for our sake, for we are dependent on you. If you are straight, we are straight ; and if you are crooked, we are crooked."
(*Tirmidhi; Ibid.*)

(3) "Part of a man's good observance of Islam is that he leaves alone what does not concern him."
(*Malik, Ahmad; Ibid.*)

(4) "A believer could be a coward, a miser, but *not* a liar." (*Malik, Baihaqi ; Ibid.*, p. 1012)

(5) "The believer is not given to cursing .. Coarse talk does not come into anything without disgracing it ; and modesty does not come into anything without adorning it."

(*Tirmidhi; Ibid.*, pp. 1010-11)

(6) "It is great treachery that you should tell your brother something and have him believe you when you are lying." (*Abu Dawud; Ibid.*, p. 1010)

(7) "No one accuses another of disobedience to God or infidelity without it coming back upon him, if the other is not as he said."

(*Tirmidhi; Ibid.*, p. 1003)

(8) "Saying something about your brother which he would dislike .. If what you say of him is true, you have *slandered* him ; and if it is not true, you have *reviled* him." (*Muslim; Ibid.*, p. 1007)

(9) "Solitude is better than an evil companion ; a good companion is better than solitude. Dictating what is good is better than silence ; and silence is better than dictating what is bad."

(*Mishkat*, Vol. III, p. 1012)

(10) " .. I enjoin you to fear God, for that will be the best adornment for everying that concerns you . . . Engage in recitation of the Quran and remembrance of God Who is great and glorious, for it will be a means of your being mentioned in heaven and will be a light for you on earth .. Observe long silence, for it is a means of driving away the devil and is a help to you in your religion .. Avoid excessive laughter, for it slays the heart and removes the light of the face .. Speak the truth, even if it is bitter .. Do not fear anyone's blame when you are serving God ..

Let what you know of yourself keep (prevent) you from blaming other people."

(*Baihaqi; Ibid.*, p. 1013)

(11) "When my Lord took me up to heaven I passed people who had nails of copper and were scratching their faces and their breasts. I asked Gabriel who these were, and he replied that they were those who were given to back-biting and who aspersed on peoples' honour."

(*Abu Dawud; Ibid.*, p. 1048)

67. We shall close this discourse on *Taharat* as that process of *purification* by which the human heart and spirit are cleansed of these soul-destroying passions (*viz. Pride, Arrogance, Vanity; Jealousy, Envy, Malice* and *Rancour; Lust, Greed, Avarice; Love of Worldly Wealth, Property, Status, Pomp and Power; Anger and Rage; Hypocrisy; Lying, Slander, Abuse, Back-Biting; Contentiousness, Idle Dispute, Disputation; Self-Praise; Cursing, Jesting, Ridiculing, Scoffing at People; being Loud-Mouthed, Empty, Noisy, Vain of Speech*). As the spirit of him who strives to be a *Muslim* is progressively cleansed of these *Passions*, the decks are simultaneously cleared for the entry of those *Virtues* which represent the positive aspect of *Taqwa*—virtues that must be cultivated for the transformation of the *Momin* into the *Muslim*, completing both his *Iman* and *Islam*.

68. We proceed to the next basic attribute of the Muslim: *Truthfulness* (*Sidq*) and *Sincerity* (*Ikhlas*).

SELECTED BIBLIOGRAPHY

1. Marmaduke Pickthall, *The Meaning of the Glorious Quran: Text and Explanatory Translation.* Accurate Printers, P. O. Box 1338, Lahore.

2. Altaf Gauhar, *Translations from the Quran.* Idara-e-Tarjumanul Quran, Ichhra, Lahore.

3. *Mishkat al-Masabih,* Translation by Dr. James Robson. Sheikh Muhammad Ashraf, Kashmiri Bazar, Lahore.

4. Al-Ghazzali, *Ihya Ulum al-Din.* Translation by Nabih Amin Faris

("Revival of the Religious Sciences"), Sheikh Muhammad Ashraf, Kashmiri Bazar, Lahore.

5. Al-Ghazzali, *Bidayat al-Hidayah*. Translation by Montgomery Watt ("The Faith and Practice of al-Ghazzali"), Sheikh Muhammad Ashraf, Kashmiri Bazar, Lahore.
6. Ali al-Hujwiri, *Kashf al-Mahjub*. Translation by R. A. Nicholson, Luzac and Co. Ltd., London.
7. Farid al-Din Attar, *Tadhkirat al-Auliya*. Translated by A. J. Arberry (' Memorial of the Saints: Muslim Saints and Mystics"), Routledge and Kegan Paul, London.
8. *Masnun Duaen (Prayers of the Prophet)*. Compilation by Maulana Anis Ahmad, translation by M. A. H. Siddiqui. Sheikh Muhammad Ashraf, Kashmiri Bazar, Lahore.
9. William Shakespeare, *Macbeth*. "Great Books of the Western World", Encyclopaedia Britannica Inc, Chicago.
10. P. B. Shelley, *Ozymandias*. Quoted by Will Durant, *Pleasures of Philosophy*, George Allen and Unwin Ltd., London.
11. *Unto Thee I Grant*, Rosicrucian Library, San Jose, California.
12. Abul Ala Maududi, *Towards Understanding Islam*. Islamic Publications, Shah Alam Market, Lahore.

THE BASIC ATTRIBUTES OF A MUSLIM

Passages from the Quran

(Ref. Page 110)

Say (O Muslims) : We believe in Allah and that which is revealed unto us and that which was revealed unto Abraham, Ishmael, and Isaac, and Jacob, and the tribes, and that which Moses and Jesus received, and that which the Prophets received from their Lord. We make no distinction between any of them, and unto Him we have surrendered. (2 : 136)

١٣٦- قُولُوا آمَنَّا بِاللّٰهِ وَمَا أُنْزِلَ إِلَيْنَا وَمَا
أُنْزِلَ إِلَىٰ إِبْرٰهِمَ وَإِسْمٰعِيلَ وَإِسْحٰقَ وَ
يَعْقُوبَ وَالْأَسْبَاطِ وَمَا أُوتِيَ مُوسَىٰ وَ
عِيسَىٰ وَمَا أُوتِيَ النَّبِيُّونَ مِنْ رَبِّهِمْ لَا نُفَرِّقُ
بَيْنَ أَحَدٍ مِنْهُمْ وَنَحْنُ لَهُ مُسْلِمُونَ ○

(Ref. Page 118)

All that is in the heavens and the earth glorifieth Allah ; and He is the Mighty, the Wise.

١- سَبَّحَ لِلّٰهِ
مَا فِي السَّمٰوٰتِ وَالْأَرْضِ
وَهُوَ الْعَزِيزُ الْحَكِيمُ ○

His is the Sovereignty of the heavens and the earth ; He quickeneth and He giveth death ; and He is Able to do all things.

٢- لَهُ مُلْكُ السَّمٰوٰتِ وَالْأَرْضِ
يُحْيِي وَيُمِيتُ
وَهُوَ عَلَىٰ كُلِّ شَيْءٍ قَدِيرٌ ○

He is the First and the Last, and the Outward and the Inward ; and He is Knower of all things.

٣- هُوَ الْأَوَّلُ وَالْآخِرُ
وَالظَّاهِرُ وَالْبَاطِنُ
وَهُوَ بِكُلِّ شَيْءٍ عَلِيمٌ ○

He it is Who created the heavens and the earth in six Days ; then He mounted the Throne. He knoweth all that entereth the earth and all that emergeth therefrom and all that cometh down from the sky and all that ascendeth therein ; and He is with you wheresoever ye may be. And Allah is Seer of what ye do.

٤- هُوَ الَّذِي خَلَقَ السَّمٰوٰتِ وَالْأَرْضَ فِي
سِتَّةِ أَيَّامٍ ثُمَّ اسْتَوَىٰ عَلَى الْعَرْشِ
يَعْلَمُ مَا يَلِجُ فِي الْأَرْضِ
وَمَا يَخْرُجُ مِنْهَا
وَمَا يَنْزِلُ مِنَ السَّمَاءِ وَمَا يَعْرُجُ فِيهَا
وَهُوَ مَعَكُمْ أَيْنَ مَا كُنْتُمْ
وَاللّٰهُ بِمَا تَعْمَلُونَ بَصِيرٌ ○

His is the Sovereignty of the heavens and the earth, and unto Allah (all) things are brought back.

٥- لَهُ مُلْكُ السَّمٰوٰتِ وَالْأَرْضِ
وَإِلَى اللّٰهِ تُرْجَعُ الْأُمُورُ ○

He causeth the night to pass into the day, and He causeth the day to pass into the night, and He is Knower of all that is in the breasts. (57 : 1-6)

٦- يُولِجُ الَّيْلَ فِي النَّهَارِ وَيُولِجُ النَّهَارَ
فِي الَّيْلِ وَهُوَ عَلِيمٌ بِذَاتِ الصُّدُورِ ○

He is Allah, than Whom there is no other God, the Knower of the invisible and the visible. He is the Beneficent, the Merciful.

٢٢- هُوَ اللّٰهُ الَّذِىْ لَآ اِلٰهَ اِلَّا هُوَ
عٰلِمُ الْغَيْبِ وَالشَّهَادَةِ
هُوَ الرَّحْمٰنُ الرَّحِيْمُ ○

He is Allah, than Whom there is no other God, the Sovereign Lord, the Holy One, Peace, the Keeper of Faith, the Guardian, the Majestic, the Compeller, the Superb. Glorified be Allah from all that they ascribe as partner (unto Him) !

٢٣- هُوَ اللّٰهُ الَّذِىْ لَآ اِلٰهَ اِلَّا هُوَ
اَلْمَلِكُ الْقُدُّوْسُ السَّلٰمُ
الْمُؤْمِنُ الْمُهَيْمِنُ
الْعَزِيْزُ الْجَبَّارُ الْمُتَكَبِّرُ
سُبْحٰنَ اللّٰهِ
عَمَّا يُشْرِكُوْنَ ○

He is Allah, the Creator, the Shaper out of naught, the Fashioner. His are the most beautiful names. All that is in the heavens and the earth glorifieth Him, and He is the Mighty, the Wise. (59 : 22-24)

٢٤- هُوَ اللّٰهُ الْخَالِقُ
الْبَارِئُ الْمُصَوِّرُ
لَهُ الْاَسْمَآءُ الْحُسْنٰى
يُسَبِّحُ لَهٗ
مَا فِى السَّمٰوٰتِ وَالْاَرْضِ
وَهُوَ الْعَزِيْزُ الْحَكِيْمُ ○

(Ref. Page 119)

Thee (alone) we worship ;
Thee (alone) we ask for help. (1 : 4)

٥- اِيَّاكَ نَعْبُدُ وَاِيَّاكَ نَسْتَعِيْنُ ○

Now, if they turn away (O Muhammad) Say : Allah sufficeth me. There is no God save Him ; In Him have I put my trust, and He is Lord of the Tremendous Throne. (9 : 129)

١٢٩- فَاِنْ تَوَلَّوْا فَقُلْ حَسْبِىَ اللّٰهُ
لَآ اِلٰهَ اِلَّا هُوَ عَلَيْهِ تَوَكَّلْتُ وَهُوَ رَبُّ
الْعَرْشِ الْعَظِيْمِ ○

Allah knoweth best (who are) your enemies. Allah is sufficient as a Friend, and Allah is sufficient as a Helper. (4 : 45)

٤٥- وَاللّٰهُ اَعْلَمُ بِاَعْدَآئِكُمْ
وَكَفٰى بِاللّٰهِ وَلِيًّا وَّكَفٰى بِاللّٰهِ نَصِيْرًا ○

(Ref. Page 119)

O mankind ! A similitude is coined, so pay ye heed to it. Lo ! those on whom ye call besides Allah will never create a fly though they combine together for the purpose. And if the fly took something from them, they could not rescue it from it. So weak are (both) the seeker and the sought !

(22 : 73)

٧٣- يَا أَيُّهَا النَّاسُ ضُرِبَ مَثَلٌ
فَاسْتَمِعُوا لَهُ ۚ إِنَّ الَّذِينَ تَدْعُونَ مِنْ
دُونِ اللَّهِ
لَنْ يَخْلُقُوا ذُبَابًا وَلَوِ اجْتَمَعُوا لَهُ ۖ
وَإِنْ يَسْلُبْهُمُ الذُّبَابُ شَيْئًا
لَا يَسْتَنْقِذُوهُ مِنْهُ ۚ
ضَعُفَ الطَّالِبُ وَالْمَطْلُوبُ ۝

(Ref. Page 120)

It was by the mercy of Allah that thou wast lenient with them (O Muhammad), for if thou hadst been stern and fierce of heart they would have dispersed from round about thee. So pardon them and ask forgiveness for them and consult with them upon the conduct of affairs. And when thou art resolved, then put thy trust in Allah. Lo ! Allah loveth those who put their trust (in Him).

١٥٩- فَبِمَا رَحْمَةٍ مِنَ اللَّهِ لِنْتَ لَهُمْ ۖ
وَلَوْ كُنْتَ فَظًّا غَلِيظَ الْقَلْبِ
لَانْفَضُّوا مِنْ حَوْلِكَ ۖ
فَاعْفُ عَنْهُمْ
وَاسْتَغْفِرْ لَهُمْ
وَشَاوِرْهُمْ فِي الْأَمْرِ ۖ
فَإِذَا عَزَمْتَ فَتَوَكَّلْ عَلَى اللَّهِ ۚ
إِنَّ اللَّهَ يُحِبُّ الْمُتَوَكِّلِينَ ۝

If Allah is your helper none can overcome you, and if He withdraw His help from you, who is there who can help you ? In Allah let believers put their trust. (3 : 159-160)

١٦٠- إِنْ يَنْصُرْكُمُ اللَّهُ فَلَا غَالِبَ لَكُمْ ۖ
وَإِنْ يَخْذُلْكُمْ
فَمَنْ ذَا الَّذِي يَنْصُرُكُمْ مِنْ بَعْدِهِ ۗ
وَعَلَى اللَّهِ فَلْيَتَوَكَّلِ الْمُؤْمِنُونَ ۝

Knowest thou not that it is Allah unto Whom belongeth the sovereignty of the heavens and earth and ye have not, besides Allah any friend or helper ? (2 : 107)

١٠٧- أَلَمْ تَعْلَمْ أَنَّ اللَّهَ لَهُ مُلْكُ السَّمَاوَاتِ
وَالْأَرْضِ ۗ وَمَا لَكُمْ مِنْ دُونِ اللَّهِ مِنْ
وَلِيٍّ وَلَا نَصِيرٍ ۝

But when they spy some merchandise or pastime they break away to it and leave thee standing. Say: that which Allah hath is better than pastime and than merchandise, and Allah is the best of providers.

(62 : 11)

١١- وَإِذَا رَأَوْا تِجَارَةً أَوْ لَهْوًا
انْفَضُّوا إِلَيْهَا وَتَرَكُوكَ قَائِمًا ۚ
قُلْ مَا عِنْدَ اللَّهِ خَيْرٌ
مِنَ اللَّهْوِ وَمِنَ التِّجَارَةِ ۚ
وَاللَّهُ خَيْرُ الرَّازِقِينَ ۝

(Ref. Page 121)

O ye who believe ! Seek help in steadfastness and prayer. Lo ! Allah is with the steadfast.

١٥٣- يٰٓاَيُّهَا الَّذِيْنَ اٰمَنُوا اسْتَعِيْنُوْا
بِالصَّبْرِ وَالصَّلٰوةِ ؕ
اِنَّ اللّٰهَ مَعَ الصّٰبِرِيْنَ ○

And call not those who are slain in the way of Allah "dead". Nay, they are living, only ye perceive not.

١٥٤- وَلَا تَقُوْلُوْا لِمَنْ يُّقْتَلُ فِىْ سَبِيْلِ اللّٰهِ
اَمْوَاتٌ ؕ
بَلْ اَحْيَآءٌ وَّلٰكِنْ لَّا تَشْعُرُوْنَ ○

And surely We shall try you with something of fear and hunger, and loss of wealth and lives and crops ; but give glad tidings to the steadfast.

١٥٥- وَلَنَبْلُوَنَّكُمْ بِشَىْءٍ
مِّنَ الْخَوْفِ وَالْجُوْعِ وَنَقْصٍ مِّنَ الْاَمْوَالِ
وَالْاَنْفُسِ وَالثَّمَرٰتِ ؕ
وَبَشِّرِ الصّٰبِرِيْنَ ○

Who say when a misfortune striketh them : Lo ! We are Allah's and Lo ! unto Him we are returning. (2 : 153-156)

١٥٦- الَّذِيْنَ اِذَآ اَصَابَتْهُمْ مُّصِيْبَةٌ ۙ
قَالُوْٓا اِنَّا لِلّٰهِ وَاِنَّآ اِلَيْهِ رٰجِعُوْنَ ○

When Allah's succour and the triumph cometh,

١- اِذَا جَآءَ نَصْرُ اللّٰهِ وَالْفَتْحُ ○

And thou seest mankind entering the religion of Allah in troops,

٢- وَرَاَيْتَ النَّاسَ يَدْخُلُوْنَ فِىْ دِيْنِ اللّٰهِ
اَفْوَاجًا ○

Then hymn the praises of thy Lord, and seek forgiveness of Him. Lo ! He is ever ready to show mercy. (110 : 1-3)

٣- فَسَبِّحْ بِحَمْدِ رَبِّكَ وَاسْتَغْفِرْهُ ؕ
اِنَّهٗ كَانَ تَوَّابًا ○

(Ref. Page 122)

Say (O Muhammad), Lo ! the bounty is in Allah's hand. He bestoweth it on whom He will. Allah is All-Embracing, All-Knowing.

قُلْ اِنَّ الْفَضْلَ بِيَدِ اللّٰهِ ۚ
يُؤْتِيْهِ مَنْ يَّشَآءُ ؕ
وَاللّٰهُ وَاسِعٌ عَلِيْمٌ ○

He selecteth for His mercy whom He will. Allah is of infinite bounty. (3 : 73-74)

۷۴- يَخْتَصُّ بِرَحْمَتِهٖ مَنْ يَّشَآءُ ؕ
وَاللّٰهُ ذُو الْفَضْلِ الْعَظِيْمِ ۝

(Ref. Page 122)

Say : O Allah ! Owner of sovereignty ! Thou givest sovereignty unto whom Thou wilt, and Thou withdrawest sovereignty from whom thou wilt. Thou exaltest whom Thou wilt and Thou abasest whom thou wilt. In Thy hand is the good. Lo ! Thou art able to do all things. (3 : 26)

۲۶- قُلِ اللّٰهُمَّ مٰلِكَ الْمُلْكِ
تُؤْتِي الْمُلْكَ مَنْ تَشَآءُ
وَتَنْزِعُ الْمُلْكَ مِمَّنْ تَشَآءُ ۫
وَتُعِزُّ مَنْ تَشَآءُ
وَتُذِلُّ مَنْ تَشَآءُ ؕ
بِيَدِكَ الْخَيْرُ ؕ
اِنَّكَ عَلٰى كُلِّ شَيْءٍ قَدِيْرٌ ۝

(Ref. Page 125)

By the morning hours.

And by the night when it is stillest,

Thy Lord hath not forsaken thee nor doth He hate thee.

And verily the latter portion will be better for thee than the former,

And verily thy Lord wilt give unto thee so that thou will be content.

Did He not find thee an orphan and protect (thee) ?

Did He not find thee wandering and direct (thee) ?

Did He not find thee destitute and enrich (thee) ?

Therefor the orphan oppress not,

Therefor the beggar drive not away.

Therefor of the bounty of thy Lord be thy discourse. (93 : 1-11)

۱- وَالضُّحٰى ۝
۲- وَالَّيْلِ اِذَا سَجٰى ۝
۳- مَا وَدَّعَكَ رَبُّكَ
وَمَا قَلٰى ۝
۴- وَلَلْاٰخِرَةُ خَيْرٌ لَّكَ مِنَ الْاُوْلٰى ۝
۵- وَلَسَوْفَ يُعْطِيْكَ رَبُّكَ
فَتَرْضٰى ۝
۶- اَلَمْ يَجِدْكَ يَتِيْمًا فَاٰوٰى ۝
۷- وَوَجَدَكَ ضَآلًّا
فَهَدٰى ۝
۸- وَوَجَدَكَ عَآئِلًا
فَاَغْنٰى ۝
۹- فَاَمَّا الْيَتِيْمَ فَلَا تَقْهَرْ ۝
۱۰- وَاَمَّا السَّآئِلَ فَلَا تَنْهَرْ ۝
۱۱- وَاَمَّا بِنِعْمَةِ رَبِّكَ فَحَدِّثْ ۝

(Ref. Page 125)

Have We not caused thy bosom to dilate,
And eased thee of the burden,
Which weighed down thy back ;
And exalted thy fame.
But Lo ! with hardship goeth ease,
Lo ! with hardship goeth ease ;
So when thou art relieved, still toil.
And strive to please thy Lord. (94 : 1-8)

١- أَلَمْ نَشْرَحْ لَكَ صَدْرَكَ ○
٢- وَوَضَعْنَا عَنكَ وِزْرَكَ ○
٣- الَّذِيٓ أَنقَضَ ظَهْرَكَ ○
۴- وَرَفَعْنَا لَكَ ذِكْرَكَ ○
۵- فَإِنَّ مَعَ الْعُسْرِ يُسْرًا ○
۶- إِنَّ مَعَ الْعُسْرِ يُسْرًا ○
۷- فَإِذَا فَرَغْتَ فَانصَبْ ○
۸- وَإِلَىٰ رَبِّكَ فَارْغَبْ ○

(Ref. Page 135)

And covet not the thing in which Allah hath made some of you excel others. Unto men a fortune from that which they have earned, and unto women a fortune from that which they have earned. (Envy not one another) but ask Allah of His bounty. Lo ! Allah is ever Knower of all things. (4 : 32)

٣٢- وَلَا تَتَمَنَّوْا مَا فَضَّلَ اللّٰهُ بِهِ بَعْضَكُمْ
عَلَىٰ بَعْضٍ لِّلرِّجَالِ نَصِيبٌ مِّمَّا اكْتَسَبُوا
وَلِلنِّسَآءِ نَصِيبٌ مِّمَّا اكْتَسَبْنَ
وَسْئَلُوا اللّٰهَ مِن فَضْلِهِ
إِنَّ اللّٰهَ كَانَ بِكُلِّ شَيْءٍ عَلِيمًا ○

(Ref. Page 136)

Rivalry in worldly increase distracteth ye,
Until ye come to the graves.
Nay, but ye will come to know !
Nay, but ye will come to know !
Nay, would that ye knew (now) with a sure knowledge !
For ye will behold hellfire.
Aye, ye will behold it with sure vision ;
Then, on that day, ye will be asked concerning pleasure. (102 : 1-8)

١- أَلْهٰكُمُ
التَّكَاثُرُ ○
٢- حَتّٰى زُرْتُمُ الْمَقَابِرَ ○
٣- كَلَّا سَوْفَ تَعْلَمُونَ ○
۴- ثُمَّ كَلَّا سَوْفَ تَعْلَمُونَ ○
۵- كَلَّا لَوْ تَعْلَمُونَ عِلْمَ الْيَقِينِ ○
۶- لَتَرَوُنَّ الْجَحِيمَ ○
۷- ثُمَّ لَتَرَوُنَّهَا عَيْنَ الْيَقِينِ ○
۸- ثُمَّ لَتُسْئَلُنَّ يَوْمَئِذٍ عَنِ النَّعِيمِ ○

(Ref. Page 143)

And of mankind are some who say : We believe in Allah and the Last Day, when they believe not.

٨- وَمِنَ النَّاسِ مَن يَقُولُ اٰمَنَّا بِاللّٰهِ وَ
بِالْيَوْمِ الْاٰخِرِ وَمَا هُم بِمُؤْمِنِينَ ○

(Ref. Page 143)

They think to beguile Allah and those who believe, and they beguile none save themselves ; but they perceive not.

۹- يُخٰدِعُوْنَ اللّٰهَ وَالَّذِيْنَ اٰمَنُوْا ۚ وَمَا
يَخْدَعُوْنَ اِلَّآ اَنْفُسَهُمْ وَمَا يَشْعُرُوْنَ ○

In their hearts is a disease, and Allah increaseth their disease. A painful doom is theirs because they lie.

۱۰- فِيْ قُلُوْبِهِمْ مَّرَضٌ ۙ فَزَادَهُمُ اللّٰهُ مَرَضًا ۚ
وَلَهُمْ عَذَابٌ اَلِيْمٌ ۙ بِمَا كَانُوْا
يَكْذِبُوْنَ ○

And when it is said unto them : Make not mischief in the earth, they say ; We are peacemakers only.

۱۱- وَاِذَا قِيْلَ لَهُمْ لَا تُفْسِدُوْا فِي الْاَرْضِ ۙ
قَالُوْٓا اِنَّمَا نَحْنُ مُصْلِحُوْنَ ○

Are not they indeed the mischief-makers ? But they perceive not.

۱۲- اَلَآ اِنَّهُمْ هُمُ الْمُفْسِدُوْنَ وَلٰكِنْ لَّا
يَشْعُرُوْنَ ○

And when it is said unto them : Believe as the people believe, they say : Shall we believe as the foolish believe ? Are not they indeed the foolish ? But they know not.

۱۳- وَاِذَا قِيْلَ لَهُمْ اٰمِنُوْا كَمَآ اٰمَنَ النَّاسُ
قَالُوْٓا اَنُؤْمِنُ كَمَآ اٰمَنَ السُّفَهَآءُ ۭ اَلَآ اِنَّهُمْ
هُمُ السُّفَهَآءُ وَلٰكِنْ لَّا يَعْلَمُوْنَ ○

And when they fall in with those who believe, they say : We believe ; but when they go apart to their devils they declare : Lo ! We are with you ; verily we did but mock.

۱۴- وَاِذَا لَقُوا الَّذِيْنَ اٰمَنُوْا قَالُوْٓا اٰمَنَّا ۚ وَاِذَا
خَلَوْا اِلٰى شَيٰطِيْنِهِمْ ۙ قَالُوْٓا اِنَّا مَعَكُمْ ۙ اِنَّمَا
نَحْنُ مُسْتَهْزِءُوْنَ ○

Allah (Himself) doth mock them, leaving them to wander blindly on in their contumacy.

۱۵- اَللّٰهُ يَسْتَهْزِئُ بِهِمْ وَيَمُدُّهُمْ فِيْ طُغْيَانِهِمْ
يَعْمَهُوْنَ ○

They are they who purchase error at the price of guidance, so their commerce doth not prosper, neither are they guided.
(2 : 8-16)

۱۶- اُولٰٓئِكَ الَّذِيْنَ اشْتَرَوُا الضَّلٰلَةَ بِالْهُدٰى
فَمَا رَبِحَتْ تِّجَارَتُهُمْ وَمَا كَانُوْا مُهْتَدِيْنَ ○

(Ref. Page 144)

Lo ! the hypocrites (will be) in the lowest deep of the fire, and thou wilt find no helper for them. (4 : 145)

۱۴۵- اِنَّ الْمُنٰفِقِيْنَ فِي الدَّرْكِ الْاَسْفَلِ
مِنَ النَّارِ ۚ وَلَنْ تَجِدَ لَهُمْ نَصِيْرًا ○

(Ref. Page 144)

Allah promiseth the hypocrites, both men and women, and the disbelievers fire of hell for their abode. It will suffice them. Allah curseth them, and theirs is the lasting torment. (9 : 68)

٦٨- وَعَدَ اللّٰهُ الْمُنٰفِقِيْنَ وَالْمُنٰفِقٰتِ وَ
الْكُفَّارَ نَارَ جَهَنَّمَ خٰلِدِيْنَ فِيْهَا
هِيَ حَسْبُهُمْ وَلَعَنَهُمُ اللّٰهُ
وَلَهُمْ عَذَابٌ مُّقِيْمٌ ○

Whether thou ask forgiveness for them or ask not forgiveness for them, Allah will not forgive them. Lo ! Allah guideth not the evil-living folk. (63 : 6)

٦- سَوَآءٌ عَلَيْهِمْ اَسْتَغْفَرْتَ لَهُمْ اَمْ لَمْ
تَسْتَغْفِرْ لَهُمْ لَنْ يَّغْفِرَ اللّٰهُ لَهُمْ
اِنَّ اللّٰهَ لَا يَهْدِى الْقَوْمَ الْفٰسِقِيْنَ ○

THE QURANIC CONCEPT OF PRAYER

INTRODUCTORY REMARKS

Two Modes of Inquiry

1. I venture to speak to you today on the "Quranic Concept of Prayer". There are two ways in which we may approach the subject : one, by way of the discursive intellect ; the other, a mode of perception known only to the devotional spirit, a mode of perception peculiar to the spirit wrapped in prayer. In my exposition, I shall attempt to journey to the centre of my subject using both modes ; for, I believe, we cannot otherwise grasp the totality of the meaning and significance of Prayer.

Complementary Modes

2. While we shall tread both paths—the path of "analytical inquiry" as well as the path of "devotional perception"—I should like to say a word or two about the mutual relationship between these two apparently divergent modes of approach. The divergence is apparent (in appearance only), not real. The two modes are, in fact, complementary ; not contradictory. The one buttresses the other. Scholarship, if it be true, must some day lead to Devotion ; and Devotion, if it be true, must spur the mind of man to further reflective enquiry. Of these two complementary modes of perception, which is the primary and which the secondary, I do not know. I only know that both are necessary ; without the one or the other, our quest of the truth must necessarily remain lop-sided and incomplete. There is *no* such thing as Ignorant Devotion, for Devotion is Love born of Understanding ; it is a seeing, not a blind Love. The devotee who approaches the altar of God without the Lamp of Knowledge, or with that lamp unlit, may no doubt pray ; but his prayer will be a prayer in the dark ; he will not "see" his Lord. And what

use is prayer if we be denied a flash of His Countenance ?[1]

3. I am not for a moment suggesting that our little lamp is enough to light up the Face that we wish to see, for that vision is an act of His grace. I am only saying that we should at least be in a position to beg for that grace. We should at least be able to say : "Lord, here is my little lamp lit and laid as an offering before You. With this feeble light I have dared to search for You, because You commanded me to do so, saying : 'Remember ye Me, and I shall remember you' (2 : 152). The seeker now is before the Sought ; breathe Your spirit into me Lord, snuff out this little flame, fill it with Your own oil, and light it with Your own light—so that through You, I may see You."[2]

Not By Scholarship Alone

4. That then is the role of reflective inquiry and scholarship—to my mind, indispensable aids to Devotion. But I would hasten to add that scholarship alone, without the gift of God's grace, is

---

1. The "vision of the Lord" is to be understood in its figurative, *not* literal sense : touching Him and being touched by Him in the spirit. To construe these words in any sense other than this would not only be obtuse and vulgar but also a cruel travesty of the truth. Allah is beyond physical vision, touch or any other mode of sensory perception but the spirit of man may perceive Him with an immediacy more intense than the physical : an awareness of His presence "closer to us than our jugular vein".
2. Prayer is prayer only when true communion is established. In that state of communion, the consciousness of the seeker is merged with the Sought. Words fail to express what only personal experience can confirm to the individual soul. Ali al-Hujwiri tries to explain :
"... in remembering Me he is enraptured by the remembrance (*Dhikr*) of Me, and his own 'acquisition' (*Kasb*) is annihilated so as to have no part in his remembrance, and the relationship of humanity (*Adamiyyat*) is entirely removed from his remembrance : then My remembrance is his remembrance... The fact is that when the Divine omnipotence manifests its dominion over humanity, it transports a man out of his own being, so that his speech becomes the speech of God. But it is impossible that God should be mingled (*Imtizaj*) with created beings, or made one (*Ittihad*) with His works, or become incarnate (*Hall*) in things : God is exalted far above that...."
See : Ali al-Hujwiri, *Kashf al-Mahjub*, p. 254.

barren, sterile, toil bound in toil and not proceeding beyond. A thousand years of analytical study and scholarship, devoid of God's grace, will *not* reveal to us the meaning and significance of Prayer—or for that matter, any other of the higher values of life. And yet, our little lamp, however dim and feeble, consecrated to one moment of devotion and surrender, one moment of prayer felt and experienced, one moment of silent communication throbbing with the joy of approach and the glory of surrender before the Lord—one such moment, covered with grace and peace and limitless light, will teach us more of Prayer than all the scholars of the world put together can.

5. Well then, in our approach towards an understanding of the meaning and significance of Prayer, we shall tread both paths : the Analytical and the Devotional, the former first. So help me Allah!

ANALYTICAL STUDY

Six Conclusions

6. My analytical study of the Quran, frighteningly limited though it is, leads me (as of now) to the following conclusions about the fundamentals relating to Prayer :—

(*a*) Firstly : that Prayer is not the privilege of the few but the prerogative of all.

(*b*) Secondly : that Prayer is a state of mind, *not* just words intoned.

(*c*) Thirdly : that Prayer is communication, two-way communication, *not* one-way traffic.

(*d*) Fourthly : that all time is prayer time and that to pray we need no ceremonies.

(*e*) Fifthly : that the way to true prayer reveals itself only after much prolonged practice.

(*f*) Finally : that prayer must be followed by acts of prayer, from prayer to prayer.

Let us examine these one by one.

Prayer : The Prerogative of All

7. The first conclusion that I presented was : that prayer is not the privilege of the few but the prerogative of all. The Lord says : "I hear the cry of every crier when he crieth unto Me" (**2** : 186). There is none among us so depraved that he may not pray. The Lord says : "O ye My servants who have transgressed against your souls, despair not of the mercy of Allah" (**39** : 53). Again : "So lose not heart, nor fall into despair ; for, ye must gain mastery if ye are true in faith" (**3** : 139). The Prophet prays, the saint prays, the common man prays, the sinner prays—all have the right to prayer on the assurance given to all : "Then do ye remember Me, and I shall remember you" (**2** : 152). The right to prayer is universal, a prerogative to be exercised by all, spilling over the borders of mankind and embracing the whole of His creation.[3] Apart from the right, there is also a need for all of us to pray ; there is none among us so exalted (the prophets of yore included) that he is above the need to pray. It is curious that those nearest to Him should pray the most ; and those that are most in need of prayer should pray the least ; but of this we may be certain that the urge is universal and eternal. It cannot be snuffed out. Consider what William James, one of the greatest of modern psychologists, has to say on this issue :—

> "It seems probable that in spite of all that science may do to the contrary, men will continue to pray to the end of time, unless their mental nature changes in a manner which nothing we know should lead us to expect. The impulse to pray is a necessary consequence of the fact that whilst the innermost of the empirical selves of a man is a

3. "Seest thou not that it is God
Whose praises
All beings in the heavens and on earth do celebrate,
And the birds (of the air) with wings outspread ?
Each one
knows its own mode of prayer and praise.
And God knows well all that they do." (**24** : 41)

self of the social sort, it yet can find its only adequate socius (its "great companion") in an ideal world .. Most men, either continually or occasionally, carry a reference to it in their breasts .. I say "for most of us", because it is probable that men differ a good deal in the degree in which they are haunted by this sense of an Ideal Spectator. It is a much more essential part of the consciousness of some men than of others. Those who have the most of it are possibly the most religious men. But I am sure that even those who say they are altogether without it, deceive themselves, and really have it in some degree."[4]

8. What William James struggles to explain in so many words (meandering as any human effort must), the Quran captures in a single sentence : " .. Those who believe, and whose hearts find satisfaction in the remembrance of God ; for, lo ! In the remembrance of God alone do hearts find satisfaction" (**13** : 28). The impulse to pray is indeed intrinsic to human nature, and the decay or erosion of that impulse is a measure of man's downward slide along that very ladder by which he may ascend to the highest fulfilment of his nature. The point, however, is that it matters little how low on the ladder we stand ; the need remains and with it, the right, the privilege, the prerogative to pray. I draw your attention once again to God's assurance :—

(*a*) "I hear the cry of every crier when he crieth unto Me .. " (**2** : 186).

(*b*) "O ye among My servants who have transgressed against your souls, despair not of the mercy of Allah. For Allah forgives all sins; for He is Oft-Forgiving, Most Merciful." (**39** : 53).

9. So much for the first conclusion : that Prayer is not the privilege of the few, but the prerogative of all.

State of Mind and Spirit, Not Words Intoned

10. Consider the second conclusion : that prayer is a state of

4. William James, *Varieties of Religious Experience.* Quoted by Iqbal, *The Reconstruction of Religious Thought in Islam*, p. 89.

mind, not just words intoned. It is a condition of the spirit, a state of absorption in God which energizes every thought and transforms every act into an act of prayer. It is one timeless extinction of our little selves, face to face with the Eternal Spirit. It is excellent when we can find the words to match the mood of this inner state of total, unconditional, complete surrender ; but the finest words are useless if they spring not from the innermost recesses of the heart. Prayer, in its highest and truest form, demands of the devotee an exclusive concentration on and in God. It is an occasion for communion, an occasion for an all-embracing surrender at the altar of God, an occasion when we may truthfully declare what God asks us to declare :—

> "Say :
> My prayer and my sacrifice,
> My life and my death,
> Are (all) for the Lord of the worlds.
> I assign no partners unto Him :
> And this I have been commanded.
> And I am (among) the first of those
> Who surrender their will to the will of God."

11. Prayer is *a state of intense, supreme concentration*—a state of mind in which the devotee gathers together every scattered strand of his being and bows down before his Lord in one, single, integrated act of self-surrender.[5] It is an all-embracing pros-

---

5. One common reason for the inefficacy of our Salat is our inability to concentrate on the Object of our prayer : Allah. We take to the prayer-mat with mind scattered, spirit divided—mundane thoughts encroaching on sacred territory. This happens because we are "without" Allah in the conduct of our daily lives and we vainly try to be "with" Him in snatches of 10-15 minutes. He who is God-oriented in *all* his actions, will find in Salat an occasion for heightened communion. Salat must not degenerate into an "extra-curricular" activity but become the nodal points of our daily existence—"bounds", you might say, on which to pause and ponder, take stock, cleanse, consolidate, re-check our bearings, re-plenish our strength at His altar and re-dedicate ourselves to His way. Only when so integrated into the stream of life, does Salat become meaningful.

[*Cont.*

tration before the Lord ; a total offering. I struggle to explain in words what I cannot ; so, you might as well hear a poet's perception of this state of mind and spirit. The poet sings and the Lord bears witness to his song :—

> "In one salutation to Thee, my God, let all my senses spread out and touch this world at Thy feet.
>
> Like a rain-cloud of July hung low with its burden of unshed showers, let all my mind bend down at Thy door in one salutation to Thee.
>
> Let all my songs gather together their diverse strains into a single current and flow to a sea of silence in one salutation to Thee.
>
> Like a flock of home-sick cranes flying night and day back to their mountain nest, let all my life take its voyage to its eternal home in one salutation to Thee."[6]

Another reason why we fail to achieve concentration in prayer is our failure to practise it in other spheres of life. We cannot suddenly achieve concentration on the prayer-mat, if being hurried and slip-shod has become a way of life with us. When every task undertaken is holy and none so small as not to demand perfection, in such a pattern of life concentration on the prayer-mat presents no insuperable problem. In the content of concentration as a constant and continuous feature of enlightened action, see : (1) Erich Fromm, *The Art of Loving*. (2) *The Bhagavad Gita*, Translation by Swami Prabhavananda and Christopher Isherwood. (3) Walter T. Stace, *The Teachings of the Mystics*, a Mentor Book, The New American Library, New York, 1960. Especially, Chap 1, pp. 10-29. (4) Richard Bach, *Jonathan Livingstone Seagull*.

Yet another reason for our failure to achieve concentration in prayer is our ignorance of even the literal meaning of all that is recited during the Salat. Shorn of understanding, devotion cannot take wing. In this context, see : Maududi, *Fundamentals of Islam*, Chapter on "Salat".

The true performance of the Wudu, with all its inner implications, is also of crucial importance. In this context, see : (1) Al-Ghazzali, *The Mysteries of Purity*. (2) Ali al-Hujwiri, *Kashf al-Mahjub*. Chapter on "Purity (*Taharat*)". (3) Al-Ghazzali, *Al-Munqidh min al-Dalal and Bidayat al-Hidayah*. (4) *Masnun Duaen* (*Prayers of the Prophet*).

6. Tagore, *Gitanjali*. The last song.

12. Prayer demands and is (I can hardly distinguish the means from the end here), Prayer demands and is a state of mind in which the devotee is engaged in *an all-else-excluded search of his Lord.* God is the goal, God is the means. There is no room here even for the self, much less for the expression of private and personal desires. Let me illustrate the point I am trying to make :—

(*a*) Abu Bakr Al-Shebli (died: A.D. 846), that great mystic whom the people of Khorasan mistook for a madman, was once seen running with a piece of burning coal in his hand.

"Where are you going ?" they asked.

"I am running to set fire to the Kaaba," he answered, "so that men may henceforth care only for the Lord of the Kaaba."

On another occasion he was holding in his hand a piece of wood alight at both ends.

"What are you going to do ?" they asked.

"I am going to set Hell on fire with one end and Paradise with the other," he replied,

"So that men may concern themselves only with God."[7]

(*b*) This single-minded, all-else-excluded, passionate search of God is again beautifully exemplified in that famous prayer one of Islam's most illustrious women-saints. Rabea al-Adawiya (died : A.D. 752).

She prayed :—

"O God, whatsoever Thou hast apportioned to me of worldly things, do Thou give that to Thy enemies; and whatsoever Thou hast apportioned to me in the world to come, give that to Thy friends ; for Thou (and Thou alone) sufficest me . .

O God, if I worship Thee for fear of Hell, burn me in Hell ; and if I worship Thee in hope of Paradise, exclude me from Paradise. But if I worship Thee for

7. Attar, *Tadhkirat al-Auliya.* Translation ("Muslim Saints and Mystics"), p. 281.

Thy own sake, grudge me not Thy everlasting beauty."[8]

(*c*) While we are still on this topic of an all-else-excluded search of God as one of the fundamental ingredients of the state of mind appropriate to prayer, I might mention the name of Bayazid of Bostam (died : A.D. 874) whose absorption in God was so intense that every day when he was called by a disciple who had been his inseparable companion for 20 years, he would ask : "My son, what is your name ?"[9]

(*d*) Again, it is narrated of Abu Said al-Kharraz of Baghdad (died : 892 A.D.) that he once saw the Prophet in his dream. "Do you love me, Al-Kharraz ?" the Prophet asked. "Forgive me, my Prophet," Al-Kharraz replied.
"Forgive me, for my love of God has preoccupied me from loving you." The Prophet said : "Whoso loveth God, loveth me (also)."[10]

13. Yet another ingredient of the state of mind appropriate to prayer is the fear and love of God, that inner restlessness which drives the devotee to *rush to prayer* whenever he hears the call to prayer. Allah calls : "O ye who believe, when you hear the call to prayer on the Day of Congregation, rush ye to the remembrance of God . . " (**62 :** 9). The state of mind appropriate to prayer is *a mind in a hurry to pray*, till it reaches the stillness of prayer. It is a mind that rises above play, sport and merchandize, for it cannot live without prayer. It is also a mind that cannot die without prayer. It is a mind that rushes to prayer, because it fears each prayer might be its last. Please let me illustrate what I am struggling to explain about this rush to prayer as an essential ingredient of the state of mind appropriate

---

8. *Ibid.*, p. 51.
9. *Ibid.*, Chapter on Bayazid of Bostam.
10. *Ibid.*, p. 220.

to Prayer :—

(*a*) It is narrated of Dawud al-Tai of Kufa (died : A.D. 777) that he was seen running to prayers.
"What is the hurry ?" he was asked.
"This army at the gates of the city," he replied. "They are waiting for me."
"Which army ?" they exclaimed.
"The men of the tombs," he replied.[11]

(*b*) It is narrated of Maruf al-Karkhi of Baghdad (died : A.D. 815) that once, hearing the call to prayer and finding himself not in a state of ritual purity, he immediately made his ablutions in sand. "Why, look !" they said to him. "There is the Tigris. Why are you making ablution in the sand ?"
"It can be," he replied, "that I may be no more by the time I get to it."[12]

(*c*) Abu Bakr Al-Shebli, whose name I mentioned before, was in a hurry not only in his rush to prayer but one day, quite strangely, during prayer itself. He was repeatedly uttering : "God, God !"
An earnest young disciple addressed him later :
"Why do you not say : There is no god but God ?"
Shebli sighed and replied : "I am afraid that if I say 'no god', I may expire before I reach 'but God'; and then I shall be utterly desolated."[13]

(*d*) It is said of Khair al-Nassaj of Samarra (died : A.D. 924) that he lived to the age of 120. When death drew nigh, it was time for the evening prayer. Azrael cast his shadow, and Khair raised his head from the pillow.
"God preserve you !" he cried. "Wait a little. You are a slave under orders ; and I am a slave under

---

11. *Ibid.*, p. 141.
12. *Ibid.*, p. 164.
13. *Ibid.*, p. 282.

> orders. You have been told to collect my soul. I have been told : 'When the time for prayer comes, pray !' That time has now come. You will have plenty of time to carry out your orders. For me it is now or never. Please be patient. Please wait until I have performed the evening prayer." Khair then washed himself and performed the prayer. Immediately afterwards, he was dead.[14]

So much, gentlemen, for the rush to prayer ("Rush ye to the remembrance of God") as an essential ingredient of the state of mind appropriate to prayer.

14. For quite some time now we have been talking about our second conclusion : that prayer is a state of mind, *not* just words intoned. It is seeking God to the exclusion of all else. It is a total offering. It is an intense, supreme concentration of our entire being and its joyous consecration at the altar of God. It is a rush to prayer that finds its stillness in it. It is a joyous submission to the will of God, an all-embracing surrender that truthfully declares :—

> "Say :
> My prayer and my sacrifice,
> My life and my death,
> Are (all) for Allah
> The Lord of all the worlds .. " (**6** : 162)

Two-Way Communication : Communion

15. It is time now to pass on to our third conclusion about the meaning and significance of Prayer : that prayer is communication, two-way communication, not just one-way traffic. Our personal and private desires, our cravings as a human animal do not become "prayer" merely because it is God Whom we ask to attend to them.[15] This is closely allied to what we discussed earlier under the attitude of mind appropriate to prayer. Prayer

---

14. *Ibid.*, p. 252.
15. Daag Hammarsjkoeld, *Markings*. Personal diary.

is *not* an occasion for a monologue. It does not stop at what *Iqbal* calls "an expression of man's inner yearning for a response in the awful silence of the universe".[16] Indeed, it must go beyond to what he describes as a "vital act by which the little island of our personality suddenly discovers its situation in a larger whole of life".[17] Prayer is not merely the "yearning for a response". The Quran tells us that it is not merely "the cry of the crier" but also "listening" to the call of the Infinite. Listen to this (again) :—

> "And when My servants
> Ask thee concerning Me,
> Lo ! I am close (to thee and them) :
> *I hear the cry of every crier*
> When he crieth unto Me.
> Let them also then (with a will)
> *Listen to My call* and believe in Me,
> If indeed they would be guided aright." (2 : 186)

16. So you see, Prayer is not merely the "cry of the crier". The Lord hears us even if we should fail to find the words to articulate our cry. By far the more important component of prayer is to "listen to His call". If we pray and hear not God echo in our soul, we have not prayed. Prayer is complete when the devotee has "netted his set", for the Lord waits saying : "Hear netting call, net now .. ". Prayer is complete when the devotee is absorbing, pulsating, radiating on the same frequency as God's. Prayer is communication, two-way communication, not one-way traffic. Prayer is silent communication, not a noisy monologue.[18]

---

16. Iqbal, *The Reconstruction*, p. 92.
17. *Ibid.*, p. 90.
18. In this context, see the Preface to *Mystics at Prayer*, Rosicrucian Library. To prevent any misunderstanding, however, I wish to draw the attention of the reader to the fact that "His call" is the Quran : a call to specific modes of thought and action covering every contingency of life. Prayer is not an occasion for a tete-a-tete with the Lord (there is no such thing), [*Cont.*

17. And talk of communion, consider the Prophet's approach to prayer. For him every prayer was an occasion for Mairaj. On that Night of Bliss, when the Prophet made his supplication : "Lord, transport me not to yonder world of affliction ! Throw me not under the sway of nature and passion !", God said : "It is My decree that thou shalt return to the world for the sake of establishing the religious law, in order that that I may give thee there what I have given thee here." And when the Prophet returned to the world, he used to say as often as he felt a longing for that exalted station : "O Bilal! Comfort us by the call to prayer." Thus, for him every time of prayer was an Ascension and a new nearness to God.[19]

18. Every prayer then, when it attains its fulness, is a flight of the soul for a moment's refuge at the altar of God. It is a baptism at His pool, so that when we return dripping wet, we may joyously proclaim :—

"(Our religion is)
The Baptism of God :
And who can baptize better than God?
And it is He Whom we worship."

"Rang lia ham ne
Apne Allah se,
Aur kaun behtar rangwa sakta hai
Sewaye Allah ke ?
Aur ham to Usi ki ebadat kartey hain." (2 : 138)

---

nor should we expect to *hear* voices out of the blue. Prayer can be said to have been truly performed only when our "cry" seeking aid or expressing a thanksgiving evokes deep within us corresponding passages from the Quran, passages that : (1) Cleanse and strengthen the spirit ; (2) Show the way to action in a specific contingency ; (3) Sustain us in His Way. I am persuaded that Prayer can be meaningful only when are soaked in "His Call'—the Quran.

19. A. J. Arberry, *Sufism : An Account of the Mystics of Islam*, pp. 30-31. Quoting from Hujwiri, *Kashf al-Mahjub.*

19. It is this communion, this merger of the individual soul with the Eternal Spirit that breathed into it, that is the essence of Prayer. It is this sense of having been touched by God, as it were, from which follow the highest fruits of Prayer : an expanded, expanding mind and spirit ; peace, stability, certitude ; a sense of power, light and liberation ; a sense of dependence on God alone and independence of all else. This is a dying away of the fevers of the flesh ; a death and a resurrection. "Prayer is the coolness of my eyes," said the Prophet, with eyes lit with faith. He also said : "Fear the insight of the believer, for verily he sees with the light of God."[20] The power of the believer comes from prayer truly performed.

20. To take on the "colour of God" : that is the end, that is the purpose of prayer. And how shall we take on God's colour, if we become not colourless ourselves ? Abol-Qasem Al-Jonaid of Baghdad (died : A.D. 910) was once asked about the nature of gnosis and the quality of the gnostic (the man who has known God). He replied : "The colour of the water is the colour of the Vessel."[21] On another occasion, he said : "Let not thy purpose in prayer be, to perform it, without taking pleasure and joy in the union with Him to Whom there is no means of approach save through Himself."[22] Prayer is an occasion to step aside from the endless loneliness of our separate selves, an occasion for a return to the Source for as long as the Source will permit, to capture for a while at least that state of the devotee which Dhol-Nun Al-Mesri (died : A.D. 861) described as : "when he is, as he was, where he was, before he was."[23]

21. Prayer then is the way to communion, an exaltation of the finite spirit at the altar of the Infinite. It is not an end in itself, but only a means to an end. It is an instrument of the faith, the foremost of the five pillars that lift us up to God. It is import-

20. Kalabadhi, *Doctrine of the Sufis*. Translation by Arberry, p. 171.
21. *Ibid.*, p. 152.
22. *Ibid.*, p. 159.
23. *Ibid.*, p. 152.

ant not to confuse the means with the end and in this context you may wish to listen to Lao Tzu, that voice of wisdom from out of the heart of ancient China :—

"Thirty spokes will converge
In the hub of a wheel ;
But the use of the cart
Will depend on the part
Of the hub that is void.

With a wall all around
A clay bowl is moulded ;
But the use of the bowl
Will depend on the part
Of the bowl that is void.

Cut out windows and doors
In the house as you build ;
But the use of the house
Will depend on the space
In the walls that is void.

So advantage is had
From whatever is there;
But usefulness rises
From whatever is not."[24]

22. Through Prayer, then, we seek God. We "adore and draw nigh" (**96** : 19). We turn to Him, for He has already turned to us (**9** : 119). We seek to move from the periphery of our lives to the centre of our being, and in the course of that pilgrimage of the heart we shed our avarice and our egoism. We draw nigh by stages, through patient perseverance in prayer. We turn our countenance full-square towards Him (**2** : 112), so that having turned once we may never *re*-turn, so that we might become (as Ibrahim Al-Daqqaq once put it) "unto God a face without a back, even as thou hast formerly been unto Him a

24. Lao Tzu, *The Way of Life*. Blakney's translation, p. 63.

back without a face."[25] Every prayer, every act of such total surrender, every such step taken towards the Lord with the dying away of nervousness and the persistence of awe,[26] must lead to renewed prayer. In the words of the Quran :

"Our Lord !
Let not our hearts deviate
After Thou hast guided us aright.
And grant us mercy from Thine own presence.
Lo ! Thou art the Giver
Of bounties without measure."

23. Prayer that leads through communication to communion, is prayer truly performed. It is such prayer that makes us a citizen of the universe, restores to us a vision of the unity of all God's creation. It is such prayer that compels us to the declaration :—

"To Allah belongeth the East and the West.
Whithersoever ye turn,
There is Allah's Countenance.
For Allah is All-Pervading, All-Knowing." (2 : 115)

24. To seek His countenance is the aim of prayer ; to see His countenance everywhere the product of it. This is the meaning of Prayer leading through communication to communion ..[27]

All Time is Prayer Time and No Ceremonies

25. The fourth conclusion that I presented was : all time is prayer-time, and to pray we need no ceremonies.

26. Our discourse on the state of mind appropriate to prayer (conclusion 2, paras 10-14) already sheds some light, I hope, on the first of the two postulates that we shall now consider : *that all time is prayer time.*

27. The concept of Prayer in Islam is an almost limitless one.

---

25. Arberry, *Doctrine of the Sufis*, p. 92.
26. *Ibid.*, p. 108.
27. Connect with Notes (1) and (2) above.

It embraces the whole of life and life-activity ; it even spills over the frontiers of the Here into the Hereafter. The English word "prayer" is much too general a term, making no distinction between "Salat" (the canonical prayers), "Dhikr-Allah" (the remembrance and recollection of God) and "Ebadat" (every good act performed "fi-sabilillah"). Talking in English most of the time as we do, we equate "prayer" with "Salat" (the canonical prayers) and forget the other two components of that generic term.

28. Salat (the canonical prayers) is indeed the foremost of the five pillars of the faith. For Salat the times are fixed : at the two ends of the day and in its middle, at night, and (with a special reminder) the "mid-most" prayer (Asr, the afternoon prayer). For Salat the times are fixed, as that absolute minimum necessary for our absorption into the stream of universal adoration. But prayer does not stop at Salat. The Quran says :

> "And when the *prayer* is over,
> Scatter ye yourselves over the face of the earth :
> And seek ye of the bounties of Allah,
> *And remember Allah much,*
> So that ye may prosper." (**62 : 10**)

29. Salat then must spill over and merge into Dhikr-Allah, from Salat to Salat. Salat is essentially prophylactic in its function, for most of us at any rate. It helps us, as the Quran says, "to ward off evil". It is essentially an act of seeking refuge, a temporary withdrawal from the fretful fever of life's earthly activity. But we return to our earthly activities, as indeed we must ; and the prophylactic function of Salat lies in this that by compelling us to return to the prayer-mat five times a day, day after day, it breaks up the continuity of whatever evil we may be engaged in. Salat is the war of attrition against evil. We have to be totally depraved, swine of the first order, to be able to pray five times a day (day after day) and yet persist in relentless pursuit of evil. I believe there are few, very few among us so totally beyond salvation.

30. Beyond Salat lies Dhikr-Allah, the connecting link between one canonical prayer and the next. Here we enter into the realm of timeless prayer, what in our formulation we called : "all time is prayer time". It is that state of the human mind's total absorption in God, so that God may say : "I am for him hearing, sight and hand, so that through Me he hears, and through Me he sees."[28] And through Him, he acts also. Whatever he thinks, whatever he does, whatever he gives to another or receives from another—he lays these also as an offering before his Lord. This is the state of perpetual prayer, the state that declares : "All time is prayer time":—

(*a*) "Men who celebrate the praises of God :
Standing, sitting and reclining (on their sides),
And contemplate the wonders of creation
In the heavens and on earth . ." (**3** : 191)

(*b*) "Lit is such a light :
In houses which God hath permitted to be raised to honour,
For the celebration in them of His name.
In them is He glorified
(Early) in the mornings and (late) in the evenings,
Again and again—
By men whom neither traffic nor merchandize
Can divert from the remembrance of God ;
Nor from regular prayer,
Nor from the practice of regular charity.
Their only fear is of the Day
When hearts and eyes will be transformed
(in a world wholly new) . ." (**24** : 36-37)

31. Dhikr-Allah, then, is celebrating the praises of the Lord while contemplating the wonders of His creation. Dhikr-Allah is the reflective inquiry of the human soul fixed on the Divine Axis. Dhikr-Allah is what transforms our pursuit of knowledge

28. Kalabadhi, *op. cit.*, p. 128. Quotation from Hadith.

from vain, idle or perverse curiosity into an act of genuine prayer. Dhikr-Allah is the tireless striving towards truth and perfection, in both the inner and the external world, in thought and deed. This is an all-time activity ; and its essential components are : Thought (based on both objective and introspective observation), Contemplation, Meditation. These are words that arouse contempt in a world grown used to blind activity ; and in this context I should like to read out to you two passages from Frithjof Schuon's *Understanding Islam*:—

(*a*) "If the outlook of today is so largely determined by social preoccupations with an evidently material basis, it is not merely because of the social consequences of mechanisation and the human condition this engenders, but also because of the absence of any contemplative atmosphere such as is essential to the welfare of man whatever his standard of living—to use an expression as barbarous as it is common. Any contemplative attitude is today labelled Escapism (in German, Weltflucht) and this includes a refusal to situate total truth and the meaning of life in external agitation. A hypocritically utilitarian attachment to the world is dignified as responsibilities and people hasten to ignore the fact that flight, even supposing that it were only a question of escape, is not always a wrong attitude."

(*b*) "The world is sick because men live beneath themselves. The error of modern man is that he wants to reform the world without having either the will or the power to reform man, and this flagrant contradiction, this attempt to build a better world on the basis of a worsened humanity, can only end in the abolition even of what is human, and consequently the abolition of happiness too. Reforming man means binding him again to Heaven, re-establishing the broken link; it means plucking him from the kingdom of passions,

> from the cult of matter, quantity and cunning, and reintegrating him into the world of the spirit and serenity—even, it might be said into the world of his own sufficient reason."

32. Yes, the exercise of "his own sufficient reason": this too is prayer. Prayer is not merely Salat but also Dhikr-Allah : reflection, contemplation, meditation on the wonders of God's creation ; to know Him by His signs : the vaulted sky, the starry heavens, the alternation of day and night, the roving clouds and the changing winds, the bird poised in mid-air, the camel, the bee, even the gnat, sheafs of corn and trees laden with fruit, the thirsty earth and the life-giving rain, the silent desert, the angry ocean, the lofty mountain, the flowing waters, the planets swimming in their orbits in the infinity of space—all these and more : signs for those who consider, reflect, understand. This is an all-embracing activity, a continuous activity, a form of prayer spanning the whole of life, connecting the devotee from Salat to Salat and leading him on to acts of prayer.

33. We do not have the time here to consider the meaning and the significance of Dhikr-Allah as expounded by the great mystics of Islam. That is a subject as vast as it is fascinating ; sadly, above and beyond the scope of this little talk. But this much I do wish to draw your attention to : that the most throbbing, intense, illuminating form of Dhikr-Allah is the recitation of the Quran : the recitation of the Quran on the lips, and the contemplation of its meaning in the heart, and reflective enquiry in the external world. It is an act of immersion in the vastness of the Quran ; emptying our vessel down-stream and filling it at the Source, so that we may be for ever empty, and He may pour into us for ever more :—

> "Say : If the ocean were
> Ink (wherewith to write)
> The words of my Lord,
> Sooner would the ocean be exhausted

Than the words of my Lord,
Even if we were to add
Another ocean the like of it
To its aid." (28 : 109)

So, what do we do ?

"Recite ye, therefore,
As much of the Quran as may be easy for you ;
And establish regular prayer
And give regular charity ;
And loan to God a goodly loan.
And whatever good ye send forth
For your souls,
Ye shall find it in God's Presence—
Yea, better and greater in reward.
And seek ye the grace of God :
For God is Oft-Forgiving, Most Merciful." (73 : 20)

34. I do not have the power, for human words are inadequate, to convey the meaning and the significance of the recitation of the Quran as that most excellent form of Dhikr-Allah. It is a thing to be experienced, even as the Prophet experienced it :—

"O, Thou, wrapped up in thy garments !
Stand (in prayer) by night,
But not all night—
Half of it,
Or a little less or a little more.
And recite the Quran
In slow, measured, rhythmic tones." (73 : 1-4)

35. We shall attempt a devotional perception of prayer when we get to the second part of this talk, but since we are still in the stage of discursive analysis, consider again what Frithjof Schuon has to say in this context :—

"Man alone has the gift of speech, for he alone among all the creatures of this earth is made in the image of God in a direct and total manner; and since it is by virtue of this likeness (provided it is actualised by appropriate means) that man is saved—by virtue, that is, of the objective intelligence associated with free will and truthful speech, whether articulated or not—it is easy to understand the capital part played in the life of the Muslim by those sublime words : the verses of the Quran. They are not merely sentences which transmit thoughts, but are in a way : beings, powers, talismans. The soul of the Muslim is, as it were, woven of sacred formulae : in these he works, in these he rests, in these he lives and in these he dies."[29]

36. Prayer, then, spills over the temporal borders of Salat and flows into the timeless ocean of Dhikr-Allah : Dhikr-Allah, whose inner aspect is concentrated reflective inquiry, contemplation, meditation; and whose external aspect is the performance of good deeds "fi-sabilillah". This second aspect we shall consider when we come to the last of our six conclusions under the analytical study of Prayer.

37. We are still struggling with Conclusion 4, of which the first postulate ("All time is prayer-time") we have partially covered. We must draw in our tentacles and close this discussion with one last observation. The occasions for paryer are without limit : in times of triumph and in times of defeat ; in times of joy and times of sorrow, and through all periods of panic and adversity. There will be occasions for thanksgiving also, when peace envelops us and life proceeds on a smooth and even tenor. Yes, all time is prayer-time : in war and in peace, in private and in congregation, in the seclusion of our homes, in the market-place, on the battle-field ; by day and night, and through all seasons ; in rest and in activity—*all time is prayer-time.*

38. As for the second postulate of Conclusion 4—*that we need no ceremonies to be able to pray*—I know of no faith and no mode (and I wish to tell you that I have tried many), I know of no mode, even for the canonical prayers, so startlingly simple and

---

29. Frithjof Schuon, *Understanding Islam*,

dignified, so rich in its inner content and so profound in its symbolism, as the mode of prayer ordained by God through the last of His prophets. We need no candle, no altar, no graven, no image, no choir, no music, no priest, no bell, no conch-shell. The human voice cries out its yearning for God, or we hear the call welling up from within even as the fiery orb runs its course alternating between night and day, and we rush to prayer in whatever state of purity we can manage : a splash of water, a touch of God's good earth. And then we stand "turning our countenance full square to God", and we bow down in one all-embracing act of total offering and self-surrender—"like a rain-cloud of July hung low with its burden of unshed showers", "like a flock of home-sick cranes flying night and day back to their mountain nest". And if we pray in a flock, in congregation, it is because we seek not merely individual but also collective salvation.

Iqbal writes :—

> "The real object of prayer is better achieved when the act of prayer becomes congregational. The spirit of all true prayer is social .. A congregation is an association of men who, animated by the same aspiration, concentrate themselves on a single object and open up their inner selves to the working of a single impulse. It is a psychological truth that association multiplies the normal man's powers of perception, deepens his emotion, and dynamizes his will to a degree unknown to him in the privacy of his individuality .. In Islam, this socialisation of spiritual illumination through associative prayer is a special point of interest. As we pass from the daily (and weekly) congregational prayer to the annual ceremony round the central mosque of Mecca, you can easily see how the Islamic institution of worship gradually enlarges the sphere of human association."[30]

---

30. Iqbal, *The Reconstruction of Religious Thought in Islam*, p. 92.

39. Nowhere in the history of the whole kingdom of God do we find a mode of prayer, whether individual or associative, which rises so powerfully above ritual, spiritualising whatever little ritual must remain behind for creatures still clothed in animality, still caught in the temporal flux. We may pray, then, "sitting, standing or reclining", or even "mounted on steeds of war"—so long as we turn our "countenance full square to God". We may pray alone or in congregation. Whatever we do : *all time is prayer time, and to pray we need no ceremonies.* Even this turning of the countenance towards God is a spiritual act, not an act of ritual :—

(*a*) "It is not righteousness
That ye turn your faces towards East or West ;
But it is righteousness :
To believe in God, and the Last Day,
And the angels, and the Book,
And the messengers;
To spend of your substance, for the love of Him,
On kinsmen, orphans, the needy,
The wayfarer, those who ask,
And for the ransom of slaves ;
To be steadfast in prayer ;
To practise charity ;
To abide by the covenants ye have made ;
And to be firm and patient in pain (suffering), adversity, through all periods of panic (despair) :
Such are the people of the truth, the God-fearing".
(2 : 177)

(*b*) "To Allah belongeth the East and the West ;
Whithersoever ye turn :
There is Allah's Countenance." (2 : 115)

To Capture the Glow, Prolonged Practice

40. We come now to our fifth conclusion : that the way to true prayer reveals itself only after much prolonged practice. It is not merely the *volume* of prayer that we engage in at any

given moment that is important, but also the *regularity* with which we practise prayer. No wonder we are asked to return to the prayer-mat five times a day, day after day, from the day our consciousness achieves a modicum of maturity to the day we die. Too often, too many of us, despair too early about the spiritual content and the efficacy of our prayers. "Where is that absorption in the stream of universal adoration ?" we complain. "Where is that communion that I seek ? I cry out in the wilderness and I hear not God echo in my soul. I lift up my little lamp, but I see not His light. I remain separate, alone, lonely and afraid. I remain bound, fettered and caught in my own flux. I pray, but of what use is this prayer ? Where is that Hand to lift me up ; where is that Source that promised to fill my vessel so that I may overflow ? The crier cries, where is the Response ? The seeker seeks, where is the Sought ? Alas, it is of no use : I return to the howling emptiness of my own soul ; I remain on the circumference of a circle without a Centre. No use, no use at all. It's been a hoax, a mirage, pointless pursuit." So we complain ..

41. Alas, how easily we give way to despair ; how soon do we give up this most excellent of pursuits ! The reason why for many of us our Salat loses or has lost its savour is easy enough to discover ; and that discovery made through reflective inquiry, remedial measures can be taken. But the first thing to do is to order Despair to wait outside, while we hold our conference with ourselves. For have we not heard the Lord say :—

(*a*) "And lose not heart ;
Nor fall into despair.
For ye must gain mastery
If ye would be true in faith." (**3** : 139)

(*b*) "O ye among My servants who have transgressed against your souls !
Despair not of the mercy of Allah .. " (**39** : 53)

Fine. Now that Despair waits outside, we can proceed with our conference,

42. *The first thing to consider is that our Salat loses its savour because our faith is not firm :—*

> "Nay, seek (God's) help
> With patient perseverance and prayer ;
> It (prayer) is indeed hard,
> Except for those :
> Who bring a *lowly spirit*,
> Who bear in mind the *certainty that they are to meet their Lord*,
> And that to Him they are to return." (2 : 45-46)

Do we bring with us a "lowly spirit" when we approach Prayer ? Have we shed vanity, pride, egoism, selfishness, self-centredness, anger, rage, greed and avarice before we take our stand on the prayer-mat ? Are we "cetrain" that one day we *are* to meet our Lord, or do we merely say it ? Are we "certain", or do we merely "think"? Is it an "attestation with the tongue" only, without an "acknowledgement with the heart"? Are there up our sleeves gods other than God ? If there are, indeed we must cry out as Iqbal cried out :—

> "Jo main sar ba-sajdah hua kabhi,
> To Zamin se aaney lagi sadaa :
> Tera dil to hai sanam-aashna,
> Tujhe kia milega namaaz mein ?"

Have we read and truly absorbed what the Quran offers to us when it proclaims :—

> (*a*) " .. Say :
> I am commanded to worship God.
> And not to ascribe partners unto Him.
> Unto Him do I call,
> And unto Him is my return". (13 : 36)

> (*b*) "Did ye then think
> That we created you in jest,
> And that ye would not be brought

Back to Us (for account) ?
Therefore, exalted be God,
The King, the Reality :
There is no god but He,
Lord of the Throne of Honour !

....

So say : O my Lord !
Grant Thou forgiveness and mercy
For Thou art the Supreme Giver of Mercy."

(**24** : 115, 116, 118)

If prayer, then, has lost its savour for us, the first remedial action to be taken is : to make our faith firm and pure, to bring to the prayer-mat a "lowly spirit" and the "certainty" that one day we are to return to our one and only Lord.

43. *The second thing to consider is that prayer is an act of supreme concentration, an all-else-excluded search for His Countenance*—points that we have already discussed under the "state of mind" appropriate to prayer (paras 11-14). If we bring to the prayer-mat only our bodies, leaving our mind and spirit behind, how shall we make that total offering that prayer demands ? Where is that "rain cloud of July hung low with its burden of unshed showers" ? Where is that "flock of home-sick cranes flying night and day back to their mountain nest" ? If we pray, it is not merely the head that must bow down : but every limb of our body, every drop of our mind, every particle of our spirit—the entire flock, the entire *Being*—in one all-embracing act of total self-surrender. This demands *concentration* : a thing to be practised every day, in every sphere of life in whatever we undertake before we can actualize it on the prayer-mat. As for seeking "His Countenance", which is the sole aim of prayer, alas, how readily we forget the aim ! We cannot turn full square to God, with a mind preoccupied with things other than God. We *say* we seek His Countenance ; but when we cry out, our cry is : for a posting abroad, a word of grace from some general or the other sitting on the Promotion Board, a merciful stroke of the CMA's

pen on the next increment due—and alas, a host of other things just as vile. This is *not* prayer ; this is *not* seeking His Countenance. And then, we are shameless enough to say : the crier hath cried, but God did not hear ! If we are to pray successfully, we must learn how to pray, with hopes and aspirations articulated through words appropriate to the Goal of prayer. This we shall consider when we come to Part II of this talk. For the while we need only note, that if prayer has lost its savour for us, the second remedial action to take is : to practise concentration, and to remind ourselves again of the aim of prayer, which is an all-else-excluded search of God.

44. *The third point to consider is that prayer becomes effective by accumulation.* We have no business to give up prayer, merely because of a given moment we feel that all our past prayers have been empty and in vain. We must steadfastly persevere in prayer ; we must bow down again and again, for the spirit of prayer grows by continuous accumulation :—

(*a*) "And be steadfast in prayer ;
Practise regular charity ;
And bow down your heads
With those who bow down (in worship)". (**2** : 43)

(*b*) "Guard your prayers,
And the most excellent prayer ;
And stand before God
In a devout frame of mind." (**2** : 238)

(*c*) "And establish regular prayers
At the two ends of the day,
And at the approaches of the night ;
For those things that are good
Remove those that are evil :
Be that the word of remembrance
To those who remember." (**11** : 114)

(*d*) "Men who celebrate the praises of God :
Standing, sitting and reclining (on their sides) . ."
(**3** : 191)

(*e*) " .. In them is He glorified,
(Early) in the mornings,
And (late) in the nights,
Again and again .. " (**24** : 37)

So then, regardless of any creeping despair, we must remain steadfast in prayer, we must guard our prayers, we must establish regular prayer, we must celebrate His praises in whatever our bodily state, day and night, again and again. So does the spirit of prayer grow in power by continuous accumulation. That is our third conclusion with regard to the remedial measures necessary to restore to our prayer the savour that it may have lost. At this stage we may conveniently interrupt our conference, go out for a while to where Despair sits huddled up on his stool, and tell him with a clear conscience to get the hell out of here ![31]

45. Despair is gone, but we may still continue our conference to round it off with *a few last observations on the prolonged practice necessary* to capture the true meaning and significance of Prayer. We all know how that most exalted of men, the last of the Prophets, devoted a life-time to capturing and concretizing the meaning of Prayer. In this context, you may wish to listen to some other accounts from Attar's *Tadhkirat al-Auliya* :—

(*a*) "For forty years Al-Jonaid persevered in his mystic course. For thirty years he would perform the prayer before sleeping, then stand on his feet repeating "Allah, Allah" until dawn, saying the dawn prayer with the ablution he had made the previous night. 'After forty years had gone by,' he said, 'the conceit arose in me that I had attained my goal' .. " And then Al-Jonaid repented, and took to the prayer-

---

31. "Say :
Truth hath come
And Falsehood hath vanished.
Lo ! Falsehood, by its very nature,
Must perish." (*Quran*)

mat again.[32]

(*b*) "It took Abu Yazid a full twelve years to reach the Kaaba. This was because at every oratory he passed he would throw down his prayer rug and perform two rakas.

'This is not the portico of an earthly king,' he would say, 'that one may run thither all at once'. "[33]

(*c*) "For twelve years," said Abu Yazid, "I was the blacksmith of my soul .. For five years I was my own mirror .. After that I gazed upon my own reflection for a year .. For five further years I laboured, till that girdle was snapped and I became a Muslim anew .. "[34]

(*d*) "How much of the Koran do you recite daily ?" Ibn Ata was asked.

"Formerly," he replied, "I used to complete the whole Koran twice every twenty-four hours. Now I have been reciting the Koran for fourteen years, and today I have just reached the Sura of the Spoils."[35]

(*e*) "You are recommended as an expert on pearls," Al-Shebli once said to Al-Jonaid, "Either give me one or sell one to me."

"If I sell you one, you will not have the price of it ; and if I give you one, having come so easily by it you will not realize its value," Al-Jonaid replied. "Do like me ; plunge head first into the Sea, and if you wait patiently you will find your pearl."[36]

(*f*) "My battle has waxed fierce, and I have no more strength to fight," Abul Hosain Al-Nuri (died :

---

32. Arberry, *Muslim Saints and Mystics*, pp. 201-202.
33. *Ibid.*, p. 103.
34. *Ibid.*, p. 113.
35. *Ibid.*, p. 237.
36. *Ibid.*, p. 278.

A.D. 908) once said to Al-Jonaid, "For thirty years, whenever He has appeared I have vanished, and whenever I appear He is absent. His presence is in my absence. For all that I supplicate Him, His answer is : 'Either I am to be, or you'."

"Look upon a man," said Jonaid to his companions, "who has been sorely tried and bewildered by God. Such must be the state of affairs," he added turning to Nuri, "that whether He is veiled by you or revealed through you, you shall no more be you, and all shall be He."[37]

46. These anecdotes, gentlemen, have a meaning spilling over the borders of our immediate discourse but they do illustrate *Conclusion* 5 *: that the way to true prayer reveals itself only after much prolonged practice.* I did not speak of the Prophet, because he is after all a prophet ; but it does seem exceedingly presumptuous on our part to hope to find a short-cut to prayer. We *cannot* condense, summarize, short-circuit, circumvent, curtail or telescope the process that took even such great men as I have mentioned so many years to discover. In truth, what makes them great is not so much the product of their prayers, as their steadfast pursuit of the Goal of all prayer.

Acts of Prayer, from Prayer to Prayer

47. We come now to the last of our six conclusions under the analytical study of the meaning and significance of Prayer : *that prayer* (*Salat*) *must be followed by the acts of prayer* (*Ebadat*), *from prayer* (*Salat*) *to prayer* (*Salat*). I spoke before about Salat spilling over into Dhikr-Allah, whose *inner* aspect (reflective enquiry directed towards God and contemplation/meditation of Him) we have already discussed. We come now to the "acts of prayer" (Ebadat) which constitute the *external* aspect of Dhikr-Allah.

48. The concept of *Ebadat* in Islam is exceedingly vast. *Every good deed done* "fi-sabilillah" (for His sake only, with no other

37. *Ibid.*, p. 226.

motive) is prayer. *Every good thing given* of our spiritual, intellectual, emotional and material "wealth" (in the most intensive and extensive meaning of that term), every good thing given to another "fi-sabilillah" (for His sake only, with no other motive) is prayer. *Every good thing received* with gratitude towards God and accepted with humble thanksgiving (whether it be the food we eat, the success that comes our way, the health we enjoy, the woman who shares the burden of our life and the children we are blessed with, the friend with whom we commune, the teacher at whose fountain our spirit drinks, the parents at whose feet our paradise lies, the book that we read and the wonders that our senses grasp)—every good thing (material or non-material) accepted with gratitude and humble thanksgiving, harnessed to the purpose of God and used to greater good, is Prayer. We are in a state of prayer, if every time some good befalls us, we involuntarily break into the Quranic refrain :—

> "Say :
> Verily all bounties are in the hands of God.
> He granteth them to whomsoever He pleaseth.
> And God careth for all things and knoweth all things.
> For His mercy he chooseth whomsoever He pleaseth,
> For God is the Lord of bounties unbounded." (**3** : 73-74)

49. It is not merely the good deed done, the good thing given and the good thing accepted with gratitude towards God that is prayer, but also *every sorrow and misfortune endured with patience and combated with perseverance.* Helen Keller prayed, when having been born blind, she struggled towards light till she became the most celebrated name in the history of education for the blind. Beethoven prayed, when being deaf, he struggled to create some of the finest music that the world has ever heard. Demosthenes prayed, when having been born a stutterer, he struggled to become one of the greatest names in the history of elocution and oratory. Carl Gustav Jung prayed when, overcoming the loneliness of his childhood and youth, he became one of the greatest seers of the human mind. Father Damiens prayed in

Molokai, Paul Gaugin in the South Sea Islands, Albert Schweitzer in the jungles of Africa, Florence Nightingale in war-torn Crimea. The list is almost endless .. To endure with patience and to combat with fortitude every misfortune that befalls us, *not* to lose heart and *not* to give way to despair in times of sorrow and adversity : this too is Prayer.

50. We are in a state of prayer "if we can meet with Triumph and Disaster, and treat those two impostors just the same".[38] We are in a state of prayer if we can take the ups and downs, the rise and the fall in our lives with the self-same stride. We are in a state of prayer, if we can recite this verse from the Quran *with equal ease in both success and failure* :—

"Say : O Allah,

Owner of all power and sovereignty !
Thou givest power unto whom Thou wilt ;
And Thou withdrawest power from whom
Thou wilt.

Thou exaltest whom Thou wilt ;
And Thou abasest whom Thou wilt.
In Thy hands is all good :
Lo ! Thou art able to do all things." (3 : 26)

51. Good deeds done "fi-sabilillah" is prayer. A good thing given and taken "fi-sabilillah" is prayer. Sorrow and adversity endured with patience and combated with perseverance is prayer. Every evil transformed into good through effort is prayer. Above all, prayer is the performance of good deeds. Prayer, without the acts of prayer, is sterile, barren, dead. Prayer, devoid of the acts of prayer, is mockery ; and God's curse is on those who so soil the fair name of Prayer :—

(*a*) "Hast thou observed him who belieth religion ?
That is he who repelleth the orphan,
And urgeth not the feeding of the needy.
Ah, woe unto worshippers who are heedless of their

38. Rudyard Kipling, *If*.

prayer !
Who would be seen (at worship),
And yet refuse small kindnesses." **(107)**

(*b*) "Enjoin ye righteousness upon mankind
While ye yourselves forget (to practise it) ?
And ye are readers of the Scripture !
Have ye then no sense ?" (**2** : 44)

52. Of all the maladies that haunt our prayers (and this I have deliberately reserved as my last observation), of all the maladies that haunt our prayers, *nothing is more destructive than the absence of the acts of Prayer and nothing is more defiling than the presence of the acts of Un-prayer.*

Summing Up Our Analytical Enquiry

53. This, gentlemen, brings us to the end of our analytical enquiry into the meaning and significance of prayer. While memory serves, let me repeat our six conclusions :—

(*a*) That prayer is not the privilege of the few but the prerogative of all.
(*b*) That prayer is a state of mind, not just words intoned.
(*c*) That prayer is communication, two-way communication, not one-way traffic.
(*d*) That all time is prayer time and that to pray we need no ceremonies.
(*e*) That the way to true prayer reveals itself only after much prolonged practice.
(*f*) That prayer must be followed by acts of prayer, from prayer to prayer.

Devotional Perception

54. So far, gentlemen, we have been engaged in an analytical enquiry into the meaning and significance of Prayer. The time has come to move over to a devotional perception of it, a unitarian experience of what prayer means and signifies. It is intrinsic to the processes of the discursive, rational intellect that

it takes things apart, breaks up a concept into its constituent components to facilitate understanding. This *analysis*, a thing at which the rational intellect excels, must eventually give way to *synthesis* if understanding is to be complete. Synthesis, the piecing (the piecing together) of the parts for a vision of the whole, is also an act of the rational intellect but not its exclusive preserve. In fact, when it comes to synthesis, the rational intellect begins to falter and fumble ; it is no longer quite sure of its ground ; it doesn't quite know how to piece together again what it has so laboriously taken apart—like a child, a still curious child striving to discover what it is that makes his toy tick. I am not for a moment suggesting that the rational intellect cannot put back the pieces together again ; it can, it does ; but it fumbles and in the process damages, here and there, the unity that it set out to examine. Furthermore, the very clarity of our perception of the individual parts seems to cloud our vision of the whole, in a way as real as it is paradoxical.

55. I have said all this not to denounce rational enquiry but to identify its limitations. Within its own orbit, it is a powerful instrument of knowledge ; and I would hasten to add an indispensable instrument. It is for this reason that I have devoted so much of this presentation to an analytical study of our subject-matter. But a time comes, when having got to the air-port by car, one must step out of the car and step into the plane—with a word of profound thanks to the car.

56. For our flight into prayer, for our search of the meaning of prayer through prayer, what plane shall we take, what airline shall we choose ? You could search, as I have searched, through the pages of the Talmud, the Bible, the Bhagavad Gita, the Upanishads, Zoroaster's Book of Light and Buddha's treatises on the Four-fold Path. You could do all this and more ; but I fear you would return, as I returned, thirst unslaked and desire heightened, despite (and who knows, also because of) the many gems gathered along the way, till you turn to the splendour of the Quran.

57. To the Quran then we shall turn, and pray even as God taught man to pray. We shall pray in the words of the Quran. There will always be a prayer to suit every occasion, and there will be many to suit all occasions. Come, let us pray together . .

58. Prayers from the Quran. Selections from the "passages in green" in my copy of the Quran.

CONCLUSION

59. I have, gentlemen, within the short span of this talk (in two parts), proceeded from an analytical study of the meaning and significance of prayer, to capture something of the spirit of the prayers that adorn the Quran. Through that and this, (*this* more than *that*), I have made a joyous attempt, however imperfect, to convey to you something of the spirit and substance of the Quranic concept of prayer. Recite these and more, again and over again, in private and in congregation, and you will find it a rewarding, enriching, expanding experience. Recite of them "as much as may be easy for you", and let your recitations over-flow into every nook and corner of your and our lives. Let our prayer wash, cleanse, soothe and strengthen ; let us rise on the wings of our prayer, till we hear His voice echo in our soul :—

> "And when My servants
> Ask thee concerning Me,
> Lo ! I am close (to thee and them).
> I hear the cry of every crier
> When he crieth unto Me.
> Let them also then (with a will)
> Listen to My call,
> If indeed they would be guided aright." (2 : 186)

SELECTED BIBLIOGRAPHY

1. Abdullah Yusuf Ali, *The Holy Quran : Text, Translation and Commentary.* Sheikh Muhammad Ashraf, Kashmiri Bazar, Lahore.
2. Abul Kalam Azad, *Tarjumanul Quran.* Sind Sagar Academy, Lahore.
3. A. J. Arberry, *The Koran Interpreted.* George Allen and Unwin Ltd., London.
4. Frithjof Schuon, *Understanding Islam.* George Allen and Unwin Ltd., London.
5. Mohammad Iqbal, *The Reconstruction of Religious Thought in Islam.* Sheikh Muhammad Ashraf, Kashmiri Bazar, Lahore.
6. Abul Ala Maududi, *Fundamentals of Islam.* Islamic Publications, Lahore.
7. Erich Fromm, *The Art of Loving.* A Bantam Book, Harper and Row, New York.
8. Richard Bach, *Jonathan Livingstone Seagull.*
9. Walter T. Stace, *The Teachings of the Mystics.* A Mentor Book, The New American Library, New York, 1960.
10. *Mystics at Prayer.* The Rosicrucian Library, San Jose (California), U.S.A.
11. Ali al-Hujwiri, *Kashf al-Mahjub.* Translation by R.A. Nicholson, Luzac and Co., London.
12. Farid al-Din Attar, *Tadhkirat al-Auliya.* Translation ("Muslim Saints and Mystics") by A. J. Arberry, Routledge and Kegan Paul Ltd., London.
13. Al-Ghazzali, *The Mysteries of Purity* (Vol. 3, *Ihya Ulum al-Din*). Translation by Nabih Amin Faris, Sheikh Muhammad Ashraf, Kashmiri Bazar, Lahore.
14. Al-Ghazzali, *Al Munqidh min al-Dalal and Bidayat al-Hidayah.* Translation ("The Faith and Practice of Al-Ghazzali") by Montgomery Watt, Sheikh Muhammad Ashraf, Kashmiri Bazar, Lahore.
15. *Masnun Duaen* (*Prayers of the Prophet*). Sheikh Muhammad Ashraf, Kashmiri Bazar, Lahore.
16. *Al-Hizb al-Azam* (*Quranic Prayers*). Islamic Book Centre 25-B, Masson P. O. Box-1625, Lahore.
17. Rabindranath Tagore, *Gitanjali.* English translation by Tagore, Macmillan and Co., Calcutta.
18. Daag Hammarsjkoeld, *Markings.*
19. A. J. Arberry, *Sufism : An Account of the Mystics of Islam.* George Allen and Unwin Ltd., London.
20. Abu Bakr Kalabadhi, *Kitab al-Taaruf li Madhub Ahl al-Tasawwuf.* Translation ("Doctrine of the Sufis") by A. J. Arberry, Sheikh Muhammad Ashraf, Kashmiri Bazar, Lahore.
21. Lao Tzu, *The Way of Life.* Translation by R. B. Blakney, a Mentor Book, New York, 1955.

THE QURANIC CONCEPT OF PRAYER

Passages from the Quran

(Ref. Page 157)

Say : O My slaves who have been prodigal to their own hurt ! Despair not of the mercy of Allah, Who forgiveth all sins. Lo ! He is the Forgiving, the Merciful.

(39: 53)

٥٣- قُلْ يٰعِبَادِيَ الَّذِيْنَ اَسْرَفُوْا عَلٰٓى اَنْفُسِهِمْ
لَا تَقْنَطُوْا مِنْ رَّحْمَةِ اللّٰهِ ۭ اِنَّ اللّٰهَ يَغْفِرُ
الذُّنُوْبَ جَمِيْعًا ۭ اِنَّهٗ هُوَ الْغَفُوْرُ الرَّحِيْمُ ○

(Ref. Page 165)

(We take our) colour from Allah, and who is better than Allah at colouring ? We are His worshippers. (2 : 138)

١٣٨- صِبْغَةَ اللّٰهِ ۚ وَمَنْ اَحْسَنُ مِنَ اللّٰهِ
صِبْغَةً ۡ وَّنَحْنُ لَهٗ عٰبِدُوْنَ ○

(Ref. Page 169)

And when the prayer is ended, then disperse in the land and seek of Allah's bounty, and remember Allah much that ye may be successful. (62 : 10)

١٠- فَاِذَا قُضِيَتِ الصَّلٰوةُ فَانْتَشِرُوْا فِي الْاَرْضِ
وَابْتَغُوْا مِنْ فَضْلِ اللّٰهِ
وَاذْكُرُوا اللّٰهَ كَثِيْرًا
لَّعَلَّكُمْ تُفْلِحُوْنَ ○

(Ref. Page 170)

Such as remember Allah, standing, sitting, and reclining, and consider the creation of the heavens and the earth, (and say) : Our Lord! Thou createdst not this in vain. Glory be to thee ! Preserve us from the doom of Fire. (3 : 191)

١٩١- الَّذِيْنَ يَذْكُرُوْنَ اللّٰهَ قِيٰمًا
وَّقُعُوْدًا وَّعَلٰي جُنُوْبِهِمْ
وَيَتَفَكَّرُوْنَ فِيْ خَلْقِ
السَّمٰوٰتِ وَالْاَرْضِ ۚ
رَبَّنَا مَا خَلَقْتَ ھٰذَا بَاطِلًا ۚ
سُبْحٰنَكَ
فَقِنَا عَذَابَ النَّارِ ○

(This lamp is found) in houses which Allah hath allowed to be exalted and that His name shall be remembered therein. Therein do offer praise to Him at morn and evening.

٣٦- فِيْ بُيُوْتٍ اَذِنَ اللّٰهُ
اَنْ تُرْفَعَ وَيُذْكَرَ
فِيْهَا اسْمُهٗ ۙ يُسَبِّحُ لَهٗ فِيْهَا
بِالْغُدُوِّ وَالْاٰصَالِ ○

Men whom neither merchandise nor sale beguileth from remembrance of Allah and constancy in prayer and paying to the poor their due ; who fear a day when hearts and eyeballs will be overturned. (24 : 36-37)

٣٧- رِجَالٌ ۙ لَّا تُلْهِيْهِمْ تِجَارَةٌ وَّلَا بَيْعٌ
عَنْ ذِكْرِ اللّٰهِ وَاِقَامِ الصَّلٰوةِ
وَاِيْتَاۗءِ الزَّكٰوةِ ۽
يَخَافُوْنَ يَوْمًا تَتَقَلَّبُ
فِيْهِ الْقُلُوْبُ وَالْاَبْصَارُ ○

(Ref. Page 173)

So recite of it that which is easy (for you), and establish worship and pay the poor due, and (so) lend unto Allah a goodly loan. Whatsoever good ye send before you for your souls, ye will surely find it with Allah, better and greater in the recompense. And seek forgiveness of Allah. Lo ! Allah is Forgiving, Merciful. (73 : 20)

فَاقْرَءُوا مَا تَيَسَّرَ مِنْهُ
وَأَقِيمُوا الصَّلَوٰةَ وَآتُوا الزَّكَوٰةَ
وَأَقْرِضُوا اللَّهَ قَرْضًا حَسَنًا
وَمَا تُقَدِّمُوا لِأَنفُسِكُم مِّنْ خَيْرٍ
تَجِدُوهُ عِندَ اللَّهِ
هُوَ خَيْرًا وَأَعْظَمَ أَجْرًا
وَاسْتَغْفِرُوا اللَّهَ
إِنَّ اللَّهَ غَفُورٌ رَّحِيمٌ ۝ ع

O thou wrapped up in thy raiment !
Keep vigil the night long, save a little.
A half thereof or abate a little thereof.
Or add (a little) thereto—and chant the Qur'ān in measure. (73 : 1-4)

١- يَا أَيُّهَا الْمُزَّمِّلُ ۝
٢- قُمِ اللَّيْلَ إِلَّا قَلِيلًا ۝
٣- نِّصْفَهُ أَوِ انقُصْ مِنْهُ قَلِيلًا ۝
٤- أَوْ زِدْ عَلَيْهِ
وَرَتِّلِ الْقُرْآنَ تَرْتِيلًا ۝

(Ref. Page 177)

Faint not nor grieve, for ye will overcome (them) if ye are (indeed) believers. (3 : 139)

١٣٩- وَلَا تَهِنُوا وَلَا تَحْزَنُوا
وَأَنتُمُ الْأَعْلَوْنَ إِن كُنتُم مُّؤْمِنِينَ ۝

(Ref. Page 178)

Seek help in patience and prayer ; and truly it is hard save for the humble-minded ; Who know that they will have to meet their Lord, and that unto Him they are returning. (2 : 45-46)

٤٥- وَاسْتَعِينُوا بِالصَّبْرِ وَالصَّلَوٰةِ وَإِنَّهَا
لَكَبِيرَةٌ إِلَّا عَلَى الْخَاشِعِينَ ۝
٤٦- الَّذِينَ يَظُنُّونَ أَنَّهُم مُّلَاقُوا رَبِّهِمْ وَ
أَنَّهُمْ إِلَيْهِ رَاجِعُونَ ۝

Say ; I am commanded only that I serve Allah and ascribe unto Him no partner. Unto Him I cry, and unto Him is my return. (13 : 36)

قُلْ إِنَّمَا أُمِرْتُ
أَنْ أَعْبُدَ اللَّهَ وَلَا أُشْرِكَ بِهِ
إِلَيْهِ أَدْعُو وَإِلَيْهِ مَآبِ ۝

(Ref. Page 180)

Establish worship, pay the poor-due, and bow your heads with those who bow (in worship). (2 : 43)

٤٣- وَأَقِيمُوا الصَّلَوٰةَ وَآتُوا الزَّكَوٰةَ وَارْكَعُوا
مَعَ الرَّاكِعِينَ ○

Be guardians of your prayers, and of the midmost prayer, and stand up with devotion to Allah. (2 : 238)

٢٣٨- حَافِظُوا عَلَى الصَّلَوٰتِ
وَالصَّلَوٰةِ الْوُسْطَىٰ
وَقُومُوا لِلَّهِ قَانِتِينَ ○

Establish worship at the two ends of the day and in some watches of the night. Lo ! good deeds annul ill deeds. This is a reminder for the mindful. (11 : 114)

١١٤- وَأَقِمِ الصَّلَوٰةَ طَرَفَيِ النَّهَارِ
وَزُلَفًا مِّنَ الَّيْلِ
إِنَّ الْحَسَنَٰتِ يُذْهِبْنَ السَّيِّـَٔاتِ
ذَٰلِكَ ذِكْرَىٰ لِلذَّٰكِرِينَ ○

(Ref. Page 186)

Hast thou observed him who belieth religion ?
That is he who repelleth the orphan,
And urgeth not the feeding of the needy.
Ah, woe unto worshippers,
Who are heedless of their prayer ;
Who would be seen (at worship),
Yet refuse small kindness ! (107 : 1-7)

١- أَرَءَيْتَ الَّذِي يُكَذِّبُ بِالدِّينِ ○
٢- فَذَٰلِكَ الَّذِي يَدُعُّ الْيَتِيمَ ○
٣- وَلَا يَحُضُّ عَلَىٰ طَعَامِ الْمِسْكِينِ ○
٤- فَوَيْلٌ لِّلْمُصَلِّينَ ○
٥- الَّذِينَ هُمْ عَن صَلَاتِهِمْ سَاهُونَ
٦- الَّذِينَ هُمْ يُرَآءُونَ ○
٧- وَيَمْنَعُونَ الْمَاعُونَ ○

TOWARDS UNDERSTANDING THE QURAN

Introductory Remarks

1. Whatever the field of education that one may choose, time is always short in relation to the field to be traversed. No education worth the name can serve everything on a plate. We cannot swallow knowledge and wisdom, as we swallow Erythromycin tablets. That being the case, the only sane course for one who dares to teach is to concentrate on fundamentals that show the way, and leave it to those who care to listen and understand to follow the way themselves : to unravel its deeper implications by personal effort and application.

2. In venturing to talk to you on Islam, I had several topics in mind ; but in accordance with what I have just said, my finest option seemed to me to start with "Understanding the Quran". This, without doubt, is fundamental to the understanding of anything whatsoever connected with Islam—whether in theory or in practice.

3. To my mind, the most malignant cancer afflicting our intellectual and spiritual lives, and eventually poisoning the totality of our individual and collective lives, is the glib talk and disputation that we indulge in with regard to Islam—without having acquired even so much as an acquaintance with the Quran. The Book lies on our shelf, neatly wrapped ; occasionally dusted and occasionally kissed ; occasionally, perhaps, read also —with little or no understanding : leave alone the contemplation and the constant resonance that it seeks in the human heart, before it finds its way into enlightened, God-oriented action in our everyday lives. A blind devotion, an ignorant reverence, blocks the way and even replaces the joy and the wonder of faith based on understanding—a faith that grows and expands, widens and deepens, maturing and ripening even as understanding and knowledge increase.

4. And so far as Islam and everything connected with it is concerned—all understanding, all knowledge, all talk and all action are hollow, if all this is not firmly anchored in an understanding of the Quran. To that primary source we must turn, in it we must soak ourselves and emerge dripping wet for our onward journey towards being a Muslim. It is this realisation, this consciousness, this compelling reason that persuades me to talk to you today on "Understanding the Quran".

Enunciation of Purpose

5. I venture to speak to you today on a methodology for the study of the Quran, a methodology particularly suited to men like us : men who do not know Arabic, men who have not yet learnt Arabic as a language.

6. For such among us, it is easy wrongly to give way to despair : to think that we shall be for ever deprived of the light of the Quran. For such among us, it is easy also to drift into reading translations of the Quran by Arberry, Pickthall or Maududi, then rest content with the wrong notion that we have thereby read the Quran.

7. The purpose of my talk today is to convince you, so help me God, that the Quran is *not* beyond the reach of our understanding, even though we have no formal grounding in Arabic. If anything, this very liability can be transformed into an asset. It can force us into that lingering concentration over the meaning of each verse, which is so essential for an understanding of the Quran. No such compulsion operates in a man well-versed in Arabic. Our very liability compels us to soak ourselves in the Quran, verse by verse—and we are saved the temptation of racing through, the disaster of reading without absorption, of reading much and retaining little, the futility of study devoid of loving, lingering contemplation.

Liability That is Also an Asset

8. We, who do not know Arabic and still strive to understand the Quran, start then with a liability that is also an asset. The

Prophet once said : "One who is skilled in the Quran is associated with the noble, upright recording angels ; and he who falters when reciting the Quran and finds it difficult for him will have a double reward."[1]

9. We, who do not know Arabic and still strive to read and understand the Quran, can take decisive steps to our goal by reference to the original through a methodology that I shall later explain and illustrate. At this stage, it is enough to note that this method enables us to progressively out-grow our dependence on translations and eventually arrive at a direct understanding of the original. This is a slow, but sure and productive process. And inherent in it is the element of individual "revelation", as the Quran gradually unfolds its meaning to the reader.[2]

10. This liability of not knowing Arabic can compel us to become, as it were, our own translators of the Quran : a stage which is reached when direct understanding of the original enables us to dispense with the very translations that help us to our goal. The joy of understanding at that stage can be as intense and given devotion, as profound, as that of a learned

---

1. Bukhari and Muslim, *Mishkat al-Masabih*, Vol. 2, p. 446. Consider the following Hadith in the context of learning/teaching and reciting the Quran :—
   (*a*) "The best among you is he who learns and teaches the Quran." (*Ibid.*, p. 446).
   (*b*) "Envy is justified only regarding two types (of men) : a man, who having been given (knowledge of) the Quran, stands reciting it during the night and during the day ; and a man, who having been given property by God, spends on others from it, during the night and during the day." (*Ibid.*).
   (*c*) "By this Book God exalts some peoples and lowers others." (*Ibid.*, p. 447).
   (*d*) "Recite the Quran, for on the Day of Resurrection it will come as an intercessor for those who recite it.." (*Ibid.*, p. 462).
2. Connect with : "*Reason, Knowledge and Faith*" paras 13-20 ; "*The Basic Attributes of a Muslim*" paras 13-18 ; "*The Quranic Concept of Prayer*" paras 54-58.

scholar. To capture the meaning of this process, I can do no better than to quote A. J. Arberry :—

> "Over a period of many months the Quran has been my constant companion, the object of my most attentive study. Though many can certainly claim to have read the Quran, indeed over and over again, and to know it well, I think it may be reasonably asserted that their understanding of the book will always fall short of what may be attained by one who undertakes to translate it in full with all possible fidelity. I had myself studied the Quran and perused it from end to end over many years, before I embarked upon making a version of it ; assuredly the careful discipline of trying to find the best English equivalent for every meaning and every rhythm of the original Arabic has profoundly deepened my own penetration into the heart of the Quran, and has at the same time sharpened my awareness of its mysterious and compelling beauty . ."[3]

The Quran Cannot be Translated

11. We, who do not know Arabic, are compelled to approach the Quran through translations. But we would do well to remember that the Quran cannot be translated. Woe unto us, if we should feel the tug of the Quran enough to take us to a translation of it, but too weak to propel us beyond to an understanding of it in the original. If Goethe's *Faust*, or Tagore's *Gitanjali*, or Iqbal's *Bang-e-Dara* cannot be translated to a degree of perfection where the translations will convey what the originals do, how infinitely more impossible must it be to translate the Quran ? If we delude ourselves into thinking that by reading a translation of the Quran we shall have read *the* Quran, then surely our error is a grievous one. In this context, you may wish to hear what Marmaduke Pickthall wrote in his foreword to *The Meaning of the Glorious Quran*:—

---

3. A. J. Arberry, *The Koran Interpreted*, Preface to Vol. 2.

> "The Quran cannot be translated. That is the belief of old-fashioned Shaikhs and the view of the present writer. The Book is here rendered almost literally and every effort has been made to use befitting language. But the result is not *the* Glorious Quran, the very sounds of which move men to tears and ecstasy. It is only an attempt to present the meaning of the Quran—and peradventure something of the charm in English. It can *never* take the place of the Quran in Arabic, nor is it meant to do so."[4]

12. For those of us who do not know Arabic, translations certainly have a value, a very elementary value, a value valid only to the extent that they enable us to understand the literal meaning of the original text. Beyond that, they have no other function. They are, in Frithjof Schuon's words, "canonically illegitimate and ritually ineffectual".[5] For a valid understanding of the Quran, we must read the original every time we read a translation ; and we must read the original many times more than the translation, till at last we outgrow our need of the translation altogether. Exactly how this may be done, we shall presently discuss ; but here, a few words more about why we must strive to read and understand the Quran in Arabic, in the original :—

(*a*) From a purely mundane, literary point of view the Quran has a rhythm, a cadence, a soul-melting resonance, an enrapturing sound that defies all translation. It baffled Arberry, as it has baffled all translators. Consider what Arberry wrote in his Preface to *The Koran Interpreted* :—

" .. it is to the rhythm that I constantly return as I grope

---

4. Marmaduke Pickthall, *The Meaning of the Glorious Quran.* Foreword, Opening para.

5. Frithjof Schuon, *Understanding Islam*, Chap. 2 (The Quran). This chapter merits very careful reading, with particular reference to the "devotional perception" of the Quran (connect with Note (1) above). As with the rest of the book, the exposition is on a plane as absorbing as it is exalted.

for a clue to the arresting, the hypnotic power of the Muslim scriptures. I was talking about this power to an Arab friend. Before I could say what I would have said, he spoke in terms that expressed exactly what was in my mind : 'Whenever I hear the Quran chanted, it is as though I am listening to music ; underneath the flowing melody, there is sounding all the time the insistent beat of a drum.' Then he added : 'It is like the beating of my heart.' .. "[6]

(*b*) Apart from, and indeed far more important than the literary aspect to which I have just referred, there is a supreme, inviolable reason for our reading and understanding the Quran in the original Arabic. When we recite the Quran, we are doing more, far more than merely absorbing the literal meaning of the text. There is, as Frithjof Schuon says, "behind the husk of the literal meaning, a concrete and active spiritual presence" to which we expose ourselves. This exposure to the power of the word of God is a vital ingredient in our understanding of the Quran. As we recite and go on reciting, we establish contact with "those sources of metaphysical and eschatological wisdom, of mystical psychology and theurgic power which lie hidden behind a veil of breathless utterances".[7] This is where the intellect dissolves ; the understanding that we seek, may at any time, and like a spark, "leap forth on mere contact with the revealed text". The translations that we read cannot replace the recitation of the Quran in the original. Even the best of translations can do no more than capture "the husk of the literal meaning" and the husk separated from the core and the whole to which it belongs is not what we seek. A translation is to the Quran, as

6. A. J. Arberry, *Ibid.*
7. Frithjof Schuon, *Ibid.*

hearsay is to evidence. Surely, the accusing finger of the Quran must not be pointed at us, when it says : "Among them are unlettered folk who know the scripture not, except from hearsay. They (do) but guess."[8] I hasten to add here that worse, far worse than the "hearsay of translations" is the empty chatter and the idle disputation of those who talk about Islam without having acquired an acquaintance with the Quran even in translation. Islam is not interested in such people, however loud their protestation of the faith and however clever their talk. "Anyone who has nothing of the Quran in him is like a house in ruins," said the Prophet ; and a house wherein there is no recitation of the Quran be likened to a "graveyard".[9]

Transcending Translations : Methodology

13. But we, who would sincerely understand the Quran but know no Arabic, how shall we go about our task ? How shall we transcend our need of translations ? The answer is as follows :—

(*a*) Take a copy of the Quran which places the translation opposite (or immediately below) each verse in Arabic, verse after verse. Even more preferable : a verse broken up into appropriate blocks, with the corresponding translation opposite each block. As one individual, I found Abdullah Yusuf Ali's and Marmaduke Pickthall's works (Ashraf Publications and Taj Company) fairly well-suited to my purpose.

(*b*) Now read the Arabic (I assume all of us know how to read Arabic), block by block, and correlate each word within each block as closely as you can to the corresponding words or phrases of the translation.

---

8. *Quran*, 2 : 78.
9. *Mishkat*, Vol. 2 ; pp. 448, 452.

(*c*) Go on doing this in intelligible blocks within each verse and eventually for the verse as a whole. Do this several times, associating the Arabic sounds that resound in your ears with the English words/phrases that your eyes *see* (but do *not* read).

(*d*) Recite the Arabic and stare at the translation. Go on doing this, till your tongue becomes fluent with the Arabic—and your mind coordinates what your tongue recites, with what your ears hear, with what your eyes *see* (but do *not* read).

(*e*) A time will soon come, far sooner than you expect, when you no longer need to stare at the translation continuously.

(*f*) Eventually, even the occasional glance becomes redundant. You can close your eyes and meditate on the *total content* of what you recite. The Quran is on your lips, in your ears and its literal meaning is clearly imbedded in your mind (without your eyes reading the translation that they see).

14. Consider three examples of the process[10] that I have outlined above :—

(1) " .. My Lord ! Relieve my mind,
And ease my task for me,
And loose the knot from my tongue :
That they may understand what I say." (**20 :** 25-28)

(2) "By the declining day,
Lo ! Man is in a state of loss,
Save those who believe,
And do good works.

---

10. "The process" is best demonstrated in three phases :—

(*a*) Visual-cum-Oral *explanation*, using a Vu-Graph or a slide-projector.

(*b*) Visual-cum-Oral *coordination*, adding the aid of a tape-recorder.

(*c*) "Closed-eye" *recapitulation*.

And exhort one another to Truth ;
And exhort one another to Endurance." **(103)**

(3) "Say : I seek refuge
In the Lord of Mankind,
The King of Mankind,
The God of Mankind ;
From the evil of the sneaking whisperer,
Who whispereth in the hearts of Mankind,
Of the Jinn and Mankind." **(114)**

15. This, then, is the first step towards our understanding of the Quran.[11] At this stage, I have found it useful to scan through the *translation* from the beginning to the end, underlining those passages of the *Arabic* which at first glance gripped my heart and mind. I used a four-fold colour scheme for my underlining : red for the passages relating exclusively to the praises of the Lord ; green for the passages that teach us how to pray ; blue for the passages relating to individual and collective conduct ; black for the rest that fell outside the first three categories.[12]

---

11. The "analytical study" of the Quran can proceed *without* the "understanding" (of the original, directly) necessary for "devotional perception". But both these modes are complementary and should be put into operation simultaneously. See : "*The Basic Attributes of a Muslim*" paras 13-18 and "*The Quranic Concept of Prayer*" paras 54-58.

12. This is the method that I evolved on my own, without any external guidance. I now perceive that a fascinating variety of "approaches" can be worked out on the basis of a "colour code". Be that as it may, it would be useful to note here the guidance that the Hadith provide on the issue of "selection of passages" from the Quran. See : *Mishkat al-Masabih*, Vol. 2 ; Chapter on "The Excellent Qualities of the Quran" (pp. 446-461). Of special significance are the following Surahs :
1 (Al-Fatihah); 2 (Al-Baqara); 3 (Aale-Imran); 11 (Hud); 18 (Al-Kahf); 20 (Ta-Ha); 32 (As-Sajdah); 36 (Ya-Sin); 44 (Al-Dukhan); 55 (Ar-Rahman); 56 (Al-Waqiah); 57 (Al-Hadid); 59 (Al-Hashr); 61 (As-Saff); 62 (Al-Jumuah); 64 (At-Taghabun); 73 (Al-Muzammil); 99 (Az-Zilzal); 103 (Al-Asr); 109 (Al-Kafirun); 112 (At-Tauhid); 113 (Al-Falaq); 114 (An-Nas); 67 (Al-Mulk).

[*Contd.*

16. Then, every day, I would recite a little (as much as was easy for me) and over the days, months, years I continue to add to the store-house in my mind. The Quran outside is transferred—step by step, little by little—to the Quran within, and my treasure house is in the throes of continuous expansion. This is the first stage and it never ceases. I hear Abu Musa al-Ashari reporting God's messenger as saying : "Keep refreshing your knowledge of the Quran, for I swear by Him in Whose hands my soul is that it is more liable to escape than camels which are tethered."[13]

17. So much for the mechanics of the first stage in our understanding of the Quran. A few words now about the manner of recitation for a rational-devotional perception of the *total content* of those passages whose *literal* meaning we have acquired a direct grasp of.

Devotional Perception

18. Let me see if I can enumerate the requirements for you, one by one :—

(*a*) The first requirement, to my mind, is to approach the Quran in the spirit of the angels ; in a spirit that places a totally empty vessel before the Lord so that He may fill it with His knowledge[14] :—

(1) " .. He said : Surely, I know that which ye know not .. " (2 : 30)

(2) " .. They said : Glory to Thee ! We have no knowledge save that which Thou hast taught us. Lo ! Thou, only Thou, art the Knower, the Wise .. " (2 : 32)

(*b*) The second requirement is to recite the Quran, even as the Prophet was directed to recite it : with under-

---

See : Particularly, *Ibid.*, pp. 449-451, 455-457 and 460.

13. *Mishkat*, Vol. 2, p. 462.

14. Also, *Quran*, 96 : 1-5.

standing and concentration ; in slow, measured, rhythmic tones—in the stillness of the night and the pregnant silence of the early hours of dawn[15]:—

(1) "O thou wrapped up in thy raiment !
Keep vigil the night, long, save a little—

---

15. In this context, consider the following :—

(*a*) *Reciting the Quran in the Stillness of the Night*

1. "Learn and recite the Quran, for to one who learns, recites and uses it in prayer at night it is like a bag filled with musk whose fragrance diffuses itself everywhere. And he who learns it and goes to sleep having it within him is like a bag with musk tied up in it."

(Tirmidhi, Nasai, Ibn Majah ;
Mishkat, Vol. 2, p. 454).

2. Like the Prophet : reciting 112 (At-Tauhid), 113 (Al-Falaq) and 114 (An-Nas) ; blowing into cupped palms and wiping body.

(*Mishkat*, Vol. 2, p. 451).

(*b*) *Concentration*

1. "Therefore, recite of it as much as may be easy for you.."

(*Quran* 73 : 20).

2. "Recite the Quran as long as you can concentrate on it ; but when your concentration flags, give it up."

(Bukhari, Muslim ;
Mishkat, Vol. 2., p. 451).

(*c*) *Recitation : Slowly, Clearly, Distinctly*

1. Tawus told in Mursal form that when the Prophet was asked who has the most beautiful voice for the Quran and whose recitation was most beautiful, he replied : "The one whom you think when you hear him recite that he fears God." Tawus added that Talq (a companion of the Prophet from Yamama) was like that. Darimi transmitted it. (*Mishkat*, Vol. 2, p. 465).

2. Al-Bara b. Azib reported God's messenger as saying : "Beautify the Quran with your voice." Ahmad, Abu Dawud, Ibn Majah and Darimi transmitted it. (*Mishkat*, Vol. 2, p. 464)

3. Al-Laith b. Sad quoted Ibn Abu Mulaika who quoted Yala b.

[*Contd.*

A half thereof, or abate a little thereof or add (a little) thereto and chant the Quran in measure,
For We shall charge thee with a word of weight.
Lo ! the vigil of the night is (a time) when impression is more keen and speech more certain.
Lo ! Thou hast by day a chain of business.
So remember the name of thy Lord and devote thyself with a complete devotion—

Mamlak as saying that he asked Umm Salma about the manner in which the Prophet recited (the Quran) and she described it in a manner by which it was explained word by word. Tirmidhi, Abu Dawud and Nasai transmitted it. (*Mishkat*, Vol. 2, p. 464)

4. 'Umar b. Al-Khattab said : I heard Hisham b. Hakim b. Hizam reciting sura Al-Furqan in a different manner from my way of reciting it, and God's messenger had taught me to recite it. I nearly spoke sharply to him, but I delayed till he had finished, and then catching his cloak at the neck I brought him to God's messenger and said : 'Messenger of God, I heard this man reciting sura Al-Furqan in a manner different from that in which you taught me to recite it.' He told me to let him go and told him to recite. When he recited it in the manner in which I heard him recite, God's messenger said : 'Thus was it sent down.' He then told me to recite it and when I had done so, he said : 'Thus was it sent down. The Quran was sent down in seven modes of reading, so recite according to what comes most easily.'" (Bukhari and Muslim; *Mishkat*, Vol. 2, p. 466).

(*d*) *Recitation and Action*

1. *Quran*, 2 : 42-44 ; 107.
2. *Hadith*, Signs of a hypocrite (*Mishkat*, Vol. 1, p. 18) and major sins (*Ibid.*, p. 68).

(*e*) *Silencing Dispute and Disputation with the Quran*

Al-Harith Al-Awar said :

While passing by the mosque I found people engrossed in talk. So I went to visit Ali and told him. He asked if that was really so, and when I assured him that it was, he said he heard God's messenger say : "Dissension will certainly come," and asked him (the Prophet) how it

[*Contd.*

Lord of the East and the West ; there is no God save Him ; so choose thou
Him alone for thy defender." (**73** : 1-9)

(2) "Establish worship at the going down of the sun until the dark of night,
And the recital of the Quran at dawn.
Lo ! the recital of the Quran at dawn is ever witnessed.
And some part of the night awake for it, a largess for thee.
It may be that thy Lord will raise thee to a praised state." (**17** : 78-79)

(3) "O ye who believe ! Remember Allah
with much remembrance ;
And glorify Him early and late." (**33** : 41-42)

(*c*) Thirdly, even as we recite the Quran (clearly, distinctly, with understanding, in measured tones) our ears must hear what our lips recite, humbly and with

---

could be avoided and he (the Prophet) replied : "God's book is the way, for it contains information of what has happened before you, news of what will happen after you, and a decision regarding matters which occur among you. It is the distinguisher and is not jesting. If any overweening person abandons it, God will break him ; and if anyone seeks guidance elsewhere, God will lead him astray. It is God's strong cord, it is the wise reminder, it is the straight path, it is that by which the desires do not swerve nor the tongues become confused, and the learned (even) cannot grasp it completely (to their full satisfaction). It does not become worn out by repetition and its wonders never come to an end. It is that of which the Jinn did not hesitate to say : 'We have heard a wonderful recital which guides to what is right, and we believe in it.' He who utters it speaks the truth, he who acts according to it is rewarded, he who pronounces judgement according to it is just, and he who invites people to it guides to a straight path."

Tirmidhi and Darimi transmitted it. (*Mishkat*, Vol. 2, p. 453).

awe, soaking ourselves in the words of the Lord as the sound overflows into every nook and cranny of our soul, our home, the vast expanse beyond. And indeed, we need not forget that the Lord Himself bears witness to our recitation and Satan is on the flight when we recite.

So, as we recite :—

(1) *Give Ear, Pay Heed*

"And when the Quran is recited, give ear to it and pay heed, that ye may obtain mercy. And do thou remember thy Lord within thyself humbly and with awe, below thy breath, at morn and in the evening. And be thou not of the neglectful."

(**7** : 204-205)

(2) *Lo ! Satan Flees*

"And when thou recitest the Quran, seek refuge in Allah from Satan the outcast.
Lo ! he hath no power over those who believe and put their trust in their Lord.
His power is only over those who make a friend of him and those who ascribe partners unto him."

(**16** : 98-100)

(3) *Rejoice ! The Lord Bears Witness*

"And put thy trust in the Mighty,
the Merciful (.) Who seeth thee when
thou standest up to pray (.) And
seeth thine abasement among those;
Lo, He, only He, is the Hearer, Knower (.)"

(**26** : 217-219)

(4) *Lamp Lit, Sound Over-flowing*

"(Lit is such a light) in houses which Allah hath allowed to be exalted and that His name shall be remembered therein.
Therein do they offer praise to Him (early) at

morn and (late into the) night." (**24** : 36)

(*d*) And when we recite the Quran, let us rejoice over the assurance that He remembers us even as we remember Him : "Therefore, remember Me ; (and) I will remember you. Give thanks to Me and reject not Me." (**2** : 152). And even as we recite the Quran, let our plea for an understanding of it seek no intercessors. Let it rather be a plea directly to Him : " .. My Lord ! Relieve my mind. And ease my task for me. And loose the knot from my tongue." (**20** : 25-27). Let us not hasten, let us not hurry ; but let our soul resound with the cry : "My Lord ! Increase me in knowledge !" (**20** : 114).

(*e*) And let us rejoice over His assurance that He hears the cry of every crier who crieth unto Him : "And when My servants ask thee concerning Me, lo ! I am nigh. I hear the cry of every crier when he crieth unto Me. Let them also, then, with a will listen to My call, and believe in Me—if indeed they would be guided aright." (**2** : 186).

(*f*) And even as we seek this guidance, this understanding, this comprehension of the Quran, let us open the gates of our soul and surrender to the peace of the recitation : "Say : Lo ! Allah sendeth whom He will astray, and guideth unto Himself all who turn to Him. Who have believed and whose hearts find rest in the remembrance of God. Verily in the remembrance of God do hearts find rest. Those who believe and do right : joy is for them and bliss their journey's end. .. Say : He is my Lord ; there is no God save Him. In Him do I put my trust and unto Him is my recourse." (**13** : 27-30).

(*g*) When we recite the Quran, we should so soak ourselves in it, that we may rise from our recitation exclaiming : "(We take our) colour from Allah, and who is better than Allah at colouring? (And) we are His worshippers." (**2** : 138).

(*h*) When we recite the Quran, we should lay our recitation along with our entire being as an offering before Him : "Say : Lo ! my worship and my sacrifice and my living and my dying are (all) for Allah, Lord of all the worlds. He hath no partner. This I am commanded, and I am the first of those who surrender (unto Him)." (**6** : 162-163). And having made such an offering before the Lord, shall we not rise in peace from our recitation, shall we not hear His voice resound in every nook and corner of our being ?— " .. But ah ! Thou soul at peace ! Return unto thy Lord, content in His pleasure ! Enter thou among My bondsmen ! Enter thou My garden !" (**89** : 27-30).

19. Alas, time keeps running out and the little that I have presented before you of the devotional perception of the *total content* of the verses of the Quran is, I am aware, woefully inadequate. This, perhaps, was inevitable. The utterances of the Quran are limitless, both as to meaning and content, intensively and extensively ; and it is enough if I have been able to convey to you that an attempt at devotional perception is necessary, that an effort of the intellect alone will not suffice. This is not to say that an analytical study of the Quran is unnecessary; indeed, I hold such study to be a necesasry complement of devotional perception, a reinforcing element. But before we go on to that, let us round off our present discourse on devotional perception with a few striking comments from A. J. Arberry :—

"I urge the view that an eternal composition, such as the Quran is, cannot be well understood if it is submitted to the test of only temporal criticism. It is simply irrelevant to expect that the themes treated in the individual Surah will be marshalled after some mathematical precision to form a rationally ordered pattern ; the logic of revelation is not the logic of the schoolmen. There is no 'before' or 'after' in the prophetic message, when that message is true ; everlasting truth is not held within the confines of time and space, but every moment reveals itself wholly and completely .. All truth was present simultaneously within the Prophet's enraptured soul : all truth, however fragmented, revealed itself in his inspired utterance. The reader of the Muslim scriptures must strive to attain the same all-embracing apprehension. The sudden fluctuations of theme and mood will then no longer present such difficulties as have bewildered critics ambitious to measure the ocean of prophetic eloquence with the thimble of pedestrian analysis. Each Surah will now be seen to be a unity within itself, and the whole Quran will be recognized as a single revelation, self-consistent in the highest degree. Though half a mortal life-time was needed for the message to be received and communicated, the message itself, being of the eternal, is one message in eternity, however heterogeneous its temporal expression may appear to be. This, the mystics' approach, is surely the right approach to the Quran ; it is an approach that leads, *not* to bewilderment and disgust—that is the prerogative of the Higher Critic—but to an ever-deepening understanding, to a wonder and a joy that have no end."[16]

20. Having quoted this at length from Arberry, I thought I would pass on to a consideration of the "analytical study" of the Quran. But I cannot proceed, without drawing your attention yet once more to that one, central idea dominating all that I have struggled to put across so far : that our understanding of the Quran must inevitably remain incomplete, if we cannot or do not expose ourselves to the miracle of the Quran in the original, as it was revealed. Indeed, in the whole of Islam there is no other miracle; and the Muslim who wishes to complete his

16. A. J. Arberry, *The Koran Interpreted,* Vol. 2, Preface.

Islam, to rise to the pinnacle of faith and understanding in a burst of glory, has no option but to expose himself to the Quran—to establish immediate and direct contact with the revealed text. Translations, commentaries, lectures, Dars all have a value but they cannot replace our own recitation of the Quran, as a vehicle to its understanding. Indeed, we do well to listen to the Quran attentively when it is recited by somebody else, but shall we deprive ourselves of the joy and the illumination of reciting it ourselves ? Nay, the Quran must be revealed to us, to each one of us personally, even as it was revealed to the Prophet—in the inner-most sanctuary of our souls, the voice of God ringing in the innermost recesses of the human spirit. "It is easy to understand," Says Frithjof Schuon : "it is easy to understand the capital part played in the life of the Muslim by these sublime words—the verses of the Quran. These are not mere sentences which transmit thoughts, but are in a way, beings, powers, talismans. The soul of the Muslim is, as it were, woven of sacred formulae : in these he works, in these he rests, in these he lives and in these he dies".[17] This is the way to the understanding of the Quran : through personal, immediate, direct, continuous contact with the revealed text. We, who are the recipients of the gift and the privilege of education, what excuse have we for not understanding and learning the Quran ? With what face shall we face the Lord on that day when we stand face to face with Him ? Shall we say : "Our Lord ! We learnt Strategy, Tactics, Staff Duties, Geopolitics, Logic and Scientific Method but we were too dull and, alas, too busy to learn the Quran." Leave the Lord alone ; let us ask ourselves, if we would accept such an excuse. And recall, then, what the Prophet of God said : "The most severely punished of all men on the Day of Resurrection will be a learned man whom God has not blessed with His knowledge."[18]

---

17. Schuon, *Understanding Islam.* See: Note (5).

18. Ghazzali, *Al-Kitab al-Ilm.* Translation, p. 1.

"Analytical Study" Deferred : Action to Complete Understanding

21. I fear I have no time, within the span of this talk, to launch into a discourse on the "analytical study" of the Quran, which however secondary, is also absolutely necessary.[19] I am compelled to close this brief, inadequate, incomplete discourse with one last observation : our understanding of the Quran will never be complete, unless our recitation of the Quran overflows into appropriate action in the concrete. The Quran, and the whole of Islam with it, is not a matter for monastic meditation or drawing-room disputation. A full understanding of the Quran demands its insertion into the stream of life, putting it to the practical test, so that the Reality that it expounds may dawn on us in the concrete, even as it suffuses our inner lives. In this context, I wish to quote to you, long though the quotation may be, from Abul Ala Maududi's *Tafheemul Quran*. In his Introduction to this work, the Maulana writes :—

> "But in spite of all these devices, one cannot grasp the inspiring spirit of the Quran .. by mere lip-service to it."[20]

---

19. Connect with Note (2).
20. Maududi, *Tafheemul Quran*, Muqaddimah, pp. 27-28.

SELECTED BIBLIOGRAPHY

1. A. J. Arberry, *The Koran Interpreted.* George Allen and Unwin Ltd., London.
2. Marmaduke Pickthall, *The Meaning of the Glorious Quran ; Text and Explanatory Translation.* Accurate Printers, Urdu Bazar, P.O. Box 1338, Lahore.
3. Abul Ala Maududi, *Tafheemul Quran (The Meaning of the Quran) : Text and Translation.* Islamic Publications Ltd., Lahore.
4. Abdullah Yusuf Ali, *The Holy Quran : Text, Translation and Commentary.* Sheikh Muhammad Ashraf, Kashmiri Bazar, Lahore.
5. Abul Kalam Azad, *Tarjumanul Quran.* Sind Sagar Academy, Lahore.
6. *Mishkat al-Masabih.* Translation by Dr. James Robson, Sheikh Muhammad Ashraf, Kashmiri Bazar, Lahore.
7. Frithjof Schuon, *Understanding Islam.* George Allen and Unwin Ltd., London.
8. Sir Muhammad Iqbal, *The Reconstruction of Religious Thought in Islam.* Sheikh Muhammad Ashraf, Kashmiri Bazar, Lahore.
9. Al-Ghazzali, *Al-Kitab al-Ilm.* Translation ("The Book of Knowledge") by Nabih Amin Faris. Sheikh Muhammad Ashraf, Kashmiri Bazar, Lahore.

TOWARDS UNDERSTANDING THE QURAN

Passages from the Quran

(Ref. Page 198)

(Moses) said : My Lord relieve my mind ;
And ease my task for me,
And loose the knot from my tongue ;
That they may understand what I say.
(20 : 25-28)

٢٥- قال رب اشرح لي صدري
٢٦- ويسر لي أمري
٢٧- واحلل عقدة من لساني
٢٨- يفقهوا قولي

(Ref. Page 199)

Say : I seek refuge in the Lord of mankind,
The King of mankind,
The God of mankind,
From the evil of the sneaking whisperer,
Who whispereth in the hearts of mankind,
Of the jinn and of mankind.
(114 : 1-6)

١- قل أعوذ برب الناس
٢- ملك الناس
٣- إله الناس
٤- من شر الوسواس الخناس
٥- الذي يوسوس في صدور الناس
٦- من الجنة والناس

(Ref. Page 203)

For We shall charge thee with a word of weight.
Lo ! the vigil of the night is (a time) when impression is more keen and speech more certain.
Lo ! thou hast by day a chain of business.
So remember the name of thy Lord and devote thyself with a complete devotion.
Lord of the East and the West ; there is no God save Him, so choose thou Him alone for thy defender. (73 : 5-9)

٥- إنا سنلقي عليك قولا ثقيلا
٦- إن ناشئة الليل هي أشد وطأ
وأقوم قيلا
٧- إن لك في النهار سبحا طويلا
٨- واذكر اسم ربك
وتبتل إليه تبتيلا
٩- رب المشرق والمغرب
لا إله إلا هو
فاتخذه وكيلا

Establish worship at the going down of the sun until the dark of night and (the recital of) the Qur'ān at dawn. Lo ! (the recital of) the Qur'ān at dawn is ever witnessed; and some part of the night awake for it, a largess for thee. It may be that thy Lord will raise thee to a praised estate.
(17 : 78-79)

٧٨- أقم الصلوة لدلوك الشمس
إلى غسق الليل وقرآن الفجر
إن قرآن الفجر كان مشهودا
٧٩- ومن الليل فتهجد به
نافلة لك
عسى أن يبعثك ربك مقاما
محمودا

(Ref. Page 203)

O ye who believe ! Remember Allah with much remembrance.

And glorify Him early and late.

(33 : 41-42)

۴۱- يٰٓاَيُّهَا الَّذِيْنَ اٰمَنُوا اذْكُرُوا اللّٰهَ ذِكْرًا
كَثِيْرًا ۝
۴۲- وَّسَبِّحُوْهُ بُكْرَةً وَّاَصِيْلًا ۝

(Ref. Page 204)

And when the Qur'an is recited, give ear to it and pay heed, that ye may obtain mercy.

And do thou (O Muhammad) remember thy Lord within thyself humbly and with awe, below thy breath at morn and evening.

And be thou not of the neglectful.

(7 : 204-205)

۲۰۴- وَاِذَا قُرِئَ الْقُرْاٰنُ فَاسْتَمِعُوْا لَهٗ
وَاَنْصِتُوْا لَعَلَّكُمْ تُرْحَمُوْنَ ۝
۲۰۵- وَاذْكُرْ رَّبَّكَ فِيْ نَفْسِكَ تَضَرُّعًا وَّ
خِيْفَةً وَّدُوْنَ الْجَهْرِ مِنَ الْقَوْلِ
بِالْغُدُوِّ وَالْاٰصَالِ
وَلَا تَكُنْ مِّنَ الْغٰفِلِيْنَ ۝

And when thou recitest the Qur'ān, seek refuge in Allah from Satan the outcast.

Lo ! he hath no power over those who believe and put trust in their Lord.

His power is only over those who make a friend of him, and those who ascribe partners unto Him (Allah). (16 : 98-100)

۹۸- فَاِذَا قَرَاْتَ الْقُرْاٰنَ فَاسْتَعِذْ بِاللّٰهِ
مِنَ الشَّيْطٰنِ الرَّجِيْمِ ۝
۹۹- اِنَّهٗ لَيْسَ لَهٗ سُلْطٰنٌ عَلَى الَّذِيْنَ
اٰمَنُوْا وَعَلٰى رَبِّهِمْ يَتَوَكَّلُوْنَ ۝
۱۰۰- اِنَّمَا سُلْطٰنُهٗ عَلَى الَّذِيْنَ يَتَوَلَّوْنَهٗ
وَالَّذِيْنَ هُمْ بِهٖ مُشْرِكُوْنَ ۝

And put thy trust in the Mighty, the Merciful,

Who seeth thee when thou standest up (to pray).

And (seeth) thine abasement among those who fall prostrate (in worship).

Lo ! He, only He, is the Hearer, the Knower. (26 : 217-220)

۲۱۷- وَتَوَكَّلْ عَلَى الْعَزِيْزِ الرَّحِيْمِ ۝
۲۱۸- الَّذِيْ يَرٰىكَ حِيْنَ تَقُوْمُ ۝
۲۱۹- وَتَقَلُّبَكَ فِي السّٰجِدِيْنَ ۝
۲۲۰- اِنَّهٗ هُوَ السَّمِيْعُ الْعَلِيْمُ ۝

TOWARDS UNDERSTANDING THE QURAN

RESPONSE TO COMMENTS ON THE TALK "ON STRIVING TO BE A MUSLIM"

Introduction

1. I was asked several questions after that talk and I heard several comments, from which I infer (with a fair measure of assurance) that some genuine interest has been aroused in this subject central to our well-being (in mind, body and spirit)—in our individual, as also collective lives.

2. The purpose of my talk, however, was not to give rise to "further talk"—but to lead to private and personal study, silent reflection, meditation and concurrent action. Questions there had to be, questions there must be; for, where there are no questions, there can be no enquiry. But I plead with you not to direct these questions at external agents, but to your own self—with the Quran as both substance and guide for your enquiry. There is no short-cut to "illumination", no substitute for self-enquiry, no means whereby the wise and the devout may wrap their wisdom and their peace in a capsule for others to swallow. Faith cannot be injected from outside; faith wells up from within—a product of personal intellectual enquiry, reflection and action.

3. I believe (and I am glad this is not my exclusive finding) that the miracle of Islam is the miracle of the Quran. To that miracle (of the Quran) we must expose ourselves, if we wish to capture a true imprint of the spirit of Islam, the system and the way of life that it advocates. I plead with you for a study of the Quran. The discussion can wait!

Study of the Quran

4. To read the Quran, we must read it in the original Arabic —with understanding. A translation of the Quran is not the Quran. Here is thought and expression, logic and language, faith and its declaration, reality and appearance inextricably inter-twined. Read the Quran in the original Arabic, with understanding.

5. This is nowhere near as difficult as you think. Start, and you will yourself find out how easy it is. This is part of the miracle of the Quran.

6. I knew no Arabic (except for a fair acquaintance with how to read the script), when I started my study of the Quran. The way I went about it was as follows:—

(*a*) I took a copy of the Quran with its English translation (it could be any language that one is proficient in) printed along-side (opposite) each verse, verse for verse.

(*b*) One day I took a foot-ruler and four ball-point pens (red, green, blue, black), scanned through the Quran and underlined the passages that made a particularly vivid impression on my mind: the passages in pure *hamd* of the Lord (in red), the prayers (in green), the injunctions for individual conduct (in blue) and the laws pertaining to our collective lives (in black).

(*c*) That done, early in the morning or late at night (day after day, without a break, for only twenty minutes or so each day), I read and re-read the passages that I had underlined, staring at the translation even as I continued with my recitation in Arabic ("in slow, measured, rhythmic tones").

(*d*) Over a period of time, effortlessly and unconscious of the miracle seeping into me, I found that I understood what I recited (word for word). And the more I recited the more I understood, eventually becoming independent of the need to "stare at the translation".

(*e*) There were days when I recited only one passage (or at best two), again and again for the full twenty minutes of so, till my mind having mastered the literal meaning, went beyond to a perception and an experience that suffused my entire being. That experience I cannot describe, much less explain.

(*f*) And there have been days, when yielding to the spirit that moved me, I read only the passages in red, or the passages in green, the passages in blue or the passages in black. I read as the spirit within me moved me, on some days finding exhilarating combinations of the red and green, the blue and black (or permutations thereof).

(*g*) And so I continued each day (for only twenty minutes or so every day) till the miracle in the Quran (external to me) found a niche inside me, in my mind and spirit —and body also. That lamp burns, all day long and all the night through. The words of the Quran reverberate—articulate on the lips or silently murmuring in the deepest recesses of the heart.

(*h*) And that is as far as I have got; but it is a good beginning. I do not know Arabic; but I understand the Quran. Where's the paradox, where the need for external aids?

7. Go to the Quran, I plead with you; find your own way to it. Seek not external aids, except such as may be necessary to master the mechanics of reading and recitation (clearly, without error). The mechanics mastered, the study is your own; as also the "illumination". Let us study first, the discussion can wait ! Let us not discuss before we study.

Prayers from the Quran

8. Someone wanted from me, written on a piece of paper, that beautiful prayer which I recited at the beginning of my talk.

I'll go beyond; I'll list below a fair sample of the many passages underlined in green in my copy of the Quran. And I shall do this not as a subsutitute for your own study of the Quran, but as a spur to it.

9. Go, buy your own copy of the Quran; and read these (and many more) so that you may not ask of others what you can yourself find, discover, reflect on, meditate and actualize through action.

10. Here, then, are some of those passages:—

(*a*) At the beginning and at the end of every task undertaken:—

(1) "*O Lord !*
Let my entry be
Through the gate of truth and honour;
And (likewise) let my exit be
Through the gate of truth and honour.
And grant thou me,
From Thy presence,
A power to aid me!" (**17** : 80)

(2) "*Say:*
My prayer and my sacrifice,
My life and my death,
Are all for Allah
The Lord of the worlds.
I ascribe no partners unto Him;
This I have been commanded.
And I am the first of those
Who submit their will to His . . ." (**6** : 162)

(*b*) At the end of every task undertaken:—

(1) "*Our Lord,*
Accept (this service) from us;
For Thou (only Thou) art
The All-Hearing, All-Knowing.
Our Lord,

Make of us Muslims (A people bowing to Thy Will),
And of our progeny a people Muslim;
And show us the way to prayer,
And turn to us in forgiveness.
Lo, Thou (only Thou) art
The Oft-Returning, Most Merciful." (**2** : 127-128).

(2) "*On no soul doth God lay a burden*
Greater than it can bear;
Each gets what it earns (of good or evil).
(Pray):
Our Lord,
Condemn us not,
If we forget or fall into error.
Lay not on us a burden
Such as Thou didst lay on those before us.
Our Lord,
Lay not on us a burden
Greater than what we have the strength
To bear.
Blot out our sins,
Grant us forgiveness,
Have mercy on us!
Lo, Thou (only Thou) art
Our Protector;
(And) help us against those
That reject Thee!" (**2** : 286)

(*c*) In Joy and Sorrow (Victory and Defeat, Success and Failure, Triumph and Disaster, Honour and Disgrace, Hope and Fear, Well-being and Adversity, Exaltation and Distress, Power and Powerlessness):—

(1) "*Say: O Allah,*
Owner of all (Power and) Sovereignty!
Thou givest power unto whom Thou wilt,
And Thou withdrawest power
From whom Thou wilt;

Thou exaltest whom Thou wilt;
And Thou abasest whom Thou wilt;
In Thy hands is all good.
Lo! Thou art able to do all things." (**3** : 26)

(2) "*Nay, but whosoever turneth his countenance*
Full square towards Allah
While doing good,
His reward is with his Lord;
And there shall no fear come upon them,
And neither shall they grieve." (**2**: 112)

(*d*) In Sorrow and Adversity (Death, Defeat, Failure, Disaster, Disgrace, Distress, Fear, Hunger, Panic):—

(1) "*O Lord,*

Pour forth constancy on us,
And make our foot-hold firm and sure
(So that we may not waver).
And come to our aid
Against those that reject Thee." (**2** : 250)

(2) "*O ye, who believe!*
Seek help and steadfastness in prayer.
Lo, Allah is with those who patiently
Persevere.
And say not of those slain in the way of Allah: 'Dead'!
Nay, they live; only ye perceive not.
And surely we shall try you
With something of fear and hunger,
And loss of wealth and lives,
And (the) fruits (of your labour).
But give glad tidings to the steadfast,
Who when sorrow and adversity strike them,
Say: Lo! We are Allah's,
And unto Him we return!" (**2** : 153-156)

(3) "*So, lose not heart,*
Nor fall into despair.

For, ye must gain mastery,
If ye are true in faith." (**3** : 139)

(*e*) In Joy and Exultation (Victory, Success, Triumph, Honour, Achievement, Power):—

(1) *"When Allah's succour and the triumph cometh,*
And thou seest mankind
Entering the religion of Allah in legions,
Hymn, thou, then
The praises of the Lord,
And seek forgiveness of Him.
Lo, He is even ready to show mercy!" (**110**)

(2) *Say:*
Verily, all bounties are in the hands of Allah.
He granteth them to whomsoever he pleaseth.
And He careth for all, knoweth all things.
For His mercy, He chooseth whom He pleaseth;
For Allah is the Lord of bounties unbounded."
(**3** : 73-74)

11. When you have begun to pray, and prayed for a while, you will discover for yourself that there is a unity in prayer which defies the artificial compartmentation that our "minor SD" seeks so arbitrarily to impose. You will experience for yourself that all time is prayer time, and a single prayer frequently spans many more than just one occasion or even a group of occasions. You will experience that prayer is not a one-way request for things mundane but a two-way communication between the devotee and his Lord: a surrender of the mind, spirit and body of man at the altar of God—pulsating, and absorbing of the same frequency as God's. For such prayer we need no ceremonies (no candles, no altar, no graven image, no music, no priest)—nothing but God and His devotee. And when we have so prayed, our prayers must lead us inexorably to the acts of prayer—the climax and the consummation of one of the finest of God's gifts to man: the ability to pray. In this context, consider the following verses from the Quran:—

(*a*) All time is prayer time (and no ceremonies required):—
"*Men who celebrate*
The praises of God:
Standing, sitting
And reclining (*on their sides*);
And contemplate
The wonders of (*His*) *creation*
In the Heavens and on Earth . . ." (**3** : 191)

(*b*) Prayer is two-way communication, not one-way traffic:—
"*And when My servants*
Ask thee (*O, Prophet*) *concerning Me,*
Lo, I am nigh unto thee,
I hear the cry of every crier
When he crieth unto me.
Let them also, then (*with a will*),
Listen to My call,
And believe in Me,
If indeed they would be guided aright." (**2** : 186)

(*c*) Prayer must be followed by the acts of prayer, from prayer to prayer:—
"*Woe to the praying ones,*
Who are unmindful of their prayers;
Who pray to be seen
And withhold small kindnesses." (**107** : 4-7)

Conclusion

11. I am grateful you came for my talk. But my talk will have reached its crowning achievement, the day you exclaim: "No, no more talks; for, lo! I am out on a search of my own—to and through the Quran!"

12. On that day, if memory serves, remember me in your prayers.

QURAN AND HADITH :
LECTURE NOTES

Introductory Remarks

1. A few words about the Quran and the Hadith: specifically, the relationship between the two and the role of Hadith in our search for a clearer, deeper and fuller understanding of the Quran. This, particularly in view of the fact there is a mistaken notion in some quarters that:—

   (*a*) The Hadith are unnecessary for an understanding of Islam; the Quran suffices.

   (*b*) The fear that the Hadith generate controversy in the Ummah and introduce an undesirable element of rigidity in the interpretation of Quranic principles and their application as a "code of life" relevant to our times.

2. To my mind, unbelief/doubts/fears are, generally speaking, products of ignorance . . . (apart from those few who, not seeking God's grace as they learn, are led by their learning into further error . . . for the Muttaqi guidance is guaranteed) . . . I believe *we* fear God . . . *We* shall dispel our doubts through knowledge.

3. The main burden of my talk is the Hadith (understanding which a little better than before, we may dispel some of our doubts and fears). But before we go on to that a few words about the Quran restricted to :—

   (*a*) A unique book; a spoken book revealed in bits and pieces to guide a movement (ref. Muqaddimah, *Tafheemul Quran*).

   (*b*) The birth of the Inductive Intellect.

   (*c*) Prophet and Quran inseparable.

4. Spoken Book revealed in bits and pieces: (importance of understanding the historical context) . . . e.g. Prohibition of interest, the change of the Qiblah, prohibition of drinking etc.

5. Inductive Intellect: from the particular to the general; from incident to principle; from nature to God.

6. Prophet's Mission: a "message" conveyed and a practical "model" established . . . e.g. Salat, Wudhu, Zakat etc.

The Prophet: Sunnah and Hadith

7. God gave the Prophet "the Book and the Wisdom" (Quran, **2** : 151; **3** : 164; **4** : 113 ; **62** : 2)—"the Book" is the Quran (the words of God); the "wisdom" is the prophetic tradition (the Prophet's words and deeds, sanctified and purified by Divine Guidance).

8. Hadith (lit. a story, a report, an account of what happened); Sunnah (lit. a practice or custom). These, within the community of Islam, related to the Prophet (what he said and did, and his reaction to things said and done in his presence) and his companions. Sunnah (what was practised) and Hadith (the record of what was practised).

9. Later: collection and compilation of "traditions"—each Hadith prefaced by a chain of authorities through whom it was transmitted (Isnad), followed by its text (Matn).

10. Shafi'i (150-204 AH) established the science of traditions. Traditions traced back to the Prophet (through an unbroken chain of reliable transmitters) came to be recognized as a basis of Islam second in importance only to the Quran.

Growth of Hadith

11. From small personal collections—accounts of the life and works of the Prophet (Ibn Hisham's edition of Ibn Ishaq's *Sirat Rasul-Allah*; *Maghazi* of Waqidi—(85-151 AH; 218 AH/130-207 AH)—first Hadith collection proper (Malik's *Muwatta*, 93-179 AH)—early collections *Musnad* of

Tayalisi (204 AH) and Ahmad bin Hanbal (164-241 AH), grouped according to "transmitters".

12. Later: a better method of compilation—"Musannaf" (classification according to subject-matter). In course of time six such works came to be recognised as the most authoritative of all: *Sahih* of Bukhari (194-256 AH); of Muslim (202-261 AH): and *the four Sunan* works of Abu Dawud (202-275), Tirmidhi (279), Nasai (303) and Ibn Majah (209-273). Note: Even the collections which rose to the rank of canonical works (Bukhari, Muslim) were not commissioned by any authoritative body, but were undertaken on the initiative of their authors. They were accepted as such by the Ummah.]

Subject-Matter of Hadith

13. Vast, covering almost every topic of life. Consider the *Sahih of Bukhari* :—

(*a*) In all: 97 books.

(*b*) First 3 (revelation, faith, knowledge).

(*c*) Next 30 (ablution, prayer, Zakat, pilgrimage, fasting).

(*d*) Next 22 (business and legal matters).

(*e*) Next 3 (Jihad, dealing with subject peoples, beginning of creation).

(*f*) Next 4 (fine qualities of the Prophet and his companions, Prophet's life unto the Hijra).

(*g*) Next 1 (Prophet's career in Medina).

(*h*) Next 2 (commentary on passages from the Quran).

(*j*) Next 3 (marriage, divorce, family).

(*k*) Books 68-95 (food, drink, clothing, seemly behaviour, medicine, invitations, vows, blood revenge, persecution, visions, civil strife, trials before the end of the world).

(*l*) Book 96 (importance of adhering to the Quran and Sunnah).

(*m*) Book 97 (unity of God).

14. *Muslim's* covers much the same ground. *The four Sunan works* confined to: matters of religious observance, law, personal relationships and eschatology. *Tirmidhi's* (sometimes called a *Sahih*) includes some commentary on the Quran and the fine qualities of the Prophet (also family and companions).

15. By the second century: the science of criticism of traditions. *Principle*: to establish the reliability of the transmitters (not so much the validity of the material itself). *Result*: detailed biographies of personalities mentioned in the Isnads. Great workers in this field: Ibn Abu Hatim Ar-Razi (327 AH), Dhahabi (1315, 1325 AH), Ibn Hajar Al-Asqalani (1325-1328), Ibn Al-Imad (1350-51).

The Great Shifting

16. To ensure authenticity:—

(*a*) *Bukhari*, 600,000—7,275 in his *Sahih* (reduced to 4000 even 2762, when repetitions eliminated). Collected from 1000 Shaykhs in the course of 16 years of travel and labour in Iran, Syria, Al-Hijaz and Egypt.

(*b*) *Abu Dawud.* 500,000—4,800 in his *Sunan.*

17. The rise of Ilm Al-Hadith: Abu Muhammad Ar-Ramahurmuzi (370 AH); Al-Hakim Abu Abdullah Muhammad Bin Abdullah an-Naisaburi (325-405 AH); and the great Ibn As-Salah (643 AH).

Classification: Grades of Reliability

18. Three main groups of traditions: Sahih (sound), Hasan (good), Daif (weak) or Saqim (infirm).

19. *Sahih*: (1) Bukhari and Muslim; (2) Bukhari, not by Muslim; (3) Muslim, not by Bukhari; (4) by neither, but up to their standard; (5) not by Bukhari, but up to his standard; (6) not by Muslim, but up to his standard; (7) considered Sahih by others, but not up to the standard of either Bukhari or Muslim (categorisation by Ibn As-Salah).

20. *Hasan*: (1) "those whose source is well-known and whose men are well-known" (*Abu Sulaiman Al-Khattabi*); (2) "those whose Isnad contains no one suspected of falsehood, which does not disagree with what is generally reported, and which has something similar transmitted by another line" (*Tirmidhi*); (3) "those which contain some very slight weakness, but are so very nearly right and admissible that they are fit to be used as a basis for legal decisions" (*Abul Faraj Bin Al-Jauzi*).

21. Ibn Salah, drawing a clearer distinction between Sahih and Hasan, says latter are of two types:—

(*a*) Those whose Isnad has someone not clearly known/capacity not fully verified but not guilty of error/deliberate falsehood; having something approximating to the text transmitted by one or more Isnads.

(*b*) Those whose transmitters have a reputation for veracity and reliability (but lower than those who transmit Sahih, because of relative weakness in memory/knowledge).

22. *Daif* (*Saqim*) traditions, though not valid for legal decisions, are not rejected out of hand (look at the contents, to justify). Various grades of weakness (from various weaknesses): links missing in the Isnad (other defectes therein); traditions which disagree with what is commonly reported; traditions which conceal defects.

The "Mishkat al-Masabih"

23. The *Mishkat* is a revision (737 AH, by Wali Al-Din Muhammad B. Abdallah Al-Khatib Al-Tibrizi) of Ibn Al-Farra Al-Baghawi's (d. 516 AH) original compilation called *Masabih As-Sunna*.

24. The original *Masabih As-Sunna* by Baghawi contained a total of 4,719 traditions: 325 from Bukhari alone, 875 from Muslim alone, 1051 from both Bukhari and Muslim and 2468 from other sources.

25. Baghawi arranged his material on the principle of Musannaf works (marshalling according to subject-matter). To save space, he omitted the Isnads because the traditions came from well-known collections where the Isnads could be found in full.

26. Within each capter, Baghawi grouped two traditions in two sections:—

(*a*) *Section I.* (Sahih: from both Bukhari and Muslim, from Bukhari alone; from Muslim alone);

(*b*) *Section II.* (Hasan: from other sources e.g., Abu Dawud, Tirmidhi, Nasai, Ibn Majah, Ahmad bin Hanbal, Darimi, Daraqutni, Abu Nuaim, Baihaqi and Razin Al-Andalusi).

27. For his great contribution to the study of Hadith, the Ummah conferred on Baghawi the titles of Muhyi As-Sunnah (the reviver of the Sunnah) and Rukn Ad-Din (the support of religion).

28. Baghawi's great work (*the Masabih As-Sunna*) was revised in 737 AH by another great servant of Islam: Wali Al-Din Muhammad. The revised work published under the name *Mishkat Al-Masabih* has earned a permanent and popular place in the literature of Islam.

29. This revised work (*the Mishkat*) differs from the original *Masabih As-Sunna* on two counts only:—

(*a*) Under each chapter a third section has been added (to give fuller information on each topic), with additional traditions from *Bukhari*, *Muslim* and other sources.

(*b*) At the end of each tradition the name of the source(s) have been quoted, frequently with comments on the quality of the tradition. Such comments as:—

(1) Gharib =with regard to Isnad (*only* tradition from a certain chain of transmitters, although the same may

		be known by other lines); with regard to both Isnad and Matn (a tradition whose exact content has only one transmitter).
(2)	Gharib Hasan (or Hasan Gharib)	=Hasan according to quality of transmitters; Matn not contradicted elsewhere but only one line of transmission.
(3)	Hasan Sahih	=isnad is Hasan, supported by another whose Insand is Sahih.
(4)	Mahjul (unknown)	=someone in the chain not clearly recognized (therefore, suspect).
(5)	Mauquf	=isnad stops at one of the companions, not all the way back to the Prophet.
(6)	Muallal	=ostensibly sound, but with some weakness not readily apparent.
(7)	Munkar	=weak transmitter, Matn disagrees with what is generally reported.
(8)	Munqati	=a link missing in the Isnad.
(9)	Mursal	=a man in the generation following that of the Prophet's companions, quoting the Prophet directly.
(10)	Shadhdh	=single transmitter, contradicting another.

30. The Mishkat consists of: 26 Books, each book having anything from 1-41 Chapters, each Chapter containing three Sections (Sahih, Hasan, Sahih/Hasan).

31. The 26 Books cover: Faith, Knowledge, Purification, Prayer (37 Chapters); Fasting. The Excellent Qualities of the Quran, Supplications, God's Names, The Rites of Pilgrimage, Business Transactions, Jihad, Game and Animals which may be Slaughtered, Food, Clothing, Medicine and Spells, Visions,

General Behaviour, Words that Soften the Heart, Fitan (41 Chapters).

Comments

32. *A Heritage to be Preserved. Not Spurned.* Shall we discard such vast scholarship and condemn it to oblivion? Here is the full blaze of the most meticulously documented history casting its searching light on the Prophet to whom the Quran was revealed. To discard these authentic traditions, would be to deprive ourselves of the historical evidence relating to the life, personality and mission of the last of the prophets of Islam, the Prophet of Islam perfected. "Were it not for these traditions, he would recede from the day-light of history into the dimness of legend, as was the case with former prophets." True, the Quran would remain to the end of time, and beyond "on tablets preserved" for the Lord Himself has undertaken to be its Guardian. And one might well argue that so long as the Quran remains (as it *will*), Muhammad and his mission cannot be effaced from the life of the universe. This I and every other Muslim unhesitatingly accepts but surely this is not adequate ground, logically speaking, to dump the Hadith into dust-bin of history. The Quran is, without doubt, the central source and the eternal flame in the life of Islam. But why should we, on that account, discard the niche, the oil and the encasing glass which throws that flame into clearer focus for the vision of all mankind? I for one, alone with the majority of Muhammad's Ummah (and his majority will never err, in principle at least), cannot and will not do so. To such an approach and attitude, some would cruelly (and I think, mistakenly) hurl the epithet: "Behold! The followers of the 'two Qurans'!" This is Zulm, to my mind gross injustice, a twisting and a travesty of the truth that we proclaim: the Quran is the ultimate, imperishable, irreplaceable, unsupplantable, unchallengeable, eternal, first and last source of Islam. The Hadith, the authentic historical record of the *concert*-isation, *actual*-isation, *real*-isation of the Quranic Sunnah by the Prophet and his com-

panions, represents a most valuable (and therefore *not* to be discarded) supplement and complement to our understanding of the Quran. We say then that the Hadith cannot supplant the Quran, nor is it co-equal with the Quran; it is only a supplement, a complement, an additional and invaluable aid to our understanding of the Quran.

33. *In the Absence of the Prophet, the Hadith.* This is particularly true for us who are separated in temporal, serial time from the Prophet and his living example. We read the Quran and the bulk of it is an open book, crystal clear. But here and there a question arises, a doubt remains, a desire for a deeper understanding haunts the mind. What do we do? The companions of the Prophet went straight to him: "O Prophet of Allah, explain!" We can do likewise; we can turn to the Hadith, the best substitute that we have of the Prophet's living presence, of explanation by demonstration (over and above further theoretical elaboration), of the Quran in practice, of the Quranic principles, laws and precepts actualised and realised in the concrete by one who understood the Quran best and his companions who modelled themselves on his model with an acuteness and a devotion unparalleled in history.

34. *Without Fear. With Sincerity.* There is no need to fear that our study of the Hadith will cause dissensions among us, so long as we are wide awake and scrupulously honest in discriminating the authentic from the spurious. And the criterion for this remains the Quran, "the cable of Allah" to which all of us must cling. There can be no 'authentic' Hadith that contradicts the Quran. We may still have "personal doubts" that remain, but these are for us to personally clear through personal effort (further study, practice and prayer)—*not* for public flouting and disputation.

35. The "companionship" of the Prophet, through the study of the Hadith.

36. Some vivid examples of "the Quran in practice."

37. Some prayers of the Prophet.

Note: These notes (paras 1-31) are based almost exclusively on Dr. James Robson's learned preface to his English translation of the *Mishkat al-Masabih*, published in four (recently in two) volumes by Sheikh Muhammad Ashraf of Kashmiri Bazar, Lahore.

APPENDICES

REFLECTIONS ON LIFE AND LONELINESS

(*Extracts from a Soldier's Diary*)

Lines from Russell

1. "Three passions, simple but overwhelmingly strong, have governed my life: the longing for *Love*, the search for *Knowledge* and unbearable *pity* for the suffering of Mankind. These passions, like great winds, have blown me hither and thither, in a wayward course, over a deep ocean of anguish, reaching to the very verge of despair.

2. I have sought *love*, first, because it brings ecstasy—ecstasy so great that I would often have sacrificed all the rest of life for a few hours of this joy. I have sought it, next, because it relieves loneliness—that terrible loneliness in which one shivering consciousness looks over the rim of the world into the cold unfathomable lifeless abyss. I have sought it, finally, because in the union of love I have seen, in a mystic miniature, the prefiguring vision of the heaven that saints and poets have imagined. This is what I sought, and though it might seem too good for human life, this is what, at last, I have found.

3. With equal passion I have sought *knowledge*. I have wished to understand the hearts of men. I have wished to know why the stars shine. And I have tried to apprehend the Pythagorean power by which number holds sway above the flux. A little of this, but not much, I have achieved.

4. Love and knowledge, so far as they were possible, led upward towards the heavens. But always *pity* brought me back to earth. Echoes of cries of pain reverberate in my heart. Children in famine, victims tortured by oppressors, helpless old people a hated burden to their sons ; and the whole world of loneliness, poverty and pain make a mockery of what human life should be. I long to alleviate the evil, but I cannot; and I too suffer.

5. This has been my life. I have found it worth living, and would gladly live it again if the chance were offered me."

(*Bertrand Russell*, "*Autobiography*")

Fugitives All

6. ND said : "Some men are *born* lonely." And then he spoke of a loneliness here on earth, even in the midst of a crowd, such as one can only have felt but cannot describe: the loneliness of outer space, of the void many light years away from this little planet and even this solar system, of a loneliness that (he said) "reverberates'' ("goonj uthti hai"), a loneliness (I think) where not even your own echo can be heard, an abysmal loneliness, the loneliness of the grave on earth and eternity in outer space...And what is our consciousness, but a frantic flight from this terrifying loneliness? We are, I think, fugitives all—each in his own way...and in that unholy scramble for a shore, for a grain of faith and a straw of certainty, for a momentary forgetfulness, we inflict our loneliness (or the products of our flight from it) on those whom we love and on those whom we hate, and even those whom we casually meet "to kill time" . . . Some seek work, some fall in love and others find a prostitute ; my father begets fourteen ehildren and devotes a life-time to their education; Bertrand Russell writes volumes on our knowledge of the external world and Adolf Hitler goes to war; Descartes exclaims: "Cogito Ergo Sum", and Einstein scribbles: "$E=MC^2$"; a prince renounces the throne seeking "The Four-fold Path" and Ghazzali goes globe-trotting; Posidonius travels to the shores of the Atlantic (the end of the then known world) to study the tides and see the sun set over the African coast and Spain; the Prophet retires to the cave and we enter the market-place . . . Fugitives all, for ever lonely, for ever on the run . . . (*Rawalpindi*, 6 *Jan*. '69)

Forever Seeking the Lonelier Way

7. Could 20th Century Man build no finer monument to his loneliness than the Apollo-8, which he flung into outer space the other day ? For a while it gridled our little globe, and

then three men in a capsule swung it out of its terrestrial orbit for an epic 147 hour, half-million-mile voyage to the moon, and back to a spectacular splash-down in the Pacific 1,043 miles from Father Damien's islands in the Hawaii. A magnificent feat that statistics could not deny : a 363-foot-tall rocket and ship with no fewer than 3½ million working parts ; swinging out of its orbit around our globe at 24,200 MPH; hurtling through space and crossing the "equigravisphere" (the "Great Divide" between earth and moon: 202,700 miles from earth ; 38,900 miles from the moon) at a more modest 2,217 MPH; approaching the moon and firing a 20,500-pound-thrust rocket engine 231,000 miles from home to circumnavigate the moon (10 times) at an altitude of 70 miles—to see her "fair" face and come back running home to tell us that wonders will never cease :

(*a*) "It is awe-inspiring, and it makes you realize just what you have back there on earth. The earth, from here, is a grand oasis in the big vastness of space." (*Lovell*)

(*b*) "I am fascinated by the lunar sunrise and sunset. They bring out the stark nature of the terrain...The sky up here is also a rather forbidding, foreboding expanse of blackness." (*Anders*)

8. Not to falsify the record, it must be admitted that these expressions of awe and wonder were communicated to earth during tke second live lunar tele-cast in the ninth orbit on Christmas Eve . . .

9. A magnificent feat, by any standard; but is magnificence all? Did Borman, Lovell and Anders have to go all that far to reaffirm our sense of awe and wonder, our loneliness in this vast, arcanc universe, our non-existence almost even with *all* mankind put together? Were we need of yet another reminder of our loneliness, of the uselessness of our strife on earth and pettiness of our quarrels? There have been reminders before and wonders without end, and yet we are no better off today than

when Socrates dared to question the presumptions of his day, In fact, we are worse off in many ways, with greater power to do evil and spread injustice . . . Hunger stalks the world, bitterness thrives and war ravages the countryside . . . And this is the hour we choose to acclaim our triumphant voyage to the moon . . . Lonely, miserable man—"forever seeking the lonelier way" and "taking its endlessness for goal" !

(*Rawalpindi*, 7 *Jan* '69)

The Hunter and the Hunted

10. The thought that we are all "fugitives"—each one of us in his own way—has been on my mind these many days . . . Now, the opposite occurs to me ; it seems to me that we are all "hunters" of a thousand hue—as individuals and communities, in an infinite variety of ways . . .

11. "Hunters and fishers often go hungry because they are never sure of their next meal,"—I still remember Mr. Hacker teaching us at school (RIMC, Dehra Dun, 1944) . . . The world is a little surer of its next meal since it took to "agriculture" ; and by some queer twist of economics, even after it took to "industry"—but our ancient love of hunting we have not yet out-grown . . . True, we have lost our relish for the big kill (except for the retention of such hobbies as fishing and bird-shooting to enrich our leisure hours) ; and verily, we have found new objects for the satisfaction of our hunting instinct . . .

12. Bertrand Russell never tires of the chase, trying to trap the truth with every ingenious weapon in his armoury of "logical analysis". Salam hunts the atom and merrily takes to the pursuit of more fundamental particles. In a thousand laboratories of the civilised world men will not leave the amoeba alone; they will hound him out to his hiding place with microscope and chemical-coated film . . .

13. In our own country today (after years of somnolent nothingness), the "Opposition" and the "Government by law established" hunt each other—nourished by the hope that the chase is

really for the capture of a more viable political order . . . Lieutenant Gerard will not relent in his pursuit of Dr. Richard Kimble, and the doctor will not give up his search of the one-armed man who killed his wife . . .

14. The Germans hunt the Jews, the Jews hunt the Arabs and the Arabs hunt among themselves which no Arab-lover approves !) . . . And occasionally, in a mighty resurgence of our ancient love of the big kill, the world goes to war and history calls it I or II . . . and my good friend Faruqi would have prospective officers exercise their imagination in an examination by writing an essay ("not more than 2000 words") on "The Pattern of the Third World War" . . .

15. Somewhere, the extending circle will find its own tail to re-establish the most perfect "form" of the Greeks, so that the hunters also become the hunted—an eternal merry-go-round that makes it impossible to distinguish one "fugitive" from the other, between the "hunter" of Sequence I and the "hunted" of Sequence II.

16. What cruel fascination is this—of the circle, this most vicious of all "forms"—that makes progress an illusion and reduces the meaning of life to that of a pantomime ? Somewhere it *must* be broken, from dizziness we must have respite . . .

(*Rawalpindi*, 31 *Jan.* '69)

"A Grin" by Ted Hughes

17. "There was this hidden grin.
It wanted a *permanent* home. It tried faces
In their forgetful moments : the face, for instance,
Of a woman pushing a baby out between her legs,
But that didn't last long. The face
Of a man so pre-occupied
With the flying steel in the instant
Of the car crash—he left his face
To itself, but that was even shorter. The face
Of a machine gunner—a long burst

but not long enough. And
The face of a steeplejack the second
Before he hit the paving. The faces
Of two lovers in the seconds
They got so far into each other, they forgot
Each other completely. That was OK.
But none of it lasted.
And the grin tried the face
Of somebody lost in sobbing ;
A murderer's face ; and the racking moments
Of the man smashing everything
He could reach, and had strength to smash—
Before he went beyond his body.

It tried the face

In the electric chair—to get a tenure

In eternal death ; but that too relaxed.
The grin

Sank back, temporarily non-plussed,
Into the skull."

18. Copied down from *The Observer Review*, 12 January 1969—faithfully, except for the punctuation which is my own. The original contains hardly any punctuation at all . . . May be, ND thought, because the poet saw several over-lapping images (as we sometimes see on the movie screen) and he reproduced the blurred whole as he saw it . . . And yet, how cruelly clear ! The lonely, lonely grin seeking *permanence* in the external world, and withdrawing "non-plussed" into its skull...Such permanence that such things may ever find will only be in a "Mona Lisa" or in a "Grecian Urn" . . . But shall we try to preserve a grin also, as Ted Hughes has done? Lonely 20th Century Man, what better can you find? The cesmic vision will never be ours, and our age drives us inexorably to the grin . . . Truth, we may capture in part but beauty we shall not find till our vision encompass the whole . . . (*Rawalpindi*, 4 *Feb*. '69)

Birth and Death

19. "The traumatic experience of birth", "the ecstasy of love experienced" and "death" (simply that, without clarification)—these, in some such words, Romain Rolland held to be the main notches in the Staff of Life . . . Of the first, we hardly remember a thing; and shorn of memory, thought can hardly proceed. Of birth, my birth, I have nothing to say for I remember nothing . . . The world (Freud included) can say what it pleases; my birth, so far as I am concerned, is an empty, emotionless "fact"—it happened: that's all there is to be said about it. Denied memory, I can hardly exalt it to the status of an "experience"—leave alone qualify it as "traumatic" or otherwise . . .

20. Will "death" be, after the event, as "emotionless" a "fact", as "birth" has been? Will memory survive, not merely to recapture the experience of death but also all that we have so intensely lived between the first notch and the last? Or is it going to be a cosmic forgetfulness—a life after "death" as *this* is oblivious of whatever we were before "birth"?

21. Beyond the notches, then, our mind—as we know it—will shed no light . . . Of life, then, we shall never gain the perspective we seek. Faith, scepticism, agnosticism—nothing helps. It would help if the mind would stop asking these questions; but it won't, knowing perfectly well that it can't get an answer . . .

22. A timid, tentative guess has been: "Life has only so much meaning as you put into it." What a weary solution! And it only leads to more questions . . . What is "meaning"? How does one pour meaning into a thing the beginning of which he does not remember and the end of which his imagination cannot comprehend—leave alone any understanding of what "was" before the beginning and what "will be" after the end? . . .

23. The memory of birth is fled, but the "forward" memory of death remains so long as we live. That thought haunts:

sometimes a spectre of fear, sometimes of loneliness, often-times a sheer, empty weariness . . . Such meaning as we can put into life must be expressed (for want of any other strategy that we know) in terms of an honourable surrender before this inscrutable, unconquerable "enemy" . . . To have lived a life, such as would enable us at the time of the surrender, to say, without fear and without arrogance, that we have found it better to have lived and died, than never to have lived at all—that seems to me the best that we can ever hope to do . . . For that, thank God, neither "perspective" nor "understanding" (in the sense that these words worried us) is really necessary...We know instinctively what will bring peace and what will not. It is quite another matter, of course, if some of us don't care two hoots for peace and wage the battle oblivious of the unconquerable "enemy". . .

(*Rawalpindi*, 5 *Feb* '69)

The Ecstasy of Love Experienced

24. "The ecstasy of love experienced", the central notch—this certainly has meaning, in itself even without reference to what precedes and what follows . . . To the traditional trial (Truth, Beauty, Goodness), I would add Love—the ultimate "good in itself", the crowning consummation of them all.

25. Words get in our way, even though the perception is clear (pity, we haven't found yet a camera to photograph the mind) . . .

26. When I said "Love", I meant it in the concrete : the love of a man and a woman for each other—of the torment of the flesh violently soothed, of children fondly reared and filling a home with memories to live by, of a drowsiness in the sun, of meals shared and feelings exchanged, of quarrels forgotten and loneliness by-passed, of souls drenched with the readiness to die...

27. Our love of Truth, of Beauty, of Goodness—of anything at all, is bound to be a little queer if that central "Love" (in all its carnality and its spiritual glow) should fail to suffuse our

lives. That denied, we must remain dwarfs whatever our line of pursuit . . .

28. Nietzsche, Schopenhauer and Otto Weininger are dwarfs by that measure. Honourable exceptions there have been: Socrates (though married), Spinoza (though celibate), Bertrand Russell (through many trials and nearly as many errors) and even Voltaire (with his patch-work of many loves !) . . .

29. True, I have read Schopenhauer with eagerness, and Tolstoy and Bernatd Shaw in their moments of bitterness, even as I have looked deep at a Degas, a Toulouse Lautrec, even a Sadequain...I have not, thank God, chosen them (in their transient or permanent moods) as my elect. They have been washed away by Tagore on my tape ("Klanti amar khoma koro probhu", "Bhuboneshworo He", "Tumi shondharo meghomala"), gently put to sleep by Will Durant in his "Pleasures of Philosophy", drowned in the colours of a Renoir or simply rendered inaudible by the conversations of Abelard and Heloise.

30. Too sweet, you think, sickeningly sweet . . . Not, if you would resist the temptation of taking it in all in one draught ! There is Russell yet to read, in the interval Einstein to understand, a pair of shoe-laces to be bought, and enough salt and wound in the external world *not* to tire of the sweet . . .

(*Rawalpindi*, 6 *Feb*. '69)

The Quotations

31. "For all the few who seek truth whole,
And take its endlessness for goal,
And steer by stars as if no shoal
Could mar their firmament.
For all the few that sing and sail,
Knowing their quest of small avail ;
Thank God Who gave them strength to fail
In finding out what He meant."

(*Lord Vansittart, quoting from "The Singing Caravan" in his book "Mist Procession"*)

32. "People of Orphalese !
The wind bids me leave you.
Less hasty am I than the wind, yet I must go.
We wanderers, ever seeking the lonelier way,
begin no day where we have ended another day.
And no sunrise finds us where sunset left us.
Even while the earth sleeps, we travel.
We are seeds of that tenacious plant, and it is
in our ripeness and our fullness of heart that
we are given to the wind and are scattered . . ."

(*Kahlil Gibran*, "*The Prophet*")

NOTES ON THE RECONSTRUCTION OF CHARACTER

(Culled from "*The Pleasure of Philosophy*" *by Will Durant* and clothed in minor SD. For the original, refer to *Chapter XII* : pages 170-187 of the tenth paper-back edition published by *Simon and Schuster, New York*).

The Elements of Character

1. Everywhere physics and chemistry, mathematics and mechanics, have remade the face of the earth nearer to the will of man. Only man himself, his will and his character, seem to have remained unchanged.

2. Three hundred years hence psychology will probably be where physics is today, still incomplete like some groping figure of Rodin's, but masterful none-the-less, with the hand of science laid at last upon "mind" and "heart" and "soul", and the raw materials of our chaotic wills slowly forged by knowledge into the strength and kindliness of a higher race.

3. The older psychology divided characters in accordance with their "humours") into ; *sanguine, melancholic, choleric and phlegmatic.*

4. Later, Bain suggested the classification of characters into : *intellectual, emotional and volitional* (depending on which one of the three functions of the mind—*thinking, feeling, willing*—happens to be the dominant one in a particular human personality). But:—

   (*a*) Since the volitional type may also be emotional (*e.g*, Alexander, Queen Elizabeth I) or intellectual *e.g.* Caesar, Napoleon),

   and

   (*b*) Even the intellectual may also be emotional *e.g.* Plato, Abelard, Voltaire, Nietzsche),

we come out by the same door wherein we went.

(*Note*: For an interesting discussion of this subject, the reader may wish to turn to CarlGustav Jung's *Psychological Types* or the appropriate chapter in Frieda Fordham's *An Introduction to Jung's Psychology*).

5. *There are two ways of studying a man*:—

(*a*) *One begins outside* with the environment, and considers man as a mechanism of adjustment. It is a point of view: advocated in philosophy by Democritus, Epicurus, Lucretius, Hobbes and even the gentle Spinoza ; it appears in the materialism of Spencer and the behaviourism of Watson; in the biology of Darwin; in the sociology of Buckle, Spencer and Marx.

(*b*) *The other way begins within*: it looks upon man as a system of needs, impulses, and desires impelling him to study, to use, and to master his environment. This is a point of view finding expression in: the "entelechy" of Aristotle; the "vitalism" of Bergson; the "pragmatism" of WIlliam James; the philosophy of Plato, Descartes, Leibniz, Kant and Schopenhauer; the biology of Lamarck; the sociology of Goethe, Caryle and Nietzsche.

6. *Character*, from the second point of view (para 5b above), *is the sum of inherent dispositions and desires; it is a mosaic of instincts coloured and rearranged by environment, occupation and experience*.

7. *See Table of Character Elements at Annex A*. Observations and deductions:—

(*a*) *Our species* and our races determine what *instincts* we shall have; *environment* determines what objects they will seek, and what habits they will generate. All experience is a process of elicitation or repression: every day some tendency is nourished by success, another is weakened by inaction or defeat. Each of us has several potential characters (habit-mosaics), one of which is gradually selected and strengthened by environment, like the iron filings drawn by the magnet from the midst of unresponsive wood. Hence, the first principle in changing one's character is to seek another environment, to let new forces play upon our unused chords, and draw from us a better music.

(*b*) Note that each *instinct* is the psychological expression of a physiological system. Each instinct is rooted in our structure, and any change of character which mutilates an instinct does injury to the body as well as the soul.

(*c*) Note again that every instinct has an emotional accompaniment, a mode of *feeling* as original and profound as the impulse to which it corresponds.

(*d*) Finally, observe that nearly every instinct has an opposite in the same person; that there is *a positive and a negative here* (as Empedocles thought there must be in everything).

8. Here, in this dichotomy of elements (as explained in Annex A and para 7 above), lies the clue to the fundamental distinction among human characters. The only distinction which nature and history accept is that between *positive and negative characters*, the strong and the weak:—

(*a*) There are persons in whom the positive impulses predominate—in whom the tendency is to approach, to seek, to overcome and to possess. Let us call them *positive characters.*

(*b*) And there are others in whom the negative impulses predominate—persons in whom the general tendency is to hesitate, to retreat, to find safety and shelter, to submit. Let us call them *negative characters.*

9. *No man or woman is entirely one or entirely the other*; the distinction is like masculine and feminine, and allows of every

gradation and every mixture. What we should note are the poles between which human character oscillates, and the ultimate constituents of every personality.

The Negative Character

10. Here is the negative character :—

(*a*) What he lacks above all is body, energy, horse-power; he has not blood enough to be strong.

(*b*) If insult or danger comes, he trembles with surprise and fear; he does not feel active anger, but is consumed with a fretful resentment. His violence is the mask of one who knows that he will submit.

(*c*) He shrinks from responsibility and trial, and longs for the quiet security and retreat of his home.

(*d*) If he succeeds in anything he credits himself ; if he fails, he is "not guilty"; it is the environment (i.e. other people) that is at fault, or the government, or the arrangement of the stars. He is a pessimist about the world; and an optimist about himself.

(*e*) Nevertheless, he may be great by the very force of that unrestrained imagination which flourishes in him because of his physical limitations. At his height here, he may become a poetic genius; at his lowest, he is an intellectual—not a thinker, but a man who only thinks. As civilisation develops, and life becomes fatiguingly complex, and physical ability becomes less vital to survival, every city is crowded with these shifting, self-gnawing souls—Don Quixotes of imagination and Hamlets of achievement.

(*f*) In such a man the instincts of action are few and weak; he is not given to play or sport, except of thought and speech; he puns, but he does not swim. If he goes to games, it is only to see, not to partake. The impulse to rest is here supreme: he never walks when he can ride, he never stands when he can sit, it never remains awake when he can sleep. And since action does not absorb his energies, and emotion for ever arouses him without finding the physical outlet which it craves, he is for ever on edge and never knows repose.

(*g*) In love he is the courted rather than the wooer; even if he appears to approach, to besiege and overcome, it is the lady who arranges it for him with the smooth invisibility of a statesman. He yields to Destiny, becomes a faithful and industrious husband, reproduces his like as often as chance dictates, and wears himself out fretfully for his children. He dies prematurely, darkened with a sense of futility, and wondering if it would not have been better had he never been born.

(*h*) These being his impulses, he is weak, above all, because they are not coordinated by some purpose that dominates and unifies his life. He is restless, though always seeking rest; he is a ship that never makes a port, while all its cargo rots. He is intense in intention and lax in application; he is given to bursts of passion that simulate strength, but they end in quick exhaustion and accepted chaos. He has a thousand wishes, but no will.

The Positive Character

11. This man is positive :—

(*a*) He has health and vigour, a sufficiency of flesh and blood to warrant him in looking straight into the eye of the world, and wearing his hat as he likes. If he looks at you, it is face to face; but he does not look at you; he is absorbed in his enterprise, intent on his goal. He is less interested in persons than in purposes.

(*b*) All the impulses of approach are strong in him. He

eats with gusto and without formality. His motto is; "To have and to hold."

(*c*) In olden days he would have been a feudal baron or a soldier, instead of an executive, a merchant, a trade union leader, or an engineer, and much of that old pugnacity remains in him, mitigated and disguised, as when it brandished a javelin. It is this pugnacity that gives power to his purposes; in him desires are not timid aspirations, they are unavoidable impulsions; for their sake he will accept responsibilities, dangers and wearing toil. He has more courage than virtue, and less conscience than pride. He has powerful ambitions; he despises limits, and suspects humility. When he is defeated, it is only after a struggle to exhaustion.

(*d*) He is curious; all processes lure him, and his mind plays actively about strange and novel things. If he is a philosopher, he engages in affairs as well as in thought; he is a Seneca rather than an Aristotle, a Bacon rather than a Berkeley, a Voltaire, rather than a Kant.

(*e*) He believes in action rather than in thought, and like Caesar he thinks nothing finished if anything remains undone. He likes a tumultous life. He is domineering and likes to feel that men are bricks to his trowel, to build with them what he likes; and they find a secret zest in being led by him: he is so certain, so confident, so cheerful.

(*f*) He enjoys life, bad as it is, and does not ponder much over the past or the future. In some of his avatars he is, nevertheless, a man of ideas. Even so, he has a hundred lives of action for one life of thought. He seldom stops to introspect; he has few "complexes", and he never talks of psychology. When his wife irritates him, he goes to his club; and when his club bores him, he forgets himself in his work.

(*g*) In love he takes the initiative, and wins his way through with a directness and despatch that endear him to all women. He marries early, because he makes up his mind quickly, and prefers curious approach to cautious retreat; it is better, he thinks, to be burdened with wife and children, than with solitude and chorus girls. He dies never doubting that life was a boon, and only sorry that he must leave the game to younger players.

(*h*) *What he has, above all, is WILL, Not wills, but WILL.* His will is disciplined; he draws a circle defining possibility, and then within it he wills the means as resolutely as the end. He produces works, not fragments and "impressions"; and he is so absorbed in his effort that he never thinks what comments it will evoke. He has passions, great ones, but they form *one passion moving to one end*, not tattered fragments blown in chaos. He knows the pleasure of self-control.

Remaking Character

12. *If we cannot find a coordinating goal*, some master purpose to which we will sacrifice every other desire of our heart, *unity is beyond us*, and we must first choose our goal and plot our road; then we must cleaver to it whate'er betide.

13. *It is achievement that makes achievement*; by little conquests we gain strength and confidence for larger ones; practice makes will. But make sure that modest victories shall not content you; on the morning after your triumph, having feasted for a day, look about you for the next and large task. Face danger and seek responsibility. If they do not kill you, they will strengthen you and lift you nearer to greatness and your goal. Make or break.

14. If you feel weak and handicapped, consider:—

(*a*) "This feeling which the individual has of his own

inferiority furnishes the inner impulse to advance". (*Alfred Adler*). It is those who were behind that forge to the front and lead the race.

(*b*) "Whoever hath anything fixed in his person that doth induce contempt, hath also a perpetual spur in himself to rescue and deliver himself from scorn. (*Francis Bacon*).

So the club-foot Byron learned to dance perfectly, and to sin sufficiently to make himself a social lion; the stuttering Demosthenes become a perfect orator; and Beethoven, losing his hearing, fought his way to incomparable music.

Recipes for the Reconstruction of Character

15. *Seek health first.* "The first requisite of a gentleman is to be a perfect animal" (Nietzsche). "Der Mensch ist was or isst" (Moleschott): a man is what he eats. And if your waste will not eliminate itself without a druggist's aid, ask yourself what evil substance is it that weakens you so shamefully; is it your beautiful white flour, or feminine cakes and sweets, or a green-less and fruit-less meal? Keep your bowels open and your mouth shut; this is the gamut of wisdom.

16. *Do some physical work and manual labour each day.* Nature did not make us for intellectuals, for clerks and journalists and philosophers; she made us to move about, to lift weights, and run and climb; she fashioned us for a life of arms and legs. The ideal career would combine physical with mental activity in unity or alternation. There must be some wisdom in a Kaiser who daily chops wood.

17. *We shall not change ourselves substantially unless we change the stimuli that beat upon our flesh from hour to hour*, and form us at last in their image. Are we living amongst unclean people, or illiterates concerned only with material and edible things?—let us go off, whatever it may cost us, and seek better company. Is there, within however distant reach, a finer soul thanours, a better furnished mind, a firmer character?—let

us ferret him out, and hitch our wagon to him for a while. And then let us look for greater men still. Better listen to greatness than dictate to fools. Caesar was wrong; it is nobler to be second in Rome than to be first among barbarians.

18. *Read a little each day the lives and thoughts of great men.* If (as you are likely to think) there is no greater one than you in the circle to which life narrows you, then make friends of genius in the past. For a penny you can buy their counsel, and listen familiarly to their speech, and mould yourself in the clear air which runs about them. It is an error to suppose that books have no influence, like flowing water carving out a canyon, but tells more with every year; and no one can pass an hour a day in the society of sages and heroes without being lifted up a notch or two by the company he has kept. There is no excuse for being small when we can sit at the table with Napoleon, or walk with Walt Whitman, or have midnight suppers with Frederick and Voltaire.

19. *The first great rule of character is unity ("to be a whole or join a whole"—Goethe). And the second is : approach, do not retreat.* That is the line of growth, from which the wise man will permit some deviations, but not so much as to let the exceptions cloud the rule.

20. *Character does not come from conspicuous consumption, it comes from construction and creation.* The strong man gives as readily as he earns, and finds his joy in building rather than owning. He makes houses for others to live in, and money for others to spend.

21. *Character comes from action.* Avoid occupations in which you will have to think, and think and think; with never a chance to do. Better play one piece of music than listen to a hundred. And play and laugh; and if, now and then (as on a stormy at sea), life seems a bitter jest, remember the jest and forgive the bitterness.

22. *Marry!* Once that elementary problem is solved, we

can move about in the world without being distracted at every turn at the flutter of a skirt; we realize that however different the garments may be, women are substantially identical; that under the varying phenomena (as a metaphysician would say) there is always the same under-lylng reality. And so we become moderately content, and even learn to love our mates after a while.

23. *Have friends.* If you cannot make them, remake yourself until you can. Solitude is a medicine, a healing fast; but it is not a food. Character, as Goethe put it once for all, grows only in the stream of the world. Friends are helpful not only because they will listen to us, but because they will laugh at us. also. Through them we learn a little objectivity, a little courtesy; we learn the rules of life and become better players of the game. If you wish to be loved, be modest; if you wish to be admired, be proud; if you wish both, combine external modesty with internal pride. Above all, do not be clever. Epigrams are odious when they pierce the skin; and our motto should be: "De vivis nil nisi bonum".

24. *Try to move forward quietly*: without arousing unnecessary hostility, always approaching, always welcoming experience, always tempting life to give you as much as you can bear of it before you walk out from the sanctuary, leaving your children to guard the flame.

25. *Reason's healthy function is to serve as an aid to action.* When it becomes an industry in itself, it makes Hamlets and Logicians; the tug-of-war remains undecided, and muscle and character rot. But when it becomes the play of desire, the criticism of impulse, the checking of passion by passion then it is that highest state of man, in which the elements that are mingled in him move hither and thither until they melt into unity, and issue in total perspective and complete response.

26. *In the play of knowledge upon desire, which is the very essence of reason, we have the source and armoury of self-discipline,*

that power of inhibition which is the last necessity of character and will. The world disciplines us, or we discipline ourselves; we have our choice.

27. *In the end, character is what John Stuart Mill called it* long since: "*a completely fashioned will*".

NOTE-WRITER'S COMMENT

28. If I had not found Will Durant interesting, stimulating and of much profit to my mind and spirit, I would not have taken the pains that I have taken to compile these notes. This grateful acknowledgement, however, does not mean that I find myself in complete agreement with him.

29. His treatment of the subject in this case (Chapter XII) suffers from some inaccuracies and over-simplifications, several broad and breezy statements—dangers inherent in any popular presentation of subjects both deep and delicate. I cannot, for example, find myself in sympathy with neither the nomenclature of "positive" and "negative" tendencies, nor some of the specific elements marshalled under them within the three categories of instincts, habits and feelings (Annex A refers):—

(*a*) Even for the common understanding, would it not have been better to substitute "positive" by "Strong-Offensive-Active" and "negative" by "Weak-Defensive-Passive"?

(*b*) From the anomaly questioned in "a" above, rise doubts about the validity of such feelings as "cruelty" and "greed" being classified as "positive"; or in the category of habits, "cleanliness" and "thought" being classified as "negative".

(*c*) Will Durant might argue that our common understanding is attaching a moral connotation of good to "positive" and bad to "negative", whereas he uses these words to indicate these tendencies mathematically (+ and —) without any moral connotaion.

> If this were to explain away the doubts raised about Annex A, the general attitude taken by him towards the "Positive Character" (despite some criticism) does express considerable moral preference for it over the "Negative Character" (See paras 10-11). Obviously, the argument as a whole, in this particular aspect, is not self-consistent.

Personally, I find Carl Gustav Jung's classification of four psychological types (the thinking, the feeling, the willing and the intuitive type), each measured on an "introversion-extraversion" scale, logically more consistent, clear and simple.

30. The criticism in para 29 above having been voiced to clear my own understanding of this particular chapter in Will Durant's *The Pleasures of Philosophy*, I would heartily recommend to you a thorough reading of the rest of this many-times-to-be-read book.

31. Will Durant is a very readable writer—mellow, compassionate, large-hearted, with a simple and robust style. His ideas are rounded by a world-historical perspective; and his language is vivid and full-blooded. In both thought and expression, he lies mid-way between the essentially cold and scientific Bertrand Russell and the intuitive, passionate Henri Bergson. To read Will Durant is delightful education: both entertainment and work.

32. Among the other books by Will Durant, three have acquired international acclaim:—

(*a*) The Story of Philosophy.

(*b*) The Story of Civilisation.

(*c*) The Lessons of History.

Enclosure

33. "The Elements of Character". See chart on page 251.

TABLE OF CHARACTER ELEMENTS

I. INSTINCTS		II. HABITS		III. FEELINGS	
Positive	*Negative*	*Positive*	*Negative*	*Positive*	*Negative*
(1) Food-getting	Avoidance	Hunting Tearing Hoarding Acquisition	Cleanliness	Hunger Cruelty Greed	Disgust
(2) Fighting	Flight	Approach Curiosity Manipulation Mastery	Retreat Hesitation Thought Submission	Anger Wonder Pride	Fear Doubt Humility
(3) Action	Sleep	Play	Rest	Buoyancy	Fatigue
(4) Association	Privacy	Speech Suggestibility Imitation Love of approval	Secretiveness	Pleasure in Society	Shyness
(5) Reproduction and Parental Care	Refusal	Courtship	Blushing	Sex desire Parental love	Modesty

NOTES ON SELF-EDUCATION

Introduction

1. No claim to distinction which entitles me to speak with authority on this subject. I am only here for the joy of being with you, glad to grasp this opportunity offered for an hour's communication with the young—so that I might wash and refresh my spirit, and in grateful return for this service that you do even without knowing, to lay before you my humble offering on what little I have learnt from life of that vast subject called "Self-Education".

2. I am no professor of moral philosophy or even educational psychology, so don't expect of me any learned talk, except such brilliance as sincerity might add to common-sense. I shall begin.

Clearing Up Our Terms

3. A few words first about "*self*" and then about "*education*"—separately—before I can venture to talk to you about "*self-education*".

4. Firstly then, about "*self*" in the context of "*self-education*". The word "*self*" here, as I understand it, has two distinct connotations:—

(*a*) Firstly, *self* as the *field* in which *education* must operate. In this sense, the term *self* embraces the *total* personality of an individual, the *entire* spectrum of *body, mind and spirit* which constitutes a *man.*

(*b*) Secondly, *self*, the *self* as *an instrument and an agency* for education: I educating myself, you educating yourself, we educating ourselves. The stress, in the context of "*self-education*", is on the *individual* educating *himself.* He is the *field*, and he is the *operator*, the *instrument*, the *agency*. It is worth remembering, that in the final analysis, whatever we learn we owe to *ourselves.* The teacher, the friend, even the enemy (every external operator or agency) can only *assist* in the process of education. These external agents can *offer* education, but they cannot *impart* it—for education is not two ccs of penicillin which I can inject into your blood or you into mine. These external agents only show us the way, like recee parties marking the route for our approach march into the unknown. They can only guide, suggest, advise, warn, to a limited measure even *assist*—but that is all. In the final analysis, we *ourselves* must march. We *ourselves* either learn or do not learn—*you your-self*, I *my-self.* Throughout this little talk on *self-education* this is the point I would constantly urge you to bear in mind . . . . So much for the first term "*self*".

5. As for the second term, "*education*", the prospect of even attempting to define it frightens me. It is too vast a subject for a small man to speak on without some fear and much hesitation. I know, however, that I cannot get away with it by saying I am scared—for I did undertake to give this talk ! So I'll have a shot: *Education,* to my mind, is the *process* by which *man* seeks to *cultivate* his *personality* (his *total self*: body, mind and spirit) and bring it to *flowering* for the benefit of his *environment,* and thereby (and *only thereby*) for his own *self* also. "*Environment*", in this context, embraces every living and inanimate thing perceptible to *man* in the external world (in the world of matter), and such fringes and corners of the physically imperceptible which can partially apprehended only by his mind and spirit.

6. Note then, that *education* is a *process* covering the entire life span of an individual—a process of *cultivation* appropriate to each stage, from the day the seed of life is sown till it grows from sapling towering tree, yielding *fruit* through many seasons and eventually dying when its purpose has been fulfilled.

7. This *process of cultivation* (of body, mind and spirit) which we call *education* (in relation to the *human personality*) has a two-fold function to perform: to *refine* (*i.e.* to set the human personality into motion through an ascending series of evolutionary stages) and to *strengthen.* The function of *refinement* is easy to comprehend; it is the role of *strengthening* the human personality (through *education*) on which I should like to say a few words.

8. You would recollect: I said the *purpose* of education is to bring the human personality to flower and to bear fruit for the benefit of the environment in which it operates. The final goal is: *to give, to be of service*, and that done, one may die. But to be able to *give*, one must be *strong*, one must *over-flow*, one must grow *beyond* one's own needs and become sensitive to the needs of others. Education that *refines* the human personality is only the fore-play in a life-time's act of love; the climax, the consummation is in the *giving*—and this requires *strength* if you are to yield fruit through many seasons before you eventually die. This is one aspect of *strength*, the capacity to *be of service* till the day one dies, which education must impart.

9. There is one other aspect of *education's* function in *strengthening* the human personality on which I would like to touch, before I go on to matters more concrete. In relation to human personality (as indeed in the entire scheme of Nature), *strength* is a product of *harmony*, of *balance* between the *parts* and their *integration* into a whole. The *strong* personality is the *rounded* personality: a personality in which *body, mind and spirit* have all grown in unison; where none has been neglected and where each has contributed to the growth of the other, in due measure, to create the symphony of the *total personality*.

10. This much I had to say on self and education, before I could venture to talk to you on "Self-Education". It also gives me the frame-work within which I might offer some pointers that I have found useful in what each one of us might

do to *cultivate* our *body, mind and spirit* so that we may *be of service* to those around us.

Pointers for Self-Education

11. Here cover the "Recipes for the Reconstruction of Character" from Will Durant's "The Pleasures of Philosophy" (Chapter XII).

12. Also touch on :—

(*a*) Training the mind in "Logical Analysis".

(*b*) Reading deeply (as opposed to widely) and writing a little each week.

(*c*) Multiplying knowledge and experience by division (the analogy of amoeba).

(*d*) The absolute concept of loyalty.

(*e*) Points from:—

(1) "The Conquest of Happiness" (Bertrand Russell).

(2) "Character and the Conduct of Life" (William McDougall).

(3) "An Introduction to Jung's Psychology" (Frieda Fordham).

(4) "The Prophet" (Khalil Gibran).

(5) "If" (Rudyard Kipling).

(*f*) The Quran; and the balance between reason and faith.

(*g*) "A Soldier's Prayer for his Son" (Douglas Macarthur).

INDEX